Globalization and Human Subjectivity

Globalization and Human Subjectivity

Insights from Hegel's *Phenomenology of Spirit*

Yun Kwon Yoo

PICKWICK Publications • Eugene, Oregon

GLOBALIZATION AND HUMAN SUBJECTIVITY
Insights from Hegel's *Phenomenology of Spirit*

Copyright © 2021 Yun Kwon Yoo. All rights reserved. Except for brief quotations in critical publications or reviews, no part of this book may be reproduced in any manner without prior written permission from the publisher. Write: Permissions, Wipf and Stock Publishers, 199 W. 8th Ave., Suite 3, Eugene, OR 97401.

Pickwick Publications
An Imprint of Wipf and Stock Publishers
199 W. 8th Ave., Suite 3
Eugene, OR 97401

www.wipfandstock.com

PAPERBACK ISBN: 978-1-7252-9709-8
HARDCOVER ISBN: 978-1-7252-9710-4
EBOOK ISBN: 978-1-7252-9711-1

Cataloguing-in-Publication data:

Names: Yoo, Yun Kwon.

Title: Globalization and human subjectivity : insights from Hegel's *phenomenology of spirit* / Yun Kwon Yoo.

Description: Eugene, OR: Pickwick Publications, 2021 | Includes bibliographical references and index.

Identifiers: ISBN 978-1-7252-9709-8 (paperback) | ISBN 978-1-7252-9710-4 (hardcover) | ISBN 978-1-7252-9711-1 (ebook)

Subjects: LCSH: Globalization—Philosophy. | Subjectivity. | Hegel, Georg Wilhelm Friedrich, 1770–1831. Phänomenologie des Geistes.

Classification: B2949 .Y65 2021 (print) | B2949 .Y65 (ebook)

Quotations from *Phenomenology of Spirit* reproduced with permission of the Licensor (Oxford Publishing Limited) through PLSclear.

Quotations from *Hegel: Lectures on the Philosophy of Religion Volume I: Introduction and the Concept of Religion* reproduced with permission of the Licensor (Oxford Publishing Limited) through PLSclear.

All the scriptural references are from the Revised Standard Version of the Bible.

To the late Dr. Anselm K. Min,
my most respected and influential teacher and mentor throughout my academic journey to date,
without whom this book would not have been possible

Contents

Acknowledgments ix
Abbreviations xi
Introduction xiii

CHAPTER 1
Globalization, Postmodernism, and Subjectivity 1
    Globalization and Its Anthropology 2
    Postmodernism and the *Death of the Subject* 14
    Beyond Postmodern Subjectivity in the Context of Globalization 27

CHAPTER 2
A Prelude to Hegelian Subjectivity 36
    The Modern Turn to the Subject 37
    Hegel's *Sublated* Concept of Subjectivity 46

CHAPTER 3
Hegel's Philosophy of Spiritual Subjectivity
in the *Phenomenology of Spirit* (I) 54
    Subjectivity in the Womb: "Consciousness" 57
    The Birth of Subjectivity: "Self-Consciousness" 69

CHAPTER 4
Hegel's Philosophy of Spiritual Subjectivity in the
Phenomenology of Spirit (II): The Growth of Subjectivity 86
    Individual-Rational Subjectivity: "Reason" 89
    Communal-Spiritual Subjectivity: "Spirit" 124
    Absolute Subjectivity: "Religion" and "Absolute Knowing" 148

CHAPTER 5
Constructive Reflections on Hegelian Subjectivity   170
    Why *God* Is Essential to Hegelian Spiritual, Universal Subjectivity   170
    A Critique of Žižek's Reading of Hegelian Subjectivity   187

CHAPTER 6
Concluding Remarks: Hegelian Spiritual Subjectivity
for the Age of Globalization   201
    A Recap of Hegelian Spiritual Subjectivity   201
    The Significance of Hegelian Subjectivity
        in the Context of Globalization   204

Bibliography   209
Index   217

Acknowledgments

THIS BOOK IS A revised version of my doctoral dissertation, which therefore would not exist without the guidance of three professors who willingly served as my dissertation committee members: Anselm K. Min, Ingolf U. Dalferth, and Philip Clayton. I would like to express my deepest gratitude for their valuable comments, profound insights, and heartfelt encouragement while pursuing this work. They are not, of course, responsible for any inadequacies of this book.

I would especially like to thank my doctoral advisor and dissertation chair, the late Professor Anselm K. Min who passed away unexpectedly three months after I completed my degree. Since I came to know him in 2011 at Claremont Graduate University (CGU), he has always been my role model and a constant source of inspiration, not only in terms of his academic passion and achievements, but also in terms of his exemplary life as a true man of character, as a true man of faith, and as a true man of scholarship. When I think of the legacy that he would want me to carry on, I believe it is none other than his lifelong, both theoretical and practical, commitment to upholding universal consciousness, sensibility, horizon, and spirituality with their historically mediated praxis. Following in his footsteps, I will proceed with my academic journey not just for my own personal interests or fame, but always for the greater common good, namely, for God, all humanity, and all creation. This should be my own way of remembering his life and death as his student and further as his last research assistant of which I am truly honored and proud.

I would also like to thank Dr. Joseph Prabhu, a seasoned Hegel scholar, for his support and helpful comments during his presence at CGU as a visiting professor. I acknowledge my special debt to all my CGU colleagues in Philosophy of Religion and Theology program with whom I suffered, learned, and grew together.

Finally, I owe more than I can acknowledge to my entire family in Korea and the United States who have always motivated me, with their full spiritual and material support, to keep in mind the source of my identity and the purpose of my study based on our common dream of realizing one family under God: my parents, Bongsang Yoo and Myungjoo Kim, my parents-in-law, Pyungrae Moon and Kyeja Oh, and all my siblings' and in-laws' families; especially for their unwavering love, endurance, and trust, I sincerely thank my wife, Soonae, and four children, Wonsik, Namsik, Jooyeon, and Okjoo.

Abbreviations

HEGEL'S WORKS FREQUENTLY CITED in this book are identified as follows:

EL *Encyclopedia of the Philosophical Sciences in Basic Outline: Part I: Science of Logic.* Translated and Edited by Klaus Brinkmann and Daniel O. Dahlstrom. Cambridge: Cambridge University Press, 2010. Cited by page number followed by paragraph number (§) and as needed with the suffix "A" for Remark (*Anmerkung*) or "Z" for Addition (*Zusatz*).

EM *Philosophy of Mind: Part Three of the Encyclopedia of the Philosophical Sciences (1830).* Translated by W. Wallace and A. V. Miller. Revised by Michael Inwood. Oxford: Oxford University Press, 2007. Cited by page number followed by paragraph number (§) and as needed with the suffix "A" for Remark (*Anmerkung*) or "Z" for Addition (*Zusatz*).

LHP I-III *Lectures on the History of Philosophy 1825–1826.* Translated by Robert F. Brown. 3 vols. Oxford: Oxford University Press, 2009.

LPR I-III *Lectures on the Philosophy of Religion.* Translated by R. F. Brown, P. C. Hodgson, and J. M. Steward. 3 vols. Berkeley: University of California Press, 1984–1987.

LPWH *Lectures on the Philosophy of World History: Manuscripts of the Introduction and The Lectures of 1822–1823.* Translated by Robert F. Brown and Peter C. Hodgson. Oxford: Oxford University Press, 2011.

PR	*Elements of the Philosophy of Right*. Translated by H. B. Nisbet. Cambridge: Cambridge University Press, 1991. Cited by page number followed by paragraph number (§) and as needed with the suffix "A" for Remark (*Anmerkung*) or "Z" for Addition (*Zusatz*).
PS	*Phenomenology of Spirit*. Translated by A. V. Miller. Oxford: Oxford University Press, 1977. Cited by page number followed by paragraph number (§).
SL	*Science of Logic*. Translated by A. V. Miller. New York: Humanities, 1969.

Introduction

THIS BOOK EXPLORES HEGEL'S philosophy of spiritual subjectivity, particularly set forth in his *Phenomenology of Spirit*, and argues that it can and should serve as a philosophical-anthropological basis for a new conception of human subjectivity for the age of globalization, that is, a sort of cosmopolitan citizen who is constantly universalizing oneself through self-transcending, self-determined ethico-political actions in solidarity with others to create a global community of co-existence and co-prosperity for all. Why, then, does globalization demand a new conception of human subjectivity at all? What constitutes the Hegelian spiritual subjectivity such that it is not only relevant but also necessary to the contemporary, postmodern context of globalization? This book largely discusses these two questions in depth.

We are living in an age of globalization that is primarily driven by global capitalism. Globalization has been creating tremendous transformations in every field of human life, including economic, political, cultural, religious, ecological, technological, etc., bringing together all parts of the globe into common space, promoting intensified contacts within, across, and beyond borders, and thereby making the world a smaller place. This seemingly exciting globalizing world as the context of our life today, however, brings about unprecedented problems we have to cope with—such as the ever-widening, ever-deepening processes of economic bipolarization, political imperialism, cultural nihilism, religious conflict, ecological crisis, technological domination, and so on.

Among the challenges posed by globalization, the most critical—underlying and overarching—one in my view is related to the anthropological question of "what it means to be *authentically human*." Today's capitalist globalization through the process of not only the commodification or commercialization of everything but also the culturalization, aestheticization, or pseudo-spiritualization of the market economy itself strongly influences, shapes, and even manipulates the very depth of our being and consciousness *as* humans. This, in turn, results in debilitating our sense of self-determination, self-reflection, self-critique, self-responsibility, self-discipline, and self-transcendence, i.e., the erosion of human subjectivity per se, even as we seem to enjoy unlimited free choices in the market. In a sense, today's postmodern consumerist society ostensibly makes us believe that we are subjects or agents who are making free choices among endlessly alternative possibilities as we wish or desire, but its *real* voice behind the veil is whispering to us, "You are a *dead* subject *without* subjectivity"; that is to say, we are rather *subjected* to some force *extrinsic* to our own interiority, namely, to the globalizing logic of capitalist materialism and sensationalism. In short, the human being that capitalist globalization is eager to promote and produce is none other than a faithful global consumer who, without critical thinking, simply succumbs to one's sensuous inclinations or desires in their sheer particularity, contingency, and arbitrariness, who is easily attracted to the external appearances and sensible images of commodities unceasingly released onto the market, and who thus is always ready to buy them both online and offline.

Furthermore, I claim, there is an implicit alliance, or unwitting conspiracy, between global capitalism and postmodernism in terms of anthropology, i.e., the anthropological conception of human subjectivity. Regardless of its real intent, postmodernism's philosophical assertion about the "death of the subject," which claims that subjectivity is merely a by-product or after-effect of the pre-subjective, extrinsic processes of language, culture, power, the unconscious, etc., could function as an ideological supplement to global capitalism which for its unrestrained development and expansion requires non-subjective agents, namely, the sheer consuming subjects who are, without critical subjectivity, subjected to the imperialism of a globalizing market and thus desire only the desire of capitalism. I believe that such an erosion of human subjectivity (the death of the subject) is fatally problematic in that its corollary is none other than the *de-ethicalization* and *de-politicization* of people because any genuine ethics and politics constitutively rely on "subjectivity," the subjective thoughts, decisions, and actions of human beings. This is all the more serious or critical given that the current epoch of globalization imperatively calls for our more ethical and political measures and practices than ever before to make globalization a new hope for human community and co-prosperity rather than a source of exacerbating chronic divisions and alienations among the peoples of the globe.

Therefore, in this postmodern context of globalization, where we humans are desperately demanded to live together in justice, harmony, peace, and solidarity by recognizing our interdependence despite our differences, I contend in this book that we are in dire need of a new conception of human subjectivity which includes following three crucial elements in their internal, constitutive relations: *self-transcending drive toward universality* ("I am/We are intrinsically driven toward the universal common good"), *self-determined or autonomous action* ("I/We decide and act myself/ourselves"), and *solidary relationship with others* ("I am/We are in a mutually dependent relationship with diverse others in the concrete context of the socio-historical world"). Without the first element (self-transcending drive toward universality) human subjectivity may lapse into nihilistic egoism, without the second element (self-determined or autonomous action) fatalistic heteronomy, and without the third element (solidary relationship with others) totalitarian imperialism. In this way, this new conception of subjectivity should also go beyond postmodernism's view of subjectivity as externally imposed *subjectivation*, reducing humans merely to their given or reified subject positions constituted by sheer otherness, without at the same time going back to modernism's atomistic or individualistic *subjectivism*. In my view, crucial to re-conceptualizing this sort of new subjectivity for today's globalizing world is to conceive of it as *sublation* (in the Hegelian sense of *Aufhebung*)[1] of the opposition between self-sufficient and hence only-constituting subjectivism (modernism) and selfless and hence merely-constituted subjectivation (postmodernism) into their dialectical totality, that is, as a self-conscious, self-determined, self-transcending movement toward an ever greater universality in and through its intrinsic, constitutive relations to others in the actual world.

I emphatically argue in this book that we can find this perspective and orientation par excellence in Hegel's philosophy of subjectivity, and more specifically in his deep and rich conception of *spiritual subjectivity*.[2] For Hegel, the term "spirit" (*Geist*), "spirituality" (*Geistigkeit*), or

---

1. For Hegel, "sublation" (*Aufhebung*) involves three inseparable moments of *negation*, *transcendence*, and *preservation*.

2. Hegel does not himself employ the term, "spiritual subjectivity" (*geistige Subjektivität*), in his works. However, in my view, it is the most proper and fitting term that represents his conception of subjectivity in its full depth and breath.

"spiritual" (*geistig*) is neither a purely abstract or mystical nor a dichotomous notion, but a truly *dialectical* concept.[3] Three moments,[4] namely, "the absolute" in the sense of absolute universality (the ultimate ground and telos), "self-conscious identity" (being-for-itself), and "concrete socio-historical relatedness" (being-for-others), are intrinsically co-constitutive of one another in the very conception of spiritual subjectivity as their dialectical totality. In this way, Hegel's concept of subjectivity *as* spirit could also be defined as a *teleological* movement of absolute negativity,[5] that is, as a restless and developmental-progressive movement of self-transcendence toward absolute universality (i.e., the unification of universal subjectivity and universal objectivity) through dialectical relations with others in history. I find paradigmatically in Hegel's *Phenomenology of Spirit* how such Hegelian spiritual subjectivity actually emerges and develops gradually—from subjectivity-in-itself (subjectivity in the womb) through subjectivity-for-itself (the birth of subjectivity) to subjectivity-in-and-for-itself (the growth of subjectivity with its ultimate culmination in absolute subjectivity).

I am inclined to claim that this Hegelian concept of spiritual subjectivity should be revisited and explored in depth in order to formulate a new conception of human subjectivity in the ethico-political context of today's globalizing world. Moreover, I believe, such a new conception could serve as an alternative to the *subjectlessness* of postmodernism, which seems the prevailing philosophical view of human subjectivity today, but without falling back on the subject-centrism (anthropocentrism) of modernism. This undertaking of exploring the Hegelian spiritual subjectivity with the purpose of envisioning a new conception of human subjectivity for the age of globalization is precisely what I would like to carry out in this book.

In a sense, what I attempt to do is a sort of "contextual philosophy," though no one seems to have used this term, which derives its formal methodology from contextual theology—the methodology that focuses

---

3. For the dialectical meaning of Hegel's concept of "spirit," see *LPR I*, 176–77; Min, "Hegel's Dialectic," 8–10.

4. "Moments" (*Momente*) here in the Hegelian sense is not a temporal/chronological but a *dialectical* term, referring to something's parts, aspects, or factors in their internal, intrinsic, constitutive relations.

5. For Hegel, simply put, "absolute negativity" means the ability to negate and transcend things as they are (the status quo); yet, unlike abstract negativity, its negation and transcendence involve a teleology, that is, a movement *toward* something, which is for Hegel the absolute.

on a dialogue between the past text and the present context.⁶ In a similar vein to what I mean by contextual philosophy, in fact, there have been quite a few literatures written by Hegel scholars that search for "what is living and what is dead"⁷ in Hegel's philosophy, under the slogan of "Hegel Today." However, it is hard to find some among them that deal specifically with the significance and relevance of "Hegelian subjectivity" to the contemporary context with all its issues and concerns, to which this book addresses itself primarily.

The book is developed in the following order. In chapter 1, "Globalization, Postmodernism, and Subjectivity," I discuss the context or background that instigates my book project. After critically examining the characteristics and challenges of "capitalist globalization" as our *Sitz im Leben* (setting in life) and "postmodernism" as a prevailing *Zeitgeist* (a sign of the times) of today and their hidden relationship particularly against the backdrop of the problem of "human subjectivity," I contend that we need to formulate a new conception of human subjectivity fitting in today's postmodern, globalized context. There are three sections to this chapter. In the first section, "Globalization and Its Anthropology," I briefly analyze some of the characteristics and problems of capitalist globalization in its economic and cultural dimensions, with a special focus on the anthropology ("what it means to be human") that global capitalism constructs and promotes for its expansion. In the second section, "Postmodernism and the *Death of the Subject*," examining the postmodernist theme of the "death of the subject" philosophized particularly by Michel Foucault and Jacques Derrida, I claim that we can find a certain junction between the anthropology of global capitalism and that of postmodernism in terms of the erosion of human subjectivity. In the third section, "Beyond Postmodern Subjectivity in the Context of Globalization," I then provide my critique of the postmodernist view of subjectivity in the context of capitalist globalization, with the help of Slavoj Žižek who is exceptionally motivated to revitalize a Hegelian subjectivity and draw its political implications for the present age of global capitalism, and advance

---

6. Stephen B. Bevans defines "contextual theology" as a way of doing theology which takes into account two things: "First, it takes into account the faith experience of the *past* that is recorded in scriptures and kept alive, preserved, defended—and perhaps even neglected or suppressed—in tradition.... Second, contextual theology takes into account the experience of the present, the *context*" (Bevans, *Models of Contextual Theology*, 5).

7. This phrase comes originally from the title of Benedetto Croce's book, *What Is Living and What Is Dead of the Philosophy of Hegel*.

my thesis that there is the need for a new, alternative, (post-)postmodern conception of human subjectivity for the age of globalization, which in turn leads me to revisit the philosophy of subjectivity presented by Hegel.

In chapter 2, "A Prelude to Hegelian Subjectivity," I present an introductory overview of Hegel's philosophy of subjectivity, beginning with the philosophical background that nurtured him in both positive and negative ways and led him to shape his own idea of subjectivity, which I present in the first section, "The Modern Turn to the Subject." Here I specifically deal with the philosophical views on subjectivity advanced by Descartes, Kant, and Fichte, and more precisely Descartes's thinking substance, Kant's transcendental self, and Fichte's absolute ego. After examining this philosophico-historical context of the modern shift to the subject that generated Hegel's philosophical concerns, I then argue in the second section, "Hegel's *Sublated* Concept of Subjectivity," that Hegel's philosophy of subjectivity *as* "spiritual subjectivity" is his critical response to or, better, his *sublation* of philosophical subjectivism and its attending subject-object dualism that issued from the modern turn to the subject in its undialectical, non-speculative manner prevalent in his times.

In chapters 3 and 4, "Hegel's Philosophy of Spiritual Subjectivity in the *Phenomenology of Spirit*," I explore the nature and content of Hegel's vision of the subject, i.e., his idea of spiritual subjectivity as a dialectical movement or process of self-transcending development toward the Absolute (Absolute Spirit and Absolute Knowing) in and through the mediation of objectivity. In terms of the structure of my analysis and argument here, as indicated earlier, I take Hegel's *Phenomenology of Spirit* as the main text. The sequence of different forms of consciousness described in the *Phenomenology* is read as the journey of the human being to find his authentic subjectivity in the process of development or maturity with a series of sublations in dialectical relations to otherness at various and different levels in the concrete world. Chapter 3 is divided into two sections: first, "Subjectivity in the Womb," where I deal with the implicit context or horizon out of which subjectivity begins to emerge, which is an interpretation of the first chapter of the *Phenomenology*, "Consciousness"; and second, "The Birth of Subjectivity," where I examine the emergence process of self-conscious subjectivity, which is an exposition of the second chapter of the *Phenomenology*, "Self-Consciousness." In chapter 4, "The Growth of Subjectivity," I investigate the process whereby the human subject develops itself into being more and more universal, which consists of three sections—starting from "Individual-Rational Subjectivity" through "Communal-Spiritual Subjectivity" to "Absolute Subjectivity," each of which is a comprehensive reading of the remaining chapters of the *Phenomenology*, viz., "Reason," "Spirit," and "Religion" and "Absolute Knowing," respectively.

Based upon this scrutiny of Hegel's philosophy of spiritual subjectivity developed in the *Phenomenology*, in chapter 5, "Constructive Reflections on Hegelian Subjectivity," I provide my reflections on the Hegelian conception of subjectivity, particularly from a religious or theological point of view. There are two sections to this chapter. In the first section, "Why *God* Is Essential to Hegelian Spiritual, Universal Subjectivity," I explore in more depth Hegel's concept of God in his trinitarian movement *as* Absolute Spirit (absolute universality per se), with its sublation of traditional theism and pantheism, and further elaborate on its significance for Hegel's philosophy of subjectivity, namely, that Hegel's concept of God is internal and essential to his concept of the human being *as* spiritual, universal subjectivity. This assertion naturally leads to the next section, "A Critique of Žižek's Reading of Hegelian Subjectivity," which is my critical reflection on Žižek's Lacan-inspired rendering of Hegelian subjectivity as radical negativity, where I argue that although I agree with Žižek in his emphasis on "negativity" as a kernel of Hegel's conception of subjectivity, he nevertheless takes it in purely formal sense and thus overlooks another very crucial aspect in the constitution of Hegelian subjectivity, namely, its teleological structure, due in large part to his failure to see the significance and gravity of the concept of God in Hegel's philosophy of subjectivity as a whole.

Lastly, in chapter 6, "Concluding Remarks: Hegelian Spiritual Subjectivity for the Age of Globalization," I reiterate the relevance and necessity of Hegelian subjectivity in the current context of globalization as a new anthropological vision about what it means to be authentically human, which consists of two sections. In the first section, "A Recap of Hegelian Spiritual Subjectivity," I briefly recapitulate Hegel's conception of spiritual subjectivity that has been discussed throughout this book, that is, a self-conscious movement of transcending itself into an ever greater universal subjectivity in and through the dialectical mediations of otherness or objectivity in history. Then in the second section, "The Significance of Hegelian Subjectivity in the Context of Globalization," I come back to the problem set up in chapter 1 and reaffirm my main argument that the Hegelian vision of spiritual subjectivity is not only relevant but also crucially necessary in the contemporary, postmodern context of globalization.

A word on the use of gender in this book. I use neutral pronouns in referring to the terms, "the (human) subject" and "(human) subjectivity"; I alternate the masculine and feminine in referring to the human being, while I consistently use masculine pronouns to refer to God.

CHAPTER 1

Globalization, Postmodernism, and Subjectivity

IN THIS BOOK, AS already indicated in the introduction, I argue that Hegelian spiritual subjectivity is relevant and necessary, as a new conception of the human subject, to the contemporary, postmodern context of globalization that imperatively calls for a sort of cosmopolitan, global citizens who are constantly universalizing themselves—in the sense of broadening their capacity for self-transcendence toward otherness and thus making themselves more open to the rest of the world—in and through their self-determined ethico-political actions in solidarity with others to build a global community of justice, peace, and mutual prosperity. My argument is motivated initially by the following questions: What does "globalization" as our *Sitz im Leben* look like today? What are the specific challenges and problems posed by the process of globalization? In what way does "postmodernism" as a *Zeitgeist* of today link itself to globalization? Is their connection something insignificant and harmless to the present and future of humanity? All these contemporary and quite existential questions are to be addressed in this chapter, and, as will become clear, the problematic of "human subjectivity" serves as the central theme around which my exploration revolves.

In what follows—as the first step in developing my argument—I will first analyze, though very briefly, some of the main characteristics and challenges of globalization, with special attention to the desired, idealized, or ideologized image of human beings that capitalist globalization advances and promotes. I will then critically examine the postmodernist theme of the "death of the subject" and its possible function to serve as a philosophical justification for the anthropology of capitalist globalization, which will be followed by my insistence on the need for a new, alternative, (post-)postmodern conception of human subjectivity for the age of globalization.

Globalization and Its Anthropology

Before we start talking about globalization in earnest, it would be worth asking ourselves the following questions, seemingly elemental yet indeed quite fundamental. First, why do we—philosophers, religious scholars, or theologians—bother with globalization at all? Why should we care about it? Echoing Anselm K. Min's insightful observation, my simple answer is that it is precisely because the current ongoing process of globalization creates and determines the *context* in which we are living today: "The global context is now *the* context of all contexts."[1] Why, then, does "context" matter in our philosophical, religious, theological studies and praxis? Given the dialectical nature, either implicitly or explicitly, of the humanities in general (including religious studies and theology) as mediating between *text* and *context*, between an array of time-honored ideals, truths, values, or traditions and a set of our present socio-historical conditions, it is necessary that our philosophical or theological enterprise seriously pay attention to, correctly point to, and so rightly respond to specific concerns and challenges engendered by the contemporary socio-historical context.

No one seems to deny that we are now living in an already-globalized and ever-globalizing world, which is our determinate context today; that is to say, we are situated in the context of globalization. What is "globalization" precisely? As Ulrich Beck points out, "Globalization has certainly been the most widely used—and misused—keyword in disputes of recent years and will be of the coming years too; but it is also one of the most rarely defined, the most nebulous and misunderstood."[2] Although globalization is a term that lacks a precise definition and has been characterized in a number of different ways by different scholars, it nevertheless might not be impossible to capture the gist of globalization-talks commonly discussed among scholars.[3] Aware of the ever-present

---

1. Min, *Solidarity of Others*, 72.

2. Beck, *What Is Globalization?*, 19.

3. Min classifies scholars and their literatures on globalization into three types of perspective: optimistic, more critical but realistic, and oppositional; see Min, "Sin," 574n3.

risk of definition with its characteristic oversimplification, we may be able to define "globalization" by drawing the commonly-implied characteristics of this term without at the same time overlooking its fluidity and complexity. I think that among globalization scholars David Held et al. provide a very comprehensive definition in an elaborate and condensed way as follows: Globalization is "*a process (or set of processes) which embodies a transformation in the spatial organization of social relations and transactions—assessed in terms of their extensity, intensity, velocity and impact—generating transcontinental or interregional flows and networks of activity, interaction, and the exercise of power.*"[4]

Transformations through the extensive, intensive, rapid, and influential process of globalization take place literally in *all* aspects of contemporary human life, and hence globalization could be best thought of as a multidimensional set of processes, including economic, political, cultural, religious, ecological, technological, and so on. It would be necessary, therefore, to analyze the transformative powers of globalization—and particularly its challenges and problems—that reach into each domain. However, in view of the purpose of this book, my research here is confined to the two important dimensions: the economic and cultural dimensions of globalization. Affecting and interpenetrating each other, as will be clarified, these two dimensions respectively represent the objective and subjective conditions that constitute the "anthropology of globalization."

Economic Globalization: Creating a World of Global Neoliberal Capitalism

Although the phenomenon of globalization is certainly not something entirely new nor exclusively contemporary,[5] the term "globalization" has

---

4. Held et al., *Global Transformations*, 16. Based upon this definition, Manfred B. Steger presents a *short* definition of globalization that "*Globalization refers to the expansion and intensification of social relations and consciousness across world-time and world-space*," from which then he draws a *very short* definition once again as follows: "*Globalization is about growing worldwide interconnectivity*" (Steger, *Globalization*, 17).

5. For instance, Held et al. identify four historical periods of globalization: premodern (around 9000 BCE–CE 1500), early modern (1500–1850), modern (1850–1945), and contemporary (since 1945); while Steger does five periods: prehistoric (10,000–3500 BCE), premodern (3500 BCE–CE 1500), early modern (1500–1750), modern (1750–1980s), and contemporary (since the 1980s). See Held at al., *Global Transformations*, 414–35; Steger, *Globalization*, 21–37.

become a buzzword describing our *Sitz im Leben,* the word that currently defines our epoch, since the 1980s and 1990s, particularly with the full-scale emergence of a new economic paradigm or theory, namely, "neoliberalism" as a dominant ideology of global capitalism.[6] Without being ignorant of the lack of any clear-cut consensus among scholars on the meaning and nature of neoliberalism, I submit that its seemingly shared central tenets are, in their interlocking relations, as follows: the primacy of economic growth and profits; the liberalization and integration of domestic and international markets, anchored in the idea of the self-regulating mechanism of the market; the inevitability and irreversibility of the globalizing economy; the centrality of free competition; the privatization of public domain/enterprise; the minimization of government intervention and regulations; the elimination of tariffs; the reduction of public/social spending, and so forth.[7]

It is these neoliberal principles of capitalism that impel the contemporary process of economic globalization which in turn serves as the *driving* force for all other aspects or dimensions of globalization—political, cultural, religious, ecological, technological, etc. There are many everyday instances which show the overriding transformative power of economic globalization today that provides impetus to the whole processes of globalization in all its dimensions. For example, in our daily lives we can most immediately see ourselves situated and living in a truly interconnected and globalized world when we look at smartphones, tablets, or computers, wherein we directly experience that information—whether it be public news or private messages—circles the globe in an instant, oftentimes with lively images and videos. Such real-time communications, primarily by means of Internet-based social media such as Facebook, Instagram, Google, YouTube, Twitter, etc., have been made possible by the Information and Communication Technology (ICT) revolution *fueled by* economic globalization, the process of integrating

---

6. See Steger, *Globalization,* 41, where he also points out that this neoliberal economic order of global capitalism received a further boost from the collapse of communism in 1989–1991. It is widely agreed that Friedrich August von Hayek (Austrian-British economist and social philosopher) and Milton Friedman (American economist) are the most famous proponents of neoliberalism whose political and economic philosophy served as a source of inspiration for the economic policies of the Thatcher and Reagan administrations.

7. For a more comprehensive, in-depth account of neoliberalism with its history and key claims, see Boas and Gans-Morse, "Neoliberalism," 137–61; Harvey, *Brief History of Neoliberalism*; Roy et al., *Neoliberalism*; Saad-Filho and Johnston, *Neoliberalism*; Steger, *Globalism*; Steger and Roy, *Neoliberalism*; Turner, *Neo-Liberal Ideology*.

national economies into the global economy. In fact, Facebook (owning Instagram too), Google (owning YouTube too), and Twitter are all *multinational* corporations whose operations are "central to processes of economic globalization."[8] It is in this sense that economic globalization is not merely one among other facets of contemporary globalizing processes but the very matrix or motivating source of them, though this does not necessarily mean that they all could be reducible simply and completely to the economic factor. Therefore, I claim, it would make reasonable sense to say that the current processes of globalization in general are indeed *driven* by the economic logic of global neoliberal capitalism, whether we like it or not.

In brief, economic globalization refers to the increasingly widening, deepening, speeding-up, and growing impact of economic connectivity and interdependence across the globe through the growing scale of cross-national transactions of goods and services and the flow of capital.[9] One of the most important and distinctive factors, which strongly accelerates the process of contemporary economic globalization, is the operation of the above-mentioned "multinational corporations" (MNCs), which is also called transnational corporations (TNCs), as the primary agent of economic globalization. According to the United Nations Conference on Trade and Development's (UNCTAD) World Investment Report 1995, MNCs already controlled two-thirds of world trade at the end of the twentieth century,[10] and obviously, their dominance has since become more extensive and intensive. This clearly exhibits the distinctive feature of contemporary economic globalization, which indeed reflects the logic of neoliberal capitalism, compared with the previous world economic order based on the Bretton Woods system designed in 1944.[11] In other words, it is *global* corporate capital, rather than nation-states, that increasingly exerts decisive influence over the organization and distribution of economic power and resources in the contemporary world economy.[12]

8. Held et al., *Global Transformations*, 236.

9. According to World Bank data, trade percent of gross domestic product (GDP) in the world, which may be seen as an indicator of the degree of economic globalization, amounts to 60 percent in 2019, whereas it was only 27 percent in 1970; see "Trade (% of GDP)."

10. Held et al., *Global Transformations*, 236.

11. One of the key architects of the Bretton Woods system was John Maynard Keynes, a British economist.

12. In fact, some MNCs are massive with market value that outweigh the GDP

No doubt, as neoliberal hyperglobalizers argue,[13] economic globalization through the operation of transnational economic networks brings benefits to the conditions of human existence across the globe. Among all the benefits from economic globalization, from the standpoint of advancing the material condition of humankind at large, there is evidence that the process of economic globalization has, to some extent, contributed to the reduction of global poverty. According to World Bank data, between 1981 and 2017 the number of people living in extreme poverty around the world (living on less than US $1.90 per day) has decreased significantly—from 42.5 percent of the world population to 9.2 percent.[14] Certainly, this continuing trend toward the overall decline in global poverty is due primarily to the growth of national economies through economic globalization.[15]

However, a question about the different effects of economic globalization on the economies of developed countries and less-developed, or developing, countries needs to be raised—that is, the question of who gains more and who gains less from the globalizing economy. Although economic globalization, as discussed above, has contributed to economic growth and the consequential reduction of global poverty, its benefits have not been equally shared: developed countries benefit from economic globalization much more than less-developed countries.[16] In fact, to the less-developed countries "globalization has not brought the promised economic benefits,"[17] and thus, as various statistics show, economic globalization has not been narrowing the gap between developed and less-developed countries. For example, according to the Bertelsmann Stiftung's study, while the gross domestic product (GDP) per capita has

---

of some small-size countries; see Steger, *Globalization*, 55. Still, it must be noted that contemporary economic globalization, whose chief agents are the MNCs, does not simply lead to the immediate demise of the nation-state. Though the role and power of nation-states are shrinking and being constrained in comparison with previous times, they still assume an important position in world economies, especially in the case of big ones such as the United States and China.

13. Held et al. categorize three broad accounts of globalization today: the hyperglobalist, skeptical, and transformationalist theses. For detailed explanations of each view on globalization, see Held et al., *Global Transformations*, 2–10.

14. See "Poverty Headcount Ratio."

15. For a more concrete, statistical understanding of the positive effect of economic globalization on the growth of national economies, see Wolf, *Why Globalization Works*, 140–49.

16. Cf. Sachs et al., *Globalization Report 2020*.

17. Stiglitz, *Globalization and Its Discontents*, 5.

increased over the last two decades in the top twenty developed countries by some €1,000 per year on average owing to globalization, it has risen in other less-developed countries by less than €100.[18] This inequality of economic benefits from globalization is also intimately linked with the uneven progress of decline in poverty between developed and less-developed countries. Still worse, statistics show that even within the group of less-developed countries, economic globalization has been impacted differently. Among less-developed countries the poverty rate of the population living below US $1.25 per day is quite different according to the regions to which they belong—particularly, three regions of East Asia and the Pacific, South Asia, and Sub-Saharan Africa that have accounted for some 95 percent of global poverty for the last several decades. In East Asia and the Pacific, for instance, the poverty rate has fallen from 78 percent to 17 percent over the period of 1981–2005; by contrast, it has not changed much in Sub-Saharan Africa and South Asia: for Sub-Saharan Africa, 54 percent to 51 percent and for South Asia, 59 percent to 40 percent.[19] Hence, though the overall poverty rate has been declining on a global scale, poverty indeed remains *concentrated* in less-developed regions and countries, and in this way the economic gap between rich countries and poor countries is rather getting wider.

Moreover, the problem of inequality in sharing the benefits of economic globalization exists not only between countries but also within countries. Within a country, the share of income going to the richest has been growing rapidly, while the share going to the less affluent has been shrinking, and consequently rich people have been getting richer, while middle-class and poor people have been getting poorer. For example, the information provided in the World Inequality Database shows that in the United States the share of national income taken by the top 1 percent has nearly doubled in recent decades from 10.3 percent in 1980 to 18.7 percent in 2019, while the share going to the bottom 50 percent has shrunk from 20.1 percent to 13.5 percent.[20] At the global level, according to Credit Suisse Research Institute, the richest 1 percent of the world's population now owns 50.1 percent of the world's wealth, up from 42.5 percent in 2008, which clearly shows that global wealth has been and will be increasingly *concentrated* among a few people at the top.[21]

18. Hellmann, "Advanced Economies."
19. Chen and Tavallion, "Developing World," 1603.
20. See "Income Inequality, USA, 1913–2019."
21. Shorrocks et al., *Global Wealth Report 2017*.

After all, though economic globalization offers some material benefits to humanity, particularly economic growth and its impact on a certain degree of reduction in absolute poverty, it also poses serious challenges for the long-term stability and prosperity of the entire human race, and the most critical one is its movement toward intensifying the polarization of wealth, bipolarization between "the haves" who are getting more and more profits from the globalizing economy and "the have-nots" who are becoming more and more excluded from its profits. Neoliberal globalists claim that the market itself can and will eventually resolve all these problems with its self-regulating mechanism, but, as seen above in statistical trends in economic inequality, such a thing as a fair distribution of benefits from economic globalization certainly does not happen *automatically* without human involvement or intervention—be it organizing or engaging in social movements or campaigns at the grassroots level or making policies and laws at the (inter-)governmental level. Thus, rather than simply expecting the workings of the invisible hand of the free market, we humans must *do something* about an increasingly entrenching "global apartheid,"[22] the widening and deepening separation between rich and poor, between included and excluded. In other words, the contemporary world of global capitalism through economic globalization urgently demands, for the peaceful co-existence and co-prosperity of *all* people, our more ethico-socio-political active measures to address and redress the issues related to economic injustice inherent in the very structure of global neoliberal capitalism.

Hence, as Stiglitz aptly points out, the real problem lies not with economic globalization as such, but with "how it has been managed" by us humans.[23] However, I suspect, neoliberal globalists and giant multinational corporations rather seek to make us insensitive, blind, and deaf to the critical challenges of contemporary economic globalization, particularly the widening gap between the haves and the have-nots caused by

22. Gernot Köher first used the term "global apartheid" as the title of his journal article in *Alternatives*. Recently, Žižek emphatically and frequently employs this term as he insists, with reference to Peter Sloterdijk's *In the World Interior of Capital*, that capitalist globalization today stands for a self-enclosed globe separating the inside from its outside. See Žižek, *Trouble in Paradise*, 63; Žižek, *Courage of Hopelessness*, 10–11.

23. Stiglitz, *Globalization and Its Discontents*, 214, where he particularly points to the dysfunction of human-made international economic institutions, such as the International Monetary Fund (IMF), the World Bank, and the World Trade Organization (WTO).

the concentration of power and wealth amongst a select group of regions, nations, corporations, and people at the expense of the general public. They seem to continuously imbue society with their ideology, their preferred norms, ideas, values, and beliefs, and thus instill into the public mind the *uncritical* connection of global capitalism with what they claim to be the universal benefits of market expansion and liberalization, liberalization particularly from the political realm. That is, for its unfettered expansion and intensification the world of global capitalism through economic globalization creates, or rather *must* create, human beings who fully conform to the symbolic order and imperatives of global neoliberal capitalism and thus act in accordance with its prescribed codes of conduct. Indeed, as will be discussed, the cultural dimension of globalization plays a key role in this undertaking, namely, in making human beings into faithful consumers in a globalized market.

Cultural Globalization: Creating a World of Global Consumers

"Cultural globalization,"[24] which refers to the increasingly widening, deepening, speeding-up, and growing impact of cultural connectivity and interdependence across the globe, is said to "lie at the very heart of contemporary globalization"[25] for the simple reason that "it is an 'in here' phenomenon . . . influencing intimate and personal aspects of our lives."[26] In other words, it is in and through culture in general and mass culture in particular that people are most immediately and powerfully experiencing globalization in their daily lives. As explained earlier, it is the process of economic globalization that accelerates cultural transmissions across the globe through the ongoing rapid transformation and development of technologies not only in the field of transportation but also, and more importantly, in the field of media and information-communications. In this regard, it seems safe to say that the neoliberal logic of contemporary

---

24. There are largely two different perspectives on cultural globalization. One of the popular views is global cultural homogenization, which is also variously expressed in terms like "McDonaldization," "Coca-colonization," "Americanization," or "Western cultural imperialism," whereas another perspective regards cultural globalization as a process of hybridization, creolization, or indigenization in virtue of the global-local dialectic. See Hopper, *Understanding Cultural Globalization*, 87–110.

25. Steger, *Globalization*, 80.

26. Giddens, *Runaway World*, 12.

economic globalization is the driving force behind the cultural dimension of globalization.

How, then, does cultural globalization operate *in favor of* global neoliberal capitalism today? Put another way, what kind of message does market globalism infuse into the popular mind by means of "culture,"[27] both in its non-material (a set of ideas, beliefs, and aspirations) and material (the physical expressions of those ideas, beliefs, and aspirations) forms? Indeed, the rapid transmission of capitalist cultural contents and products around the world, which *contain* certain meanings, ideas, beliefs, interests, norms, attitudes, and values, increasingly affects the (re)shaping of the perceptions, sensibilities, aspirations, identities, and lifestyles of people *as* human beings.[28] In consideration of such decisive, crucial impact of cultural globalization on human consciousness and praxis in their depth, I argue, our concern must lie with *what* message it conveys to us, implicitly as well as explicitly, in terms of its constitutively transformative power that defines what it means to be human in this globalizing world—the anthropology of globalization.

As with economic globalization, there are obviously some benefits that cultural globalization can bring to humankind.[29] One of the major advantages, from the standpoint of uplifting the spiritual/cultural condition of human existence, is that cultural globalization could offer us more opportunities to acknowledge our common humanity beyond long-standing cultural, religious, national, racial, ethnic boundaries, which have been a recipe for conflicts and wars throughout human history, by allowing us to broaden the range of cultural experiences that we can have. This is all the more so today when the revolutionary development of ever faster and far-reaching media and information-communications technologies (such as the Internet, digital devices, social networking service (SNS), cable television, etc.) are proceeding rapidly, through which cultural flows across the globe are getting much more extended and intensified.

---

27. Admittedly, "culture" is so notoriously contested and complicated a concept that it does not lend itself to a consensus definition. For a variety of debates related to the concept of culture, see Hopper, *Understanding Cultural Globalization*, 37–43.

28. For a critical analysis on how capitalist culture strongly influences the construction of human nature and subjectivity, see Dean, *Capitalism and Citizenship*.

29. For a succinct explanation about the benefits of cultural globalization, see Min, "Deconstruction and Reconstruction," 38–39.

However, it must be seriously noted that this spiritual/cultural benefit from cultural globalization is not something *already* real or given but rather something *yet* imaginary or, at best, *still* ideal or potential. Put differently, the actuality of so-called global community, where we all live together in peace and harmony irrespective of differences in nationality, gender, language, race, religion, etc. by recognizing our shared identity and common aspirations as the same human beings, does not come *naturally* from the increasing extent and frequency of cross-cultural encounters and exchanges. That is to say, the mere *formal* fact that people of different nationalities, genders, languages, or religions communicate with each other—either virtually (online) or physically (offline)—and enjoy different cultural forms and traditions together does not necessarily guarantee the uplifting of their spiritual/cultural consciousness as cosmopolitan or global "citizenship."[30] Rather, as is often the case with any ideological claims, such beautiful yet reified images or metaphors of cultural globalization (e.g., "global community" or "global village") may hide its real problems, particularly in terms of *content*; namely, the messages or meanings expressed and diffused in a variety of forms in the process of cultural globalization, in effect, pose serious but often unrecognized threats to the depth of our being-human.

More specifically, the most serious problem of contemporary cultural globalization in terms of content is that what it is to globalize is, simply put, "the capitalist culture of nihilism," to borrow a phrase from Min,[31] which indeed informs the anthropology of globalization, i.e., the view of human subjectivity in the globalizing context. In what sense, then, can it be said that contemporary capitalist culture is *nihilistic* with respect to anthropology? Current globalization processes, as we have discussed repeatedly, are essentially driven by the globalization of the neoliberal capitalist economy, and accordingly the culture that is to be globalized primarily is nothing else than the consumerist culture of capitalism: "Consumerism represents the fundamental doctrine of contemporary capitalism: a cultural ideology founded on the idea and the imperative of consumption."[32] Along the same lines, to achieve with-

---

30. As Dean points out, "citizenship" here should be conceived of not merely as little more than "taxpaying and consumption," but as "public-spiritedness," which yet now "seems impossible because our lives are wholly dependent on a culture (capitalism)" (Dean, *Capitalism and Citizenship*, xi, 5).

31. Min, "Sin," 575.

32. Xavier, *Subjectivity*, 2.

out much difficulty its sole goal of maximizing economic profits, most of which go to a few giant MNCs and big capitalists, global capitalism first and foremost requires the multitude as what Erich Fromm once called "*Homo Consumens*,"[33] who are preoccupied with consumption and thereby willing to buy everything that captures their immediate attention and instinctive desire. Global neoliberal capitalism marked by consumerism seeks to create globalized societies where consumption is the highest principle and categorical imperative, and thus favors human beings who change themselves according to all external, sensible stimulations with no consistency in their own interiority because the more changeable and inconsistent they are, the more things they can buy. Therefore, in the world of global neoliberal capitalism,

> [t]he human being is no longer a subject of self-determining intellect and will who can shape an identity of his or her own with an intellectual power to make independent judgments and a volitional power to determine his or her own actions and life accordingly. Instead, the human subject is reduced to a mere succession of the moments of desire in all its difference, multiplicity, fragmentation, relativity, and rootlessness.[34]

This kind of "global consumer" as a passive victim of *extrinsic* desires beyond one's control—who is, without self-determining subjectivity, *subjected* to mere sensuous feelings or contingent, irrational inclinations aroused by external stimuli (such as sight of new commodities endlessly released onto the market) and thereby always ready to buy commodities in store and online—is precisely what the contemporary culture of capitalist globalization is eager to produce and cultivate, combined with ongoing techno-digital developments in global mass media and information-communications.[35] Furthermore, global capitalism today not only

---

33. Fromm, *Revolution of Hope*, 38; Fromm, *On Disobedience*, 95; Fromm, *To Have*, 176.

34. Min, "Deconstruction and Reconstruction," 40.

35. The French philosopher Bernard Stiegler characterizes this process of turning people into uncritical, uncreative, passive slaves of capitalist culture fed by advanced technology as the "proletarianization of the consumer," which is the distinctive feature of "consumer capitalism" today, in contrast with the productive capitalism of the eighteenth century based on the proletarianization of workers; see Stiegler, *For a New Critique*. For a research pertaining to the intimate link between contemporary processes of subjectivation and consumerism, see Baudrillard, *Consumer Society*; Bauman, *Consuming Life*; Davis, "Commodification of Self," 41–49; Dufour, *Art of Shrinking Heads*; Xavier, "Subjectivity Under Consumerism," 207–16.

commodifies or commercializes everything including culture, but also, and more importantly, *culturalizes* or *aestheticizes* commodities themselves—making them as sensuously attractive and appealing as possible to buyers—in close tandem with a variety of new strategic anthropological devices for *subjectivation*, "a psychological colonization of subjectivity,"[36] such as the psychologies of advertising, marketing, commodity branding, etc.[37] In this way, "self-formation is in fact exteriorized, since the locus is not on an inner self but on an outer world of objects and images valorized by commodity culture."[38] Put differently, capitalist globalization with this aestheticization of the market itself both "produces our very subjectivity and kills it in the process."[39] It is in this very sense of reducing and degrading human beings to *mere* consumers, for whom there is no deeper meaning to the world than the extent of their own sensations, feelings, emotions, desires in all their particularity and contingency, and thus eroding the very *subjectivity* of the human subject, that the culture of global capitalism, in essence, amounts to the global culture of nihilism.

In conclusion, as mentioned earlier, globalization as such is neither good nor bad; rather, it is "Janus-faced"[40] in the sense that it can either "bolster the potential for universal human development" or "bring about conditions that would result in the unprecedented impoverishment of humankind on a global scale."[41] Indeed, it is *we humans* that are responsible for its directions and consequences; in other words, globalization does not proceed outside the realm of human intellect, will, and action. Nevertheless, as we have discussed so far, in the currently prevailing anthropology of globalization there is or, more precisely, there should be no room for such responsible human subject because contemporary capitalist globalization—for its limitless expansion, intensification, velocity, and impact—necessarily demands humans *without* subjectivity, the capacity

36. Xavier, "Subjectivity Under Consumerism," 209.

37. Apple co-founder Steve Jobs's famous statement about Apple's DNA is a notable example of the culturalization of commodities. At the end of the launching event of the iPad 2 in March 11, 2011, he said: "It's in Apple's DNA that technology alone is not enough—it's technology married with liberal arts, married with the humanities, that yields us the result that makes our heart sing." For an in-depth study on advertising and marketing in terms of the culturalization of commodities, see Goldman and Papson, *Sign Wars*.

38. Davis, "Commodification of Self," 44.

39. Min, "Sin," 576.

40. Das, *Two Faces of Globalization*, 90.

41. Hebron and Stack, *Globalization*, 5.

for self-transcendence effected by self-determination. They are meant to be the subjects of slavish, consumerist nihilism, who always accommodate themselves *unthinkingly* to the ideological claims of global neoliberal capitalism, thereby immersing themselves in immediate, particular, and contingent, yet insatiable and endless, desires for commodities or commodified images and symbols, without moral, ethical, social, or communal sensibilities. To produce such global consumers, contemporary capitalist globalization strategically disseminates powerful cultural-ideological messages and images that promote neoliberal consumerist values and lifestyles, especially via the mass media and the Internet, thereby creating collective meanings and shaping people's identities in accord with the capitalist culture of consumerist nihilism. Consequently, in the world of global capitalism today, human beings are more and more *forced* to constitute and construct their humanness under the globalizing domination of capitalist powers, with culture-ideology control in everyday life through specific—both online and offline—forms of global consumerist rhetoric and practice, which then ultimately determine the very subjectivity of the human subject *as* a global consumer, *as* the nihilistic, aesthetic (in the Kierkegaardian sense) state of existence.[42]

Interestingly and arguably, it is quite revealing to note that this anthropology of contemporary capitalist globalization apparently goes hand in hand with, and gets reinforced or inspired by, the anthropology of postmodernism famously characterized by the "death of the subject"—though many postmodern intellectuals seem to be very critical of global capitalism as such—to which then the focus of our discussion must now turn.

Postmodernism and the *Death of the Subject*

The word "postmodernism" is not an unequivocal term to describe for various reasons. One of them is related to the fact that it is still a contemporary phenomenon; that is to say, we are very much in the middle of this movement. The claim to know the contemporary is often criticized as committing a sort of conceptual violence, a way of fixating the fluid and volatile *now* into a confined, regulated form. Another noticeable reason

42. According to Kierkegaard, there are three chief stages of existence as three existential possibilities: the aesthetic, the ethical, and the religious (pagan and Christian). The aesthetic stage of existence is characterized by the lack of self-determined commitment and decision as well as the preoccupation with sensual pleasures.

is that postmodernism is by no means a single, unitary movement, far from forming a unified school of thought. In fact, it is hardly the case that even those usually referred to as prominent postmodern thinkers, such as Jacques Derrida, Michel Foucault, Gilles Deleuze, and others, declare themselves as postmodernists. Nonetheless, it is both necessary and inevitable for us—especially, but not exclusively, as philosophers, religious scholars, or theologians—to carefully read and properly respond to the sign of the times (*Zeitgeist*) that defines the cultural/spiritual ethos and context in which we are living, i.e., the ideals, beliefs, attitudes, values, and aspirations that are so pervasive in our contemporary culture as to touch our everyday lives. Therefore, despite such difficulties in defining postmodernism, it is imperative to identify and make sense of a set of its important and essential claims that are commonly recognized among so-called postmodern thinkers.

As the name, *post*-modernism suggests, it signifies something that comes *after* and/or *against* the modern era.[43] Specifically, it involves a reaction against, or a rejection of, the assumptions that have been perceived for the last several centuries as constitutive of modern culture and civilization: "*Postmodernism* refers to an intellectual mood and an array of cultural expressions that call into question the ideals, principles, and values that lay at the heart of the modern mind-set."[44] Accordingly, there are some *anti-modern* characteristics that unify the otherwise diverse strands of postmodernism, and, in my view, those can be categorized roughly into two positions or perspectives, each in terms of its way of looking at "subjectivity" and "objectivity" respectively which indeed served in the modern Western world as *the* distinctive, overriding categories in pursuit of rational truth[45] in both theoretical and practical spheres. Postmodernism attacks the modern ideals relating to subjectivity and objectivity, namely, philosophical subjectivism and scientific objectivism. Postmodernism abandons the modernist assumption that reality (the objective world) is ordered according to timeless, universal truth, such as the laws

---

43. For a survey of the archaeology of the term *postmodernism*, see Best and Kellner, *Postmodern Theory*, 5–16; Rose, "Defining the Post-Modern," 119–36.

44. Grenz, *Primer on Postmodernism*, 12.

45. This modern searching for rational truth operates with what is called "the correspondence theory of truth" inherited from the classical notion of truth, that is, the correspondence or conformity between our proposition/judgment (subject) and reality (object). Yet, contrary to the classical tradition, modernity posits the subject at the center and criterion of truth, i.e., the conformity of object *to subject*, instead of the conformity of subject *to object* in the classical tradition.

of nature, which human reason (the subjective self) can fully discover, grasp, and act upon *as* the final arbiter of truth; postmodernists even go to the extent of blurring the very modern distinction between subject and object.[46]

More specifically, postmodernism, with respect to objectivity, rejects the modernist assertion of scientific objectivism, that is, the modern assumption that the objective world, a mechanistic, orderly, harmonious, rational *uni*verse, exists out there, independent of any particular perspectives or methods, and thus waits to have its inherent truth discovered or unlocked only by means of universal scientific procedures.[47] Against the modern scientific, realist, objectivist understanding of *the* world, postmodernism argues that it is in fact an ever-changing human construction which is not objectively real and true, namely, that different groups of people construct different discourses about the world they experience.[48] Hence, postmodern thinkers dismiss "the possibility of constructing a single correct worldview and are content simply to speak of many views and, by extension, many *worlds*."[49] Along these lines, they argue for the end of universalizing, totalizing grand theory, the one true, unified body of knowledge based on scientific-rationalistic foundationalism, which theorizes about the single, integral, objective world; indeed, they rather favor micro-discourses or stories about worlds in all their particularity, multiplicity, fragmentation, and plurality—as witness Lyotard's "incredulity toward metanarratives."[50]

Along with the rejection of the modern ideal of scientific objectivism, postmodernism also attacks the modernist insistence on

---

46. This postmodern blurring of the subject-object distinction extends to the obliteration of distinctions between truth and fiction, reality and fantasy, and so forth.

47. For the postmodern worldview as a rejection of the modern realist, objectivist view, see Anderson, *Reality*. In fact, the modern scientific, realist, objectivistic worldview has been greatly challenged within the field of science itself and particularly by the early twentieth-century developments of new theories in physics, such as Relativity Theory and Quantum Theory; see Bohm, "Postmodern Science," 386–88.

48. Anderson, *Reality*, x–xi. Friedrich Nietzsche, who is widely hailed as the forerunner of postmodernism, is the first philosopher to *radically* call into question the modern enterprise of rationalistic and objectivistic knowledge and truth about reality, arguing that reality or the world is a purely human creation like a work of art, which comes from our own perspective; see Nietzsche, *Will to Power*, 14–15; Nietzsche, "On Truth and Lie," 15–49.

49. Grenz, *Primer on Postmodernism*, 40. Emphasis mine.

50. Lyotard, *Postmodern Condition*, xxiv.

philosophical subjectivism which has been generally said to be inaugurated by Descartes, particularly with his well-known dictum that *Cogito ergo sum* ("I am thinking therefore I exist"), and to culminate in Kant's Copernican revolution in philosophy and Fichte's subjective idealism. From Cartesian subjectivity as a thinking substance (*res cogitans*) through Kantian subjectivity as the transcendental self to Fichte's subjectivity as the absolute ego, modernity places *rational* human beings at the center of the world and history in place of God, exalting appraisal of the human capacity to attain objective truth, both theoretical/epistemological and practical/moral.[51] Although the notion or idea of subjectivity has been employed in many different ways, most of the postmodern intellectuals share a common interest in being highly critical of, and even hostile to, this modern philosophical subjectivism which, they believe, has been ideologically used to suppress, totalize, domesticate, or colonize the otherness and difference of others. In this context, they pronounce or even celebrate the "death of the subject," arguing that, contrary to the modernist contention, the human subject is neither a self-identical rational, autonomous ego nor a constituting soul of the other, but, rather, a radically de-centered and structurally constituted product by otherness—whether it be language, discourse, culture, power, ideology, or the unconscious. For them, in other words, subjectivity is merely the effect from, or even the invention by, some exteriority foreign to itself.[52] In this regard, it is not a coincidence that some postmodernists often invoke the etymological root of the word "subject," identifying it as a derivative of the Latin word *subjectum*, which literally means *that which lies under* or "one who

51. The modern philosophical views on the subject from Descartes through Kant to Fichte will be further explicated in the first section of the next chapter (chapter 2).

52. This dissolution of the Enlightenment's autonomous, rational "subject" into the social, cultural structure and context became evident for the first time in what is known as "structuralism" whose major proponents are Ferdinand de Saussure (linguistic structuralism), Claude Lévi-Strauss (anthropological/cultural structuralism), early Jacques Lacan (psychoanalytic structuralism), Louis Althusser (ideological structuralism), and Roland Barthes (literary structuralism). In fact, most of the prominent postmodern philosophers, also known as "post-structuralists," that include Lyotard, Foucault, Derrida, and others, are all affected by structuralism in one way or another, particularly in terms of their anti-modern views on human subjectivity. Concerning the relationship between structuralism and post-structuralism (postmodernism), it could be said that there is a key difference between them, though the one has its roots in the other: namely, that post-structuralism emphasizes the incoherence, contingency, fluidity, and volatility of structure itself, while structuralism focuses on its coherence, systematicity, totality, and universality.

is under the dominion of a sovereign, etc."[53] Thus, they argue that the subject, as the root of the word suggests, always-already presupposes the precedence of some external power over which it can scarcely exert any control—that is to say, the subject in this sense denotes "subjection."[54]

Structure-wise, this postmodern outlook, with its claiming of the death of the subject in the sense of subjection or subjugation seems suspiciously similar to, and even intimately connected with, the anthropology of capitalist globalization that we have discussed earlier, i.e., the human being who is, *without* subjectivity, *subjected* to the imperialism of a globalizing market as a faithful global consumer. This being the case, it would be necessary to further explore the postmodern view of the subject as *subjectlessness* or *subjectivation*. To this end, since postmodernism is not just a general discourse of social, cultural phenomenon, but rather it has been buttressed and justified by powerful philosophical arguments,[55] I would like to briefly survey the deconstructive views of human subjectivity, particularly advanced by two prominent postmodern philosophers: Michel Foucault and Jacques Derrida.

Michel Foucault: The Death of Man

Discussions about the death of the subject in postmodernism are often carried out with reference to the work of Foucault. Throughout his life and works,[56] Foucault was preoccupied with a comprehensive and thoroughgoing critique of modernity, particularly problematizing modern forms of rational and universal subjectivity as totalitarian and domineering in the sense that it reduces the other to an object of knowledge, a sheer moment of its own immanent activity.[57] Not being satisfied with Nietzsche's death of God, therefore, he insists on the anticipation of the

---

53. Onions et al., *Oxford Dictionary of English Etymology*, s.v. "Subject."

54. Cf. Butler, *Psychic Life of Power*.

55. It seems very ironical that postmodernism, which is anti-philosophical in nature, is undergirded by a very rigorous philosophical movement called "post-structuralism." For deeper discussions on this matter, see Baynes et al., *After Philosophy*.

56. For a biographical information about Foucault, see Eribon, *Michel Foucault*, and Miller, *Passion of Michel Foucault*.

57. Cf. Foucault, "Subject and Power," 777: "I would like to say . . . what has been the goal of my work during the last twenty years. . . . My objective . . . has been to create a history of the different modes by which, in our culture, human beings are made subjects."

"death of man," precisely because, in his estimation, the real oppressive force in the modern world is not God but human beings or, more exactly, the very conception of "man" as the rational subject of the Enlightenment. As sarcastically stated in the following passage, Foucault sees the modern advocacy of *man* in a very critical way:

> To all those who still wish to talk about man, about his reign or his liberation, to all those who still ask themselves questions about what man is in his essence, to all those who wish to take him as their starting-point in their attempts to reach the truth, to all those who, on the other hand, refer all knowledge back to the truths of man himself, to all those who refuse to formalize without anthropologizing, who refuse to mythologize without demystifying, who refuse to think without immediately thinking that it is man who is thinking, to all these warped and twisted forms of reflection we can answer only with a philosophical laugh—which means, to a certain extent, a silent one.[58]

Central to Foucault's attack on subjectivity is the focus on the *formation* of the modern subject, tracing the birth of the very idea of "man" as such by using an archeological-genealogical method.[59] Specifically, his key strategy in this genealogy of man (the modern subject) is to de-center or dismantle the Enlightenment's vision of autonomous, rational, universal subjectivity by paying special attention to the socio-historical aspects of *discourses*—meaning "ways of constituting knowledge, together with the social practices, forms of subjectivity and power relations which inhere in such knowledges and the relations between them"[60]—which

---

58. Foucault, *Order of Things*, 342–43.

59. It is generally agreed that Foucault's philosophical method made some transition from archaeology to genealogy in 1970s, particularly with his major work *Discipline and Punish* (1975), which is also characterized as a shift to the later Foucault (genealogist) from the early Foucault (archeologist). It is true that Foucault's use of the term genealogy is distinguished from archeology, but this does not necessarily mean that his archaeological method was forsaken and then replaced by a genealogical method. Rather, this transition is better understood as a methodological expansion and enrichment, as Foucault himself says: "'archeology' would be the appropriate methodology of the analysis of local discursivities, and 'genealogy' would be the tactics whereby on the basis of the descriptions of these local discursivities, the subjective knowledges which were thus released would be brought into play" (Foucault, *Power/Knowledge*, 85). In this book I use these two terms interchangeably to refer to the Foucauldian method at large that raises questions about *how* current conceptions, categories, practices, institutions, etc., came to be the way they are.

60. Weedon, *Feminist Practice*, 108. The term "discourse" has many different

he inherited, to some extent, from structuralists.[61] Following their lead, Foucault claims that "man" is neither an independent, transcendental self with an unchanging essence nor a constituting subject, but rather, deep down, a socio-historical construct constituted by extrinsic factors that we nevertheless take for granted and thus unconsciously incorporate into ourselves, namely, the mechanisms of *power* inscribed and operated in various modern knowledge and social practices which fundamentally affect our day-to-day living experiences. That is, the notion of the human subject is constitutively bound up with, and inseparable from, the discursive workings of social structures, institutions, and practices in all their power relations.[62]

Foucault conducts throughout his scholarly life a series of intensive studies of modern discourses about "man" as diverse as psychiatry (madness),[63] medicine (clinic),[64] criminology (penal system),[65] sexology (sexuality),[66] and especially the human sciences (economics, biology, psychology, sociology, philology, linguistics, literature, etc.),[67] questioning how they have emerged and how they have been tied to the complex operations of power in modern Western society, particularly in terms of the formation of "man" (the human subject). Having carried out these archeological-genealogical studies, Foucault seems to conclude that "man" is a modern *invention* as a discursive construct to regulate and discipline people as "economically useful" and "politically conservative"[68] members of society. For example, Foucault shows in his first book, *Madness and Civilization*, how psychiatry, a discourse practiced in the institution of the mental hospital, employs scientific knowledge to make distinctions between the sane and the insane, the normal and the abnormal, the sick

---

meanings according to who is using it. For Foucault, as Weedon defines, discourse refers not only to a general aspect of language use, but also to specific social institutions, practices, forms of subjectivity, and power relations involved in it. For Foucault's own in-depth discussions on discourse, see Foucault, *Archaeology of Knowledge*.

61. For a discussion about Foucault's relation *with and beyond* structuralism, see Dreyfus and Rabinow, *Michel Foucault*; Megill, *Prophets of Extremity*, 203–19.

62. Grenz, *Primer on Postmodernism*, 127.

63. See Foucault, *Madness and Civilization*.

64. See Foucault, *Birth of the Clinic*.

65. See Foucault, *Discipline and Punish*.

66. See Foucault, *History of Sexuality*.

67. See Foucault, *Order of Things*.

68. Foucault, *History of Sexuality*, 37.

and the healthy, so as to normalize, naturalize, and objectify humanity. Foucault argues that all these judgmental distinctions, which he also refers to as "dividing practices,"[69] are, in fact, historically contingent, socially constructed, culturally variable, and thus subject to change.

Consequently, for Foucault, the subject as rational "man" is nothing more than a *fiction* made up and disseminated by modern discourses which indeed strategically function as, to use Althusser's terms, *ideological apparatuses* of power and domination, as opposed to neutral and objective vehicles of truth, progress, and emancipation.[70] In other words, it is various ideological and power-laden discourses—as the systems of domestication, categorization, marginalization, and exclusion—that themselves produce the very idea of "man" (the human subject) and not the other way around. In short, our picture of humanity as rational and universal subjectivity is merely a product of modern Western systems of knowledge as *power*, and these came into being in the age of the Enlightenment with the birth of modern discourses about man, including the human sciences, which in turn objectify, categorize, and domesticate the other or otherness. In this context, Foucault proclaims the "death of man" in the emerging postmodern *episteme*:[71] "As the archaeology of our thought easily shows, man is an invention of recent date. And one perhaps nearing its end . . . one can certainly wager that man would be erased, like a face drawn in the sand at the edge of the sea."[72]

Jacques Derrida: The Deconstruction of Subjectivity

Derrida is unquestionably one of the most influential, rigorous philosophers of postmodernism.[73] He does not attempt to construct something new on the foundation of the old either by endorsing it or by criticizing it; nor does he simply destruct or destroy it from the outside. He rather calls into question the very idea of "foundation" in its universality,

69. Foucault, "Subject and Power," 777.

70. Best and Kellner, *Postmodern Theory*, 41. For more details, see Foucault, *Order of Things*, 344–87.

71. "Episteme" here refers to the knowledge system of a particular time. Foucault defines it as "the total set of relations that unite, at a given period, the discursive practices that give rise to epistemological figures, sciences, and possibly formalized systems." Foucault, *Archaeology of Knowledge*, 191.

72. Foucault, *Order of Things*, 387.

73. For a biographical information about Derrida, see Powell, *Jacques Derrida*.

coherence, stability, fixation, and *presence*—from which all texts, arguments, theories, and practices are believed to be derived—by showing that it is *always-already* drifting, unstable, incoherent, and endlessly opening. For Derrida, as for Foucault, the "subject" is certainly one of the signs or names that points to such foundational grounding, especially in the modern Western tradition. The strategy Derrida develops to accomplish the goal of dismantling this modernist foundationalism is called "deconstruction." Thus, to find out how Derrida proceeds to denude and emasculate the concept of the subject, we should first understand what Derrida means by *deconstruction*—the aims and workings of Derridean deconstruction.[74]

Derrida's deconstruction primarily attacks the modern claims to objective truth grounded on trust in *logos* (reason) by launching a ruthless investigation into the nature of language and its relation to the world. He challenges the modern confidence that our linguistic statements are representations of the world in its essential nature and thus unfold definitive truth, with the assumption that language—as a transparent vehicle or tool for the expression of our thoughts rooted in reason—has a single meaning immediately corresponding to a fixed reality as objective presence. To problematize this modern belief based on a representational theory of language, he first puts two distinctive dimensions of language under scrutiny, that is, "speech" and "writing."[75] According to Derrida, all Western thinking can be characterized by its tendency of devaluing "writing" in favor of "speech" on the grounds that writing is less dependent upon the presence of its origin than speech—in terms of the subjective presence of rational thought or mind (logos) as unmediated knowledge of the objective presence of the world—and thus farther removed from the immediacy of meaning that speech holds.[76] Derrida critically labels this tendency "logocentrism" or "phonocentrism," meaning "absolute proximity of voice and being, of voice and the meaning of being, of voice and the ideality of meaning,"[77] which he also calls the "metaphysics of presence."[78] The fundamental problem of logocentrism

---

74. For a readable introduction to Derrida's project of deconstruction, see Caputo, *Deconstruction in a Nutshell*.

75. See Grenz, *Primer on Postmodernism*, 140–41.

76. See Derrida, *Of Grammatology*, 6–44.

77. Derrida, *Of Grammatology*, 11–12.

78. Derrida, *Of Grammatology*, 22–23. Leonard Lawlor defines what Derrida means by "presence" in its three interlocking aspects: "(a) the distance of what is over

and the metaphysics of presence inherent in the Western philosophical tradition, Derrida argues, consists in its necessary search for what he calls the "transcendental signified," some ultimate, unchanging foundation or center for our thought, language, meaning, and experience (such as God, Absolute Spirit, Subject, Reason, Being, and so forth), which then tends to function as the source of violence, oppression, domination, and exclusion.[79]

As he deconstructs this modern inclination toward logocentrism/phonocentrism and the metaphysics of presence, Derrida first sets out to appeal to Saussure's structuralist "thesis of *difference* as the source of linguistic value"[80] that "in language there are only differences. . . . Whether we take the signified or the signifier, language has neither ideas nor sounds that existed before the linguistic system, but only conceptual and phonic differences that have issued from the system."[81] In other words, contrary to the traditional and modern claim, language—for Saussure, language here still refers primarily to the spoken language (phonic signifier) though[82]—does not represent or point to something other than itself, a definite referent for meaning; rather, its meaning (signified) is produced only by the *difference* between signifiers *within* the system of linguistic relations. Derrida agrees with Saussure on this point. Consequently, they both reject the role and significance of the human subject in the creation of meaning as the bearer or producer of language, arguing that signification, the operation of language, depends solely on its inner structure of signifier-signified relations in their arbitrariness beyond, and prior to, subjectivity.[83]

Yet Derrida's deconstructive project goes one step further by *deconstructing* Saussure's linguistic structuralism that still holds on to the

and against (object and form, what is iterable), what we would call 'objective presence,' (b) the proximity of the self to itself in its acts (subjective intuition or content), what we would call 'subjective presence,' and then (c) the unification of these two species of presence, that is, presence and self-presence, in the present (in the 'form of the living present,' which . . . mediates itself through the voice)." Lawlor, *Derrida and Husserl*, 2.

79. Derrida, *Of Grammatology*, 49.

80. Derrida, *Of Grammatology*, 52.

81. Saussure, *Course in General Linguistics*, 120.

82. For Derrida's critique of Saussure's limitations in terms of logocentrism or phonocentrism, see Derrida, *Of Grammatology*, 29–44.

83. "Language is not a function of the speaking subject" (Saussure, *Course in General Linguistics*, 14). "Writing can never be thought under the category of the subject" (Derrida, *Of Grammatology*, 68).

inseparable, though arbitrary and conventional, connection or unity between signifier and signified based on its faith in a basic order and stability beneath the surface of signifying movement.[84] More specifically, Derrida radicalizes Saussure's linguistics by adding a strategic twist to the term "difference"; that is, difference becomes "*différance*." His own neologism *différance*, whose etymological root lies in the Latin verb *differre* (*différer* in French), involves not only "differing" but also "deferring."[85] Derrida argues that language is an *eternal* self-referring, self-regulating system, in the sense that language is a chain of signifiers where a signifier refers to another signifier which "itself is not simply present" and thus refers to another signifier in the same manner, and in that way each signifier becomes in turn what is signified by another signifier, and so on *ad infinitum*.[86] This means that signifiers or signs always-already contain *traces* of each other, and therefore that they have no essential, fixed signified of their own. In other words, no meaning is free from the free, perpetual *play* of signs, and thereby meaning can never be static, determined, absolute, or timeless; instead, it is always-already slithering (or *playing*) and subject to change as signifiers themselves ceaselessly provide new connections and correlations. Thus, Derrida insists, meaning must be indefinitely *deferred*.[87] In this way, with "*différance*" as the interplay of the *spacing* of being different and the *temporalization* of deferring, Derrida seeks to subvert the modern attempt to impose the sense of objective, fixed meaning on the flux of reality and experience which is based fundamentally on its presumption that language and meaning are attributed to human consciousness, mind, reason, or thought (subjectivity).

---

84. Simply put, this "going one step further" is what differentiates Derrida as a *post*-structuralist from Saussure as a structuralist.

85. For Derrida's own semantic analysis of *différance* as the intertwining movement of difference and deferral, see Derrida, *Margins of Philosophy*, 1–27, where he also points out another strategic function in changing "difference" to "*différance*," that is, a strategy for deconstructing the phonocentrism of the Western tradition that writing is simply the representation of speech, which is foundational, by saying that "this graphic difference (*a* instead of *e*), this marked difference between two apparently vocal notations, between two vowels, remains purely graphic: it is read, or it is written, but it cannot be heard. It cannot be apprehended in speech" (Derrida, *Margins of Philosophy*, 3).

86. Derrida, *Positions*, 26. See also Derrida, *Of Grammatology*, 50; Grenz, *Primer on Postmodernism*, 144.

87. See Derrida, *Positions*, 28–29.

In short, for Derrida, *"there is nothing outside of the text,"* that is to say, there is no such thing as a transcendental subject or a univocal meaning external to the free play of linguistic signifiers themselves.[88] Therefore, he argues, we must stop the logocentric search for some foundation, origin, center, or metaphysical anchor that exists outside and beyond *différance*, the differential and deferring play of language within the text. Derrida then expands this constitutive role of *différance* in grammatology (the science of writing) to all realms of human life, including all scientific disciplines,[89] thereby deconstructing the very foundation of modern Western culture, particularly of its all-embracing yet hierarchical, oppressive system of binary oppositions, such as signified/signifier, speech/writing, presence/absence, truth/non-truth, logos/mythos, rational/irrational, philosophy/literature, eternal/temporal, culture/nature, soul/body, male/female, and, most fundamentally, subject/object.[90]

Hence, Derrida's deconstruction targets the concept of subjectivity as well as of objectivity so that the binary opposition between subject and object itself may be fractured. How, then, can Derrida specifically insist that just as the modern claims to objective truth are a myth, so is the modern idea of subjectivity? What is the basis of his argument? For Derrida, the deconstruction of the subject is not only possible but also inevitable, precisely because *différance*, as discussed above, is so primordial or, to use his own vocabulary, "originary"[91] that it exceeds all present things or facts including subjectivity.[92] Put another way, the subject, too, cannot be immune from the deconstructive force or play of *différance*, and therefore the modern conception of autonomous, self-identical, self-present subjectivity as the transcendental foundation for the text in both its meaning (signified) and language (signifier), which exists outside of the text (a network of linguistic relations and activities), must be deconstructed. The following long paragraph conspicuously shows Derrida's argument for the priority and superiority of *différance* over the subject as well as the object:

88. Derrida, *Of Grammatology*, 158.

89. See Derrida, *Of Grammatology*, 92–93.

90. The problem Derrida and other post-structuralists have with this system of binary oppositions is that in it there is always a wider power structure involved in a way that one term is always seen as superior to and more primary, original, essential than the other and thus becomes privileged and powerful.

91. Derrida, *Of Grammatology*, 23.

92. See Heartfield, *Death of the Subject*, 17–18.

> What differs? Who differs? What is *différance*? If we answered these questions . . . before suspecting their very form . . . we would immediately fall back into what we have just disengaged ourselves from. In effect, if we accepted the form of the question, in its meaning and its syntax ("what is?" "who is?" "who is it that?"), we would have to conclude that *différance* has been derived, has happened, is to be mastered and governed on the basis of the point of a present being, which itself could be some thing, a form, a state, a power in the world . . . a *what*, or a present being as a *subject*, a *who*. And in this last case, notably, one would conclude implicitly that this present being, for example a being present to itself, as consciousness, eventually would come to defer or to differ . . . But in neither of these cases would such a present being be "constituted" by this *différance*.[93]

In this connection, Derrida claims that our experience of existing as the subject in its modern sense is an illusion; what we actually experience about ourselves is the result or product of a complex web of language that is constantly both differing and deferring. That is, it is not the human subject that constructs the world, or the text, as the modern mind maintains, but it is the text of *différance* that constitutes the subject, and in this sense subjectivity refers thoroughly to subjection or subjectivation: "the subject (in its identity with itself, or eventually in its consciousness of its identity with itself, its self-consciousness) is *inscribed* in language, is a 'function' of language."[94] Since Derrida's deconstruction of the subject is so profound and radical in this way, he even calls into question socio-political discourses on "democracy" or "human rights," for example, "their opposition to racism, totalitarianism, to Nazism, to fascism, etc.," because all this—inasmuch as it is advocated "in the name of spirit, and even of the freedom of (the) spirit," whether it be the freedom (emancipation) of people or the freedom (Heideggerian *Gelassenheit*) of the Spirit of the West—paradoxically relapse into the very source of racism, totalitarianism, Nazism, and fascism, namely, the "metaphysics of *subjectivity*."[95]

In conclusion, the point I am trying to make here in this section is that, whether postmodernists (including Foucault and Derrida) would agree or not, whether they recognize it or not, their common assertion of the *death of the subject*—for instance, Foucault's "death of man" and

---

93. Derrida, *Margins of Philosophy*, 14–15.
94. Derrida, *Margins of Philosophy*, 15. Emphasis mine.
95. Derrida, *Of Spirit*, 39–40. See also Heartfield, *Death of the Subject*, 18–19.

Derrida's "deconstruction of subjectivity"—is possibly used, or misused, as the logic of contemporary global capitalism, as Fredric Jameson seemed already to anticipate about two and a half decades ago.[96] To be specific, my critical observation is that, as we have examined thus far, there is a common thread running through both capitalist globalization and postmodernism in terms of the erosion of human subjectivity. Both have a very similar view on human beings, even though the former promotes it in a normative way ("should be") and the latter explains in a descriptive way ("is"), in the sense that human subjectivity, which involves not only our actions, status, and associations but also our identity and value system, is *constituted* by some extrinsic forces over which we can yet hardly exercise any control: the consumerist logic of the aestheticizing market in the case of capitalist globalization and the structure of ideologies, discourses, or language in the case of postmodernism. After all, the postmodern thesis of the death of the subject may serve as a theoretical/philosophical basis and ideological justification for global capitalism's disgraceful reduction of human beings to mere consumers who are enslaved by sheer capitalistic desires.

Beyond Postmodern Subjectivity in the Context of Globalization

It is certainly appropriate and praiseworthy that postmodern intellectuals make every effort to unearth the kernel of modern subjectivity *as* a reified substance in the sense of the purely self-identical, self-sufficient and hence likely totalitarian, colonizing subject, and thus to deconstruct its evilness in the philosophical and concomitant ethico-social planes. However, in the end, the postmodern assault on the modern subject has thrown out the baby together with the dirty water. *Insofar as* postmodern philosophers are reluctant and hesitant to provide any "alternative" to the modern conception of the subject that they are anxious to reject and deconstruct, their strategic undertaking of the "death of the subject," regardless of their real intentions, tends to lapse into the demise of human subjectivity *as such*—not limited to some inadequate features of peculiarly modern subjectivity as *subjectivism*. In my view, one of the biggest problems with the postmodern project of the death of the subject, which

---

96. See Jameson, *Postmodernism*.

I would call the *abstract* negation[97] of human subjectivity at the risk of over-generalization, is that it ultimately precludes ethical and political possibilities, for there is no subject or agent who can indeed make them happen through one's self-determined actions. What is worse, as already alluded to earlier, it is even quite possible that postmodern *subjectlessness* could function as an ideology or a philosophical anthropology for capitalist globalization that requires for its omnipotent, omnipresent performance sheer sensuous, arbitrary, atomistic, capricious, contingent, non-self-reflective, uncritical consumers who are, without critical subjectivity, purely enthralled by the logic of global capitalism.

To support my critique of the postmodernist-deconstructionist view on subjectivity (the death of the subject) in the context of globalization that I have just presented, I would like to take a look at Žižek's challenges to postmodernism, which, I believe, could be very instructive for and relevant to our discussion here.

Žižek's Critique of Postmodernism in the Context of Capitalist Globalization

Žižek criticizes today's postmodernism for "performing the ultimate service for the unrestrained development of capitalism by actively participating in the ideological effort to render its massive presence invisible."[98] Let me briefly present his critique of postmodernism along these lines, particularly with reference to the problematic of human subjectivity. From my readings of his works, I have come to find that his criticisms can be formulated in three distinctive yet interrelated dimensions: philosophical (against post-structuralism), cultural (against liberal-multiculturalism), and religious (against New Age spiritualism and Western Buddhism).

Philosophically, Žižek advances criticisms of the ideas of the leading post-structuralist philosophers such as Judith Butler,[99] Gilles Deleuze,[100]

---

97. Here I use the term "abstract negation" in the Hegelian sense. For Hegel, as opposed to "determinate negation" which is a relative or relational negation, "abstract negation" just affirms the sheer nothingness (*Nichtigkeit*) of something x.

98. Žižek, *Ticklish Subject*, 261.

99. See Žižek, *Ticklish Subject*, 291–373.

100. See Žižek, *Organs without Bodies*.

Jacques Derrida,[101] Michel Foucault,[102] Emmanuel Levinas,[103] and others. In accordance with its relevance to my research focus, as well as due to space constraints, I will only introduce the gist of Žižek's critique of Derridean deconstructionism here. Žižek's fundamental problem lies with Derrida's later notion of "pure Messianic Otherness," that is, the reduction of otherness (difference) to the forever, impossible "to-come" (*à venir*) of the wholly Other, which in turn implies that contemporary determinate, positive, real differences are rather considered as *betraying* the transcendent principle of the impossible, the absolute purity of difference-to-come (*différance*).[104] This means, after all, that in our relationship with the other we must denounce and renounce any determinate structure involving real others in real circumstances here and now, and instead embrace a "primordial passivity, sentiency, of responding, of being infinitely indebted to and responsible for the call of an Otherness that never acquires positive features but always remains withdrawn, the trace of its own absence."[105] For Žižek, Derrida's insistence on this "messianic structure of 'to come,'" which, against Hegel, argues for "the irreducible excess in the ideal concept which cannot be reduced to the dialectic between the ideal and its actualization,"[106] cannot but ultimately arrive at an improper conclusion: that our "principal ethico-political duty" is not so much to deal with actual, concrete occurrences in the present as to maintain "the gap between the Void of the central impossibility and every positive content giving body to it—that is, never fully to succumb to the enthusiasm of hasty identification of a positive Event with the redemptive promise that is always 'to come.'"[107] Furthermore, Žižek argues that this move can inevitably makes for depoliticization. Facing "the messianic promise of justice" *as* the impossible, we may justly do away with any demand for "its 'ontologization,' its transposition into a set of positive

---

101. See Žižek, *Puppet and the Dwarf*, 139–41; Žižek, "Real of Sexual Difference," 65–70.

102. See Žižek, *Ticklish Subject*, 296–304.

103. See Žižek et al., *Neighbor*, 134–90.

104. Žižek, *Puppet and the Dwarf*, 139–40. Concerning the word "messianic," Derrida distinguishes it from the various historical messianisms; see Caputo, *Prayers and Tears*, 117–18.

105. Žižek, "Real of Sexual Difference," 65.

106. Žižek, *Puppet and the Dwarf*, 140.

107. Milbank et al., *Paul's New Moment*, 80.

legal and political measures."[108] Along the same lines, Žižek condemns as a sort of the "pessimistic wisdom of the failed encounter"[109] postmodern hesitation in general and Derrida's deconstructive hesitation of hope in particular—hope in the promise of justice-to-come that always remains "absolutely undetermined" and "eschatological."[110]

As indicated in the preceding section, I suspect, this Derridean messianic impossibility and hesitation marked by the structure of the *to-come* is closely linked to his stress on the deconstruction of subjectivity. In the same vein, Žižek also maintains that there is no "messianic time" outside the intervention, engagement, and commitment of the subject, individual and collective, irreducible to the objective historical time and process. This means that things can take a messianic turn at any point; if we wait for the time, the time will never come.[111] For Derrida, however, subjectivity itself is always-already deconstructed into the play of *différance* as discussed earlier, which, on Žižek's view, accounts for the constant deferral of decisive political actions. In short, the heart of Žižek's critique of Derridean deconstructionism is that it closes off radical political possibilities particularly in this age of global capitalism by philosophically deconstructing the very concept of the subject that can strive toward making the impossible possible in and through its ethico-political actions.[112]

108. Žižek, "Real of Sexual Difference," 65. See also Min, *Solidarity of Others*, 40–44, where he provides a succinct critique of Derrida's lack of "political" horizon.

109. Milbank et al., *Paul's New Moment*, 80.

110. Derrida, *Specters of Marx*, 65.

111. See Žižek, *Puppet and the Dwarf*, 134–35. In a similar vein, Žižek answers to the question of "When is the right time for revolution?" in the following manner. The time for revolution never becomes objectively ripe, for it is only the subject's intervention itself that reveals the previous stage *as* premature. Therefore, one must "take a leap, throwing oneself into the paradox of the situation, seizing the opportunity and *intervening*, even if the situation was 'premature,' with a wager that *this ever 'premature' intervention would radically change the 'objective' relationship of forces itself, within which the initial situation appeared 'premature'*" (Žižek, *Did Somebody Say Totalitarianism?*, 114).

112. It might be debatable whether Žižek's critical interpretations of Derrida could be fully legitimized or not—particularly whether Derrida's idea of the "messianic structure of *to-come*" (justice-to-come, democracy-to-come, etc.) indeed causes depoliticization. In any event, despite Derrida's own occasional forays into political issues, it seems at least safe to say that he fails to provide a substantial political theory of his own and positive political projects, and this failure is not something accidental but rather something *constitutive* of and *inherent* to his own philosophy of deconstruction which radically rejects any attempts at the metaphysical grounding of the political.

Culturally, Žižek criticizes the postmodern emphasis on multicultural tolerance in connection with liberalism. There are mainly three interrelated reasons in his critique of multiculturalism.[113] First and foremost, multiculturalism is a cultural logic of global capitalism, devised and operated as a fantasy for simply furthering the interests of today's capitalist global market. Along these lines, Žižek claims that "the problematic of multiculturalism (the hybrid coexistence of diverse cultural life-worlds) which imposes itself today is the form of appearance of its opposite, of the massive presence of capitalism as *global* world system: it bears witness to the unprecedented homogenization of today's world."[114] Inasmuch as the globalization of capital creates the conditions for the spreading discourse of cultural diversity and particularities, the very attempt at celebrating multiculturalism and identity politics is nothing but an ideological cover-up for the social reality reigned by the totalizing force of global capitalism. Second, multiculturalism today turns out to be a form of racism or, more precisely, *reflected* (or *reflexive*) racism which paradoxically articulates itself in terms of respect for the other's culture. In other words, "multiculturalist respect for the Other's specificity is the very form of asserting one's own superiority" by positioning oneself at the "privileged *empty point of universality* from which one is able to appreciate (and depreciate) other particular cultures properly."[115] In so doing, today's reflexive multicultural tolerance has within itself its opposite, namely, a hard kernel of fundamentalism and imperialism, of irrational, excessive enjoyment.[116] In this regard, Žižek claims, the concrete realization of rational inclusivity and tolerance coincides with contingent, irrational exclusivity and violence. Third, multiculturalism inhibits politics proper by blurring fundamental political questions and thus trivializing subjective engagement in political actions. In multicultural liberalism, Žižek observes, diversity, multiplicity, and plurality are highly stressed and appreciated on condition that the most basic political order is not brought into question.[117] The vision of horizontal, cultural differences

---

113. I borrow this framework from Dean, *Žižek's Politics*, 115–20.

114. Žižek, *Ticklish Subject*, 261.

115. Žižek, *Ticklish Subject*, 258.

116. For Žižek's examples for this reflected racism, see Žižek, *Fragile Absolute*, 3–11.

117. "Why are so many problems today perceived as problems of intolerance, rather than as problems of inequality, exploitation, or injustice?" (Žižek, *Violence*, 140).

obfuscates the reality of vertical, political antagonism that cuts through the social body:

> [T]he *class* problematic of workers' exploitation is transformed into the *multiculturalist* problematic of the "intolerance of Otherness," and so on, and the excessive investment of multiculturalist liberals in protecting immigrants' ethnic rights clearly draws its energy from the "repressed" class dimension.[118]

What Žižek tries to criticize here is that when "political differences—differences conditioned by political inequality or economic exploitation—are naturalized and neutralized into 'cultural' differences" as something given beyond our control or our choosing, what we can do is only tolerance toward them, remaining "at a safe distance from others."[119]

In short, as Žižek clearly expresses in his conversation with Glyn Daly, his criticism lies not in "multiculturalism as such," but in "the idea that it constitutes the fundamental struggle of today."[120] Specifically, contemporary multiculturalism functions as a tool of depoliticization, and more precisely the depoliticization of the economy in the context of global capitalism by directing people's attention to cultural differences, tolerance for different cultures. In this way, it legitimizes the fantasy that the current order is politically neutral so that there is no need for politically engaged, active citizens as the subjects of politics.

Religiously, Žižek urges that in today's postmodern return of the religious dimension we should fight together particularly against New Age spiritualism (gnosticism, neo-paganism) and Western Buddhism. New Age spiritualism and Western Buddhism assume "the Void as the only true Good"[121] and have the fantastic image of society as a harmonious, organic unity, which, for Žižek, occludes the recognition of irreducible antagonism inherent in real society. In this regard, Žižek contends, New Age spiritualism and Western Buddhism serve today as ideological supplements to global capitalism, operating as a fetish that allows adherents to believe themselves that they are somehow detached from the ruthless capitalist system while they, in fact, fully participate in it in their everyday lives. Especially, in *The Puppet and the Dwarf*, Žižek makes poignant remarks about Western Zen Buddhism, asserting that it is not only

118. Žižek, *Fragile Absolute*, 10.
119. Žižek, *Violence*, 140, 41.
120. Žižek and Daly, *Conversations with Žižek*, 144.
121. Žižek, *Puppet and the Dwarf*, 23.

"the paradigmatic ideology of late capitalism" (the example of "corporate Zen") but also of fascism (the example of Japanese "militaristic Zen" in 1930s), for its meditation technique is "an ethically neutral instrument, which can be put to different sociopolitical uses, from the most peaceful to the most destructive."[122]

According to New Age spiritualism and Western Buddhism, it is the excess of human subjectivity or anthropocentric hubris that disturbs the cosmic balance and harmony of the universe and thereby gives rise to today's social, ecological crises. The only solution, therefore, consists in restoring human beings to their legitimate, constrained place in the global order of Being. In contrast to this postmodern cliché, Žižek emphasizes that we should rather assert "the excess of subjectivity" as the only solution to the current global catastrophe, for "true evil lies not in the excess of subjectivity as such," but "in its reinscription into some global cosmic framework," i.e., the existing capitalist world order that is imagined to be harmonious and peaceful.[123]

In conclusion, as we have examined, Žižek is aggressively opposed to postmodernism, precisely because it functions today as the implicit-obscene ideology of global capitalism which contributes to maintaining the status quo (the capitalist global order) and thus ruling out people's politicization. More fundamentally, I should emphasize that his criticisms against postmodernism in its philosophical, cultural, and religious dimensions target its deconstruction and victimization of subjectivity (the death of the subject) and the ensuing preclusion of the possibility of radical political thoughts and actions (the depoliticized subject) within the liberal societies of contemporary global capitalism.

A Call for a New (Post-)Postmodern Conception of Subjectivity

As discussed in the first section of this chapter, globalization as the context of our life today is not some neutral phenomenon taking place in the spheres of economy, politics, culture, religion, ecology, technology, etc. beyond the interests of specific individuals, groups, or nations and beyond their control and domination. Rather, it is fundamentally driven by the excesses of capitalist desires overwhelmingly performed by some few individuals, groups, and nations, and consequently most other people

---

122. Žižek, *Puppet and the Dwarf*, 26–31.
123. Milbank et al., *Paul's New Moment*, 78.

today have to confront unprecedented levels of social division, conflict, oppression, and alienation on a global scale. This current orientation and movement of capitalist globalization needs to be *rethought, resisted*, and *reformed* with the ultimate hope and goal of making it "work not just for the rich and the more advanced industrial countries but also for the poor and the least developed countries,"[124] to wit, reorienting globalization toward peaceful co-existence and co-prosperity *for all*. Such new orientation and movement absolutely require people to work together with more ethico-political sensibilities, thoughts, and actions than ever before. However, as examined in some detail, the anthropology of capitalist globalization rather promotes uncritical and thoughtless people (global consumers) who are blindly obedient to the imperialist logic of a globalizing market, particularly by means of various kinds of cultural apparatuses. To make matters worse, this, suspiciously enough, seems to have been further backed up and empowered theoretically or philosophically by the contemporary intellectual movement known as postmodernism with its claiming of the death of the subject. In this regard, I argue, we desperately need a new *philosophical* conception of subjectivity fitting in this postmodern context of globalization.

What, then, should this new subjectivity look like? How is it possible to deconstruct and reconstruct postmodern subjectlessness without simply returning to the modern sense of self-identical, self-sufficient subjectivity? In my view, it is necessary to *sublate* (in the Hegelian sense of the term) postmodernism's prevalent view of subjectivity for today's globalizing world. That is, the postmodernist thesis of the death of the subject in its sense of abstract negation is to be *negated* and *transcended* into a more authentic form of (post-)postmodern subjectivity that is proper and necessary to the context of globalization, in which at the same time the appropriateness and relevance of postmodernism's critical gesture toward modern subjectivism is to be *preserved*—particularly in terms of revitalizing sensitivity to and recognition of "relation," "difference," "diversity," and "otherness." In this way, newly refined or reformed postmodern subjectivity could be conceived as a dialectical movement of identity with itself (modernism) and its relation to the other (postmodernism) toward creating a new global order and community as non-alienating, liberating, concrete universality. Put another way, a new conception of subjectivity needs to become constituted as a dialectical totality of three

---

124. Stiglitz, *Globalization and Its Discontents*, 253.

intrinsic elements in their interrelating movement, which I would call "self-transcending drive toward universality," "self-determined or autonomous action," and "solidary relationship with others." I insist that globalization exigently demands people who are equipped with these three aspects in their dynamic interpenetration. They are, in other words, universal subjects or cosmopolitan citizens who are immanently driven by an irresistible, irrepressible longing—springing forth from their innermost being—to transcend themselves toward the universal common good and always try to act autonomously in solidarity with others for the benefit of all people and, by extension, of all entities that *are*. Importantly, it should be emphasized, this cosmopolitan subjectivity absolutely requires for its realization the *process* of cultivation, development, discipline, or education—not only in terms of cognitive learning but also, and more crucially, in terms of experiential enrichment.

The call for such new subjectivity in the postmodern context of globalization compels me to search for philosophical resources from which we can draw the form and content that help in conceptualizing it. In this respect, I would like to argue that we need to discuss in depth Hegel's philosophy of subjectivity, for I find in it the above-stated features or characteristics par excellence which are required for new subjectivity. In what follows, then, I will explore Hegel's view of the subject, with special emphasis on his conception of *spiritual* subjectivity.

CHAPTER 2

A Prelude to Hegelian Subjectivity

BEFORE UNDERTAKING A DETAILED, in-depth study on Hegel's philosophy of subjectivity, it seems necessary to give an overview of it, which begins with looking into some philosophical-historical context from which it arose. As Hegel himself states, philosophy is "*its own time comprehended in thoughts*,"[1] and this statement unquestionably holds true for his own philosophical enterprise too. In this sense, Hegel's philosophy in general, and his philosophy of subjectivity in particular, should be seen as his own perspective on and response to the concerns of his own time. What, then, are the major concerns with which modern philosophers were confronted? How did Hegel come to grips with them on his own terms? This chapter deals with these questions as a prelude to Hegel's philosophy of subjectivity, which will in turn allow us to envision a general picture of what a new, post-postmodern subjectivity proper should look like for the age of globalization beyond its typically modern conception.

In addressing those questions above, I will first delineate the philosophical background that provoked Hegel, in both positive and negative ways, to philosophize about his own vision of subjectivity, that is, the ethos of modern philosophy generally characterized by its "turn to the subject"—the subject as the ultimate reference point for all knowledge and values. I will then introduce the basic structure of Hegel's conception of subjectivity *as* spirit that is his critical response to or, more precisely, his *sublation* of philosophical subjectivism and its attending subject-object dualism that issued from this modern shift to the subject.

1. *PR*, 21.

The Modern Turn to the Subject

The history of philosophy, roughly speaking, consists of a series of attempts to pursue truth, true knowledge of all that *is*—including nature, human beings, and a divine being. One of the fundamental distinctive features of "modern philosophy" in general that marks it off from the classical tradition (Greek-Roman and Medieval philosophies) lies in its *turn to the subject* in searching for truth; in other words, modern philosophy considers the human subject to be *the* source of truth. More specifically, contrary to the classical tradition according to which true knowledge relies on and proceeds from objective reality itself as the source of intelligibility without a sharp separation between being (object) and thought (subject),[2] modern philosophy claims that the human subject, conceived as self-defining[3] and autonomous, is the principle and constitutive power from which derive all knowledge and values about the objective world. In the same vein, since most modern philosophers believe that the human mind is structured in such a way that it can discover, or even construct, the essence of reality and thereby control the world, they are preoccupied with an examination of the structure of the human subject, especially with reference to its own epistemological capacity to know the objective world which is now regarded as "disenchanted" or "desacralized."[4]

To make sense of how the turn to the subject was carried out in modern philosophy, I will single out three representative modern philosophers and present their views on subjectivity: Descartes's "thinking substance," Kant's "transcendental self," and Fichte's "absolute ego." This is certainly a huge topic in itself; given the limitation of space, however, I will only focus on a few essential elements of their epistemologies that are relevant to my argument here.[5]

---

2. In the classical tradition, in fact, the human subject was perceived as part of the entire world or creation and thus always "defined in relation to a cosmic order" (Taylor, *Hegel*, 6).

3. The "self-defining" subject refers to that which defines itself for itself without reference to things other than itself.

4. Taylor, *Hegel*, 9.

5. A further justification for my focus on their epistemologies is as follows. The modern turn to the subject is epitomized primarily in the realm of epistemology—this is why it is also called the "epistemological turn"—and thus its workings in the areas of moral philosophy and others can also be properly grasped only from the standpoint of the epistemological turn, that is, as its derivatives. In this regard, it seems not too inappropriate that I will confine myself here to these philosophers' views of theoretical

Descartes's Subject as Thinking Substance

It was the philosophy of René Descartes, who has been usually called the "father of modern philosophy,"[6] that inaugurated the modern turn to the subject. Descartes attempts to rebuild the systematic edifice of true knowledge upon a firm and solid foundation of absolute certainty. To discover such a certain foundation with absolute clarity and distinctness, he employs the method of universal, radical doubt, i.e., the methodological imperative that "we must doubt everything" (*de omnibus est dubitandum*).[7] Descartes sets out to doubt everything that can possibly be doubted until he can discover something that can no longer be doubted. In the end, by intuition in the very act of doubting, he finds out that there is only one thing that is absolutely certain and indubitable, which is the proposition that "I am thinking, therefore I exist" (*Cogito ergo sum*).[8] Consequently, for Descartes, the subject ("I") *as* a thinking substance (*res cogitans*),[9] "whose *essence* or nature resides only in thinking, and which, in order to exist, has no need of place and is not dependent on any material thing,"[10] becomes the only ultimate reference point (the Archimedean point) for philosophy that has absolute certainty, from which then truths of all things, except *my own existence that thinks*, are to be derived by deduction. In other words, Descartes claims, the subject serves as *the* justifying criterion of both the existence and knowledge of the entire realm of things other than itself, including God as an infinite substance and physical reality (including human body) as an extended substance (*res extensa*).

However, with Descartes's conception of subjectivity as *res cogitans* that is substantially separated from objectivity (*res extensa*), there emerged an apparently unbridgeable gulf between mind and body, thought and sense, the I and the world, and so forth.[11] This Cartesian

---

or epistemological subjectivity.

6. Cf. *LHP III*, 104: "Now we come for the first time to what is properly the philosophy of the modern world, and we begin it with Descartes."

7. *LHP III*, 108.

8. Descartes, *Discourse on the Method*, 28–29.

9. "Substance" here is defined in the modern sense as "that which requires nothing but itself in order to exist."

10. Descartes, *Discourse on the Method*, 29.

11. For Descartes's dualism on mind and body in particular, see his Second Meditation in Descartes, *Meditations on First Philosophy*, 17–24.

subjectivistic move thereafter dominated Western philosophy throughout the seventeenth and eighteenth centuries, in the sense that modern philosophy in general after Descartes grappled with the epistemological problem arising from his strict subject-object dualism, i.e., the dilemma of how the subject, which is *substantially* independent of and separate from the object, could attain truth (true knowledge of the object). Yet, as we will see later in Kant and Fichte as its typical examples, post-Cartesian philosophy tried to resolve this problem not in a way that simply returns to the classical worldview of objectivistic non-dualism, but rather in a way that *radicalizes* the modern turn to the subject into more philosophically sophisticated and refined forms.

Kant's Subject as Transcendental Self

The philosophy of Immanuel Kant could be seen, in a proper sense, as the culmination of this Cartesian legacy. On the one hand, for Kant, as for Descartes, the human subject (the "I think") forms the basis of all knowledge of reality.[12] Along these lines, it is well known that his entire philosophical enterprise is characterized by the Copernican revolution in philosophy in the sense of a revolutionary, radical shift to the subject in seeking true, objective knowledge. Yet, on the other hand, Kant also tries to overcome the limitations of Cartesian solipsistic, atomistic subjectivism and its consequent subject-object dualism by instituting the *transcendental* relations of the subject to the object. Since, in my view, Kant's theory of knowledge both represents the pinnacle of the modern subjective turn and discloses its limits, and since this notably prefigures what Hegel's sublation of modern subjectivity looks like, it would be worthwhile to go over it in some detail.[13]

The distinctive epistemological turn of modern philosophy finds itself truly radicalized and culminating in Kant's *Critique of Pure Reason*. As explicitly stated in the Preface to its second edition, Kant rejects the traditional proposition that the object discloses itself to the subject, and instead claims that the subject itself is fully equipped to impose its

12. "The *I think* must *be able* to accompany all my representations." Kant, *Critique of Pure Reason*, B131, which is henceforth abbreviated as *CPR*; as is standard, I refer to passages by indicating the page number(s) of the first (A) and second (B) original German editions (e.g., A428/B456).

13. In fact, Hegel sees Kant as his most important interlocutor in developing his own philosophical system. See Rockmore, *Before and After Hegel*, 4–5.

own forms on the object prior to its being given to the subject.[14] In other words, Kant focuses on true knowledge that is "occupied not so much with objects but rather with our mode of cognition of objects insofar as this is to be possible *a priori*"—this is what he calls "transcendental."[15]

According to Kant, there are two originally different sources of cognition, intuitions and concepts, each corresponding to distinct faculties of human mind, namely, "sensibility" (*Sinnlichkeit*) as the receptivity of our mind through which objects are given to us and the "understanding" (*Verstand*) as the activity or spontaneity of our mind through which they are thought, judged, and known.[16] For Kant, our knowledge is possible only through a cooperative unification between these two sources, the material and formal aspects of cognition.[17] Kant agrees with empiricists who claim that our knowledge begins with experience (sensibility), but he adds the important proviso that "although all our cognition commences *with* experience, yet it does not on that account all arise *from* experience."[18] This is the point that empiricists overlook, for they claim that all of our knowledge consists only of a series of intuitions or impressions given through our senses. For Kant, these intuitions through sensibility are the mere formless contents of the object upon which the forms (concepts) of the understanding should be imposed to make them *determinate* and hence *known*. In this regard, Kant argues, the function of sensibility consists in producing intuitions of objects and so invoking the activity of the understanding, whereas the function of the understanding lies in transforming these sensible intuitions into knowledge with universal validity and objectivity.

With this overview of Kant's epistemology in mind, let us examine in more detail the *transcendental* elements of cognition presented in his *Critique of Pure Reason*, which precisely accounts for the conception of Kant's subject as "transcendental self," i.e., as that which makes the experience and knowledge of objects possible. Kant first deals with the faculty of "sensibility" in the Transcendental Aesthetic. Here the primary question that concerns Kant is not "what is intuition or sensation?" but rather "*how* is such intuition *possible*?" That is, he asks, "what are the conditions

14. *CPR*, Bxvi.
15. *CPR*, A11/B25.
16. *CPR*, A50/B74.
17. "Thoughts without content are empty, intuitions without concepts are blind" (*CPR*, A51/B75).
18. *CPR*, B1.

necessary for the possibility of sensing objects?" Kant's answer is that there are *a priori* forms of sensibility belonging to the human subject, which are "two pure forms of sensible intuition as principles of *a priori* cognition, namely, space and time."[19] For Kant, "space" and "time" are not features of external objects, but rather necessary elements built into the structure of the human subject—like the "irremovable lens" through which the subject perceives objects—"wherein all of the manifold of appearances is intuited in certain relations."[20] In short, according to Kant, we cannot intuit, sense, or perceive an object *as* an appearance without assigning it a position in time and space that are indeed the *a priori* forms of the subject's sensibility; that is, the subject is equipped with the transcendental "conditions of the possibility of objects as appearances."[21]

Having discovered the transcendental foundations of sensibility, Kant then turns to the "understanding" in the Transcendental Logic, especially in the Transcendental Analytic, which is indeed part and parcel of what renders the Kantian subject truly *transcendental*. Once again, Kant begins not by asking, "What is knowledge of objects?" but rather "*How* is such knowledge *possible*?" That is, he asks, "what are the conditions necessary for the possibility of knowing objects?" He then observes that it is grounded in the transcendental foundations of the understanding as a faculty of thinking or judging, which he calls "the pure concepts of the understanding" or "categories."[22] According to Kant, these categories are the "pure concepts of synthesis that the understanding contains in itself *a priori*" by which we can "understand something in the manifold of intuition."[23] In other words, these pure forms of the understanding (categories) are not deduced from the object; on the contrary, they are

---

19. *CPR*, A21–22/B35–36.

20. *CPR*, A20/B34. In this respect, Kant informs us that even in the sphere of sensibility there has already been a glimpse of "transcendental deduction"—a deduction not as a Cartesian deductive reasoning, but as a *justification* of the application of the a priori forms of the subject to the formless content of the object, which finds its fully explicit operation in the sphere of the understanding; see *CPR*, A85–86/B117–18.

21. *CPR*, A89/B121.

22. *CPR*, A76/B102. According to Kant, the categories of the understanding, discovered through exhaustively exhibiting its functions of unity in judgments, include those of quantity (unity, plurality, totality), quality (reality, negation, limitation), relation (substantiality, causality, reciprocity), and modality (possibility, actuality, necessity); see *CPR*, A80/B106.

23. *CPR*, A80/B106.

built into and derived from the subject's own structure and activity,[24] so that the subject brings them to objects and thereby makes knowledge of objects possible. Kant calls the explanation of "how these categories as *a priori* concepts can relate necessarily to objects" the *transcendental deduction* of the categories.[25] Put another way, Kant's transcendental deduction shows how "*subjective conditions of thinking* should have *objective validity*, i.e., yield conditions of the possibility of all cognition of objects."[26] In short, according to Kant, we cannot understand, think, or know an object *as* a particular, determinate object without imposing upon its formless contents (intuitions) from sensibility the categories that are indeed the *a priori* forms of the subject's understanding; that is, the subject, and not the object as such, constitutes the transcendental conditions of the possibility of knowledge of objects which are at the same time "conditions of the *possibility of the objects of experience.*"[27]

In the Transcendental Dialectic (the second part of the Transcendental Logic), Kant then deals with pure or speculative reason (*Vernunft*)[28] and its "*transcendental ideas*" of the infinite or the unconditioned (the soul, the world as a whole, and God) as the *a priori* representations of an absolute unity and an unconditioned totality.[29] He first criticizes the misuse of pure reason in its spurious inferences with regard to the transcendental ideas: the paralogisms about the nature of the soul, the antinomy about the origin of the world as a whole, and the ideal about the existence of God.[30] According to Kant, these are yet inescapable and ineradicable illusions,[31] inasmuch as reason *necessarily* claims to provide cognitive

---

24. This is what makes Kant's *a priori* categories different from the Platonic-Cartesian theory of innate ideas. Kant does not argue that the human subject is born with innate ideas, but that the human subject is *structured* in such a way that it necessarily synthesizes or unifies a manifold of intuited data by means of a set of categories; see *CPR*, A79–80/B105–6.

25. *CPR*, A85/B117.

26. *CPR*, A89–90/B122.

27. *CPR*, A158/B197.

28. Kant distinguishes reason from the understanding in such a way that the former is "the faculty of principles" (a syllogistic reasoning only through concepts), whereas the latter is the faculty of rules; see *CPR*, A299/B356.

29. *CPR*, A334/B391.

30. *CPR*, A341–405/B399–432, A405–567/B432–595, A567–642/B595–670.

31. For Kant's meaning of "illusion," see *CPR*, A298/B354. Here it does not refer to a sort of empirical misapprehension but "transcendental illusion." According to Kant, it is a "*natural* and unavoidable *illusion* which itself rests on subjective principles and passes them off as objective."

knowledge of these transcendental ideas, the unconditioned and the infinite, by applying the categories of the understanding. However, Kant does not simply reject the value and function of those transcendental ideas of pure reason per se, but rather, by clearly pointing out the limits of their legitimate *use*, he indeed opens the way for their *immanent* use to perform. According to Kant, transcendental ideas can and should be used as a "regulative principle," not as a constitutive principle which pertains to the faculty of the understanding.[32] That is, they do not give the subject some knowledge of corresponding objects; instead, they direct "the understanding to a certain goal respecting which the lines of direction of all its rules converge at one point,"[33] bringing as much as possible a systematic totality or unity—yet "only a *projected* unity"—into the understanding's particular cognitions.[34] In this respect, this is also called the "hypothetical" use of reason which regards transcendental ideas only as "problematic concepts," i.e., a projected criterion for "the manifold and particular uses of the understanding" in its endless progress toward systematic totality or universality.[35] For Kant, then, transcendental ideas operative within the subject's reason in their theoretical (immanent, regulative, hypothetical, or *negative*) use play a *positive* role in the systematization and universalization of empirical cognitions.[36] In short, according to Kant, we can organize our knowledge more systematically by virtue of the transcendental ideas of the subject's pure reason, which can be *thought*, though not properly *known*, as regulative ideas.

To sum up, Kant argues that the object of cognition is constituted by the subject in the sense that the *a priori* forms of cognition exist *within* the subject of cognition. That is, the content coming from the object is put in order by the *a priori* forms of the human subject, i.e., "space and time" as the pure forms of sensibility, "categories" as the pure forms of

32. See CPR, A642–68/B670–96.
33. CPR, A644/B672.
34. CPR, A647/B675.
35. CPR, A647/B675.
36. Not only in the theoretical dimension but also in the practical dimension are the transcendental ideas of pure reason used; in fact, for Kant, their practical use has primacy over their theoretical use. This practical aspect is beyond the scope of the present study, so suffice it here to say that the transcendental ideas of pure reason in their practical use are not hypothesized but *postulated* for morality. In other words, the transcendental ideas of theoretical reason are shifted to the "postulates" of practical reason which encourage the subject to obey the inward moral law. See Kant, "Critique of Practical Reason," 236–46.

the understanding, and "transcendental ideas" as the pure problematic concepts of speculative reason only in their regulative use for the understanding.[37] According to Kant, these are the "transcendental" elements and foundations of the human subject, namely, the necessary and universal conditions of the possibility of cognition which are always and already operative in and through the subject's relations to the objects of experience. In this connection, Kant's notion of the subject in his epistemology can be construed as something like a transcendental activity[38] that at once "intuits" an object through the *a priori* forms of space and time, "imposes" upon its intuitions the *a priori* forms of categories, and "uses" the *transcendental* ideas as regulative principles for the systematization of empirical cognitions. This is what Kant means by the human subject as "transcendental self."

Fichte's Subject as Absolute Ego

Johann Gottlieb Fichte declares that his philosophy is nothing other than Kant's transcendental philosophy *properly* understood.[39] For Fichte, as for Kant, subjectivity is *the* first principle of the philosophical system as the science of knowledge.[40] However, Fichte, in a sense, becomes more Kantian than Kant himself by radicalizing his project, i.e., by pushing the Kantian revolutionary shift to the subject *to the end*.[41] In this way, Fichte transforms Kant's transcendental subject into the "absolute ego."

Against Kant's contemporaries, including Jacobi, who simply interpret Kant's view of cognition from a *representationalist* perspective,[42]

---

37. In this regard, Hegel sees Kant's philosophy as a "*subjective idealism*, insofar as the *I* (the cognitive subject) supplies the *form* as well as the *matter* of knowing, the one qua *thinking*, the other qua *sensing*." EL, 87; §42 Z(3).

38. For an argument about Kant's view of the subject as an activity in his epistemology, see Melnick, *Kant's Theory of the Self*.

39. See Fichte, *Science of Knowledge*, 3–5.

40. Fichte has the same viewpoint as Kant in terms of the Copernican revolution in philosophy: "the object shall be posited and determined by the cognitive faculty, and not the cognitive faculty by the object" (Fichte, *Science of Knowledge*, 4).

41. According to Hegel, "The relationship of Fichte's philosophy to this Kantian position is that it should be regarded as a more consistent presentation and development of Kant's philosophy" (*LHP III*, 178).

42. See Jacobi, "On Transcendental Idealism," 173: "I must confess that this impasse has hampered me more than a little in my study of the Kantian philosophy, so that for several years running I had to repeatedly start the *Critique of Pure Reason* from

Fichte seeks to reformulate it from a thoroughly *constructivist* perspective. To this end, he sharply rejects the Kantian inconsistent and ambiguous sort of idea of the "thing-in-itself" (*Ding-an-sich*) that indeed leaves room for the possibility of representationalist interpretations about Kant's critical philosophy, according to which the thing-in-itself as the mind-independent, eternal, unchangeable object beyond experience is the fundamental yet unknowable causal source of an empirical object whose knowledge is in turn its mere representation.[43] In this way, Fichte advances beyond the Kantian duality of cognitive sources—material and formal—and its concomitant distinction between noumena and phenomena, between object-in-itself and object-as-appearance. He does so precisely by thoroughly giving a *first-person*, not a Kantian third-person, account of experience and thus radically making the subjective ego *the* first, irreducible, absolute condition, ground, and principle of all experience, objectivity, and knowledge.

According to Fichte, the self-conscious subject as pure consciousness is constituted only by virtue of its "own positing of itself," i.e., by "its own pure activity,"[44]—an act of what Fichte calls "intellectual intuition."[45] He goes on to argue that this self-positing ego (I = I) *necessarily* posits or produces out of itself the object as the non-ego in absolute opposition to itself.[46] This object primarily functions as a "check" (*Anstoss*), in

---

the beginning because I continued to be confused by the fact that *without* this presupposition [the presupposition that there are things-in-themselves], I could not find my way into the system, whereas *with* it I could not stay there."

43. For instance, see *CPR*, A42/B59: "What may be the case with objects in themselves and abstracted from all this receptivity of our sensibility remains entirely unknown to us. We are acquainted with nothing except our way of perceiving them."

44. Fichte, *Science of Knowledge*, 97, where he proceeds to say, "The *self posits itself*, and by virtue of this mere self-assertion it exists; and the self *exists* and *posits* its own existence by virtue of merely existing. It is at once the agent and the product of action." Thus, for Fichte, there is no need of other conditions for the existence of the subject, such as Descartes's "I am thinking."

45. Fichte, *Science of Knowledge*, 38: "This intuiting of himself that is required of the philosopher in performing the act whereby the self arises for him, I refer to as *intellectual intuition*. It is the immediate consciousness that I act, and what I enact: it is that whereby I know something because I do it. We cannot prove from concepts that this power of intellectual intuition exists, nor evolve from them what it may be. Everyone must discover it immediately in himself, or he will never make its acquaintance."

46. See Fichte, *Science of Knowledge*, 102–5. Fichte believes that the realization of Kant's critical project can only be achieved by showing that the subject is not passive but *always* active even in the determination of the intuitive element of knowledge as well.

the sense of an external constraint on the ego's spontaneous autonomous activity, whereby the ego's self-positing can be continuously motivated or activated so that it can express its own infinite subjectivity as the absolute ego.[47] Therefore, from the subject's first-person perspective, the object, which is possible only through the opposition to the subject, is merely the product of the subject's self-positing or counter-positing activity and thus no more nor less than the subject itself in external form. From the perspective of the subject, then, the object (the divisible non-ego) is merely what is opposed to the subject (the divisible ego) within itself (the absolute ego). In this way, Fichte insists, the distinction between subject and object is nothing but a distinction internal to and posited by the subject itself called the absolute ego. Along the same lines, Fichte's absolute ego is a unity of the theoretical and practical aspects of subjectivity that Kant keeps separate, in that, for Fichte, there is no such Kantian world of noumena or things-in-themselves which cannot be known by theoretical reason but nonetheless must be postulated by practical reason for morality.

In short, Fichte's subjectivity can be viewed as the radicalization of both the self-defining Cartesian *res cogitans* and the object-constructing Kantian transcendental self. As the self-positing activity, rather than merely a thinking substance of Descartes, Fichte's absolute ego is the sole constituting source of objectivity or objective knowledge, without ever relying on a mind-independent noumenon (thing-in-itself) as Kant inconsistently does, and thereby takes itself to be the very unity of subject and object, i.e., the absolute.[48]

Hegel's *Sublated* Concept of Subjectivity

As we have seen from the examples above, the "turn to the subject" is *the* hallmark of modern philosophy in a very real sense. The subject, be it a Cartesian thinking substance, a Kantian transcendental self, or a Fichtean absolute ego, is counted as the starting point and the center for knowledge, i.e., the fundamental source of all truth as well as the constitutive norm for all objectivity. This is the very context that serves to stimulate Hegel to establish his own philosophy of subjectivity.

---

47. Fichte, *Science of Knowledge*, 190–91.

48. It is in this sense that Fichte's philosophy is generally called "subjective idealism."

Put simply, I argue that Hegel's philosophy of subjectivity *as* "spiritual subjectivity," "spiritual" in the sense of teleological, dialectical, sociohistorical *movement*, is his response to, or better yet, his *sublation* of the modern project of turning to the subject. That is to say, Hegel's philosophy of spiritual subjectivity *transcends* the typical modernist understanding of the subject—either Cartesian rationalist or Lockean empiricist, either Kantian representationalist or Fichtean constructivist—into a "developmental" view in its dialectical sense, in Hegel's own technical language, a "conceptual" approach to the view of human subjectivity. This Hegelian transcending of modern subjectivity constitutively requires two seemingly opposite moments in their internal relatedness: first, *negating* the general tendency of modern philosophy to simply absolutize, reify, or substantialize subjectivity without thereby providing a satisfactory explanation of how to overcome its necessary outcome, i.e., the dualism of subject and object, and secondly, at the same time *preserving* the ontological status and epistemological role of human subjectivity in the constitution of knowledge which has been importantly discovered and emphasized by post-Cartesian modern philosophers. What, then, does Hegel mean by the *conceptual* grasp of subjectivity as the *sublated* view of modern subjectivity? In what sense can we say that Hegelian subjectivity goes beyond modern philosophical subjectivism and its attendant subject-object dualism? How does Hegel preserve the self-determination of the I without cutting the subject off from the object? In what follows, all these questions are to be addressed.

Hegel's Critique of Philosophical Subjectivism and Dualism

Surely, Hegel's philosophy of subjectivity is significantly influenced by and draws upon the thoughts of his predecessors, especially Descartes, Kant, and Fichte.[49] Yet, as mentioned above, Hegel inherits "the turn to the subject" of modern philosophy in a very *critical* way. From Hegel's point of view, there are some problems with the modern conception of subjectivity, and, first and foremost, it could not get away from subjectivism that leads necessarily to all kinds of dichotomous bifurcations of modernity, such as thought and being, finite and infinite, human and divine, individual and social, reason and faith, intellect and sensibility,

---

49. For instance, Hegel thinks highly of Kant's transcendental self ("transcendental unity of apperception") as the important basis for his own philosophy, saying that it is one of Kant's great speculative discoveries; see *SL*, 584.

and so on, which are all possibly subsumed into one category, namely, the dualism of subject and object. Hegel seems to insist that insofar as the subject is, from the very outset, dogmatically posited and defined *as* a self-identical, self-sufficient substance, thus relating itself to things other than itself only in an external or extrinsic way, the opposition between subject and object can never be overcome. In Hegel's eyes, even Kant and Fichte, not to speak of Descartes, are not fully immune from this subjectivist account of the "I." Although both Kant and Fichte rightly characterize the subject as an *activity* in relation to the object—"transcendental activity" for Kant and "absolute self-positing activity" for Fichte—their views are still infected with subjectivism in that the subject's activity in cognition and the presumed unification of subject and object take place *only within* the subject,[50] left with "the residue of a thing-in-itself [in the case of Kant], an infinite check [in the case of Fichte], as a beyond."[51]

Fundamentally, the apparent subjectivism and dualism of modern philosophy, according to Hegel, is due to its inability to go beyond "natural consciousness" which is also called the "understanding" (*Verstand*)—or "reflective understanding"—in Hegel's technical use of the term. For Hegel, the peculiarity of the understanding as a natural, instinctive way of thinking is that it "*determines*, and holds the determinations fixed,"[52] turning things into self-sufficient substances, and hence simply looks at relations among things only in terms of pure externality and opposition, a mere temporal succession (one after another) as well as a mere spatial connection (side by side), without seeing any internal, constitutive relationship among them with a vision of the whole or the absolute. Furthermore, Hegel insists, the philosophy of the understanding, or reflective philosophy,[53] which separates the subject from the object in their opposition, is bound to be concerned about falling into error—whether or not the subject can claim to have true knowledge of the object—so that it *necessarily* demands, out of fear of error, that before we embark

50. See *EL*, 85; §41 Z(2): "even the Kantian objectivity of thinking itself is in turn only subjective insofar as thoughts, despite being universal and necessary determinations, are, according to Kant, *merely our* thoughts and distinguished from what the thing is *in itself* by an insurmountable gulf"; Hegel, *Difference*, 117: "the identity of subject and object, established as absolute in the system [Fichte's system], is a *subjective* identity of subject and object."

51. *SL*, 51.

52. *SL*, 28.

53. According to Hegel, "reflective philosophy" refers to a philosophy claiming that what we know is indeed a *reflection* of our mind's own subjective categories.

upon actual knowing we must first investigate the nature of our cognitive capacity itself and see what objects we can or cannot know.[54]

Hegel interprets Kant's transcendental self and Fichte's absolute ego as still caught up in this realm of the understanding, i.e., a subjectivist way of thinking that separates subject and object in their stark opposition and that resolves this separation and opposition only on the side of the subject. That is, the Kantian-Fichtean unity of subject and object—the transcendental unity of subjective concepts (categories) and objective sensible intuitions in Kant and the absolute identity of subjective ego and objective non-ego in Fichte—is circumscribed within the sphere of the subject, rather than transpires in a real, genuine relation between subject and object. The necessary effect of this is to merely reconfirm the unbridgeable gap between subject and object by saying either that we know phenomena (appearances) but cannot know noumena (things in themselves) as Kant does or that we cannot achieve the highest unity of subject and object but ought to strive toward it *ad infinitum* as Fichte does.[55]

It is how to overcome these ingrained subjectivism and dualism of modern philosophy that constitutes Hegel's primary concern in doing his own philosophy[56]—not, of course, in the direction of a pre-Cartesian realism, but rather in a more improved way to subject-object unification while approving of the general direction of modern philosophy. What, then, does the "Hegelian improvement" exactly mean here? According to Hegel, roughly speaking, every subjectivism and dualism can and should be overcome by introducing a *spiritual*—that is, teleological, dialectical, socio-historical—dimension that other modern philosophical systems, including those of Descartes, Kant, and Fichte, lack; more precisely, they were unable to explain how subjectivity *gradually* appears and grows toward its telos in its dialectical relationship with objectivity in actuality (*Wirklichkeit*).

---

54. Hegel remarks that this is the same demand as declaring that one will not go into the water until he has learned to swim; see *LPR I*, 138–39, and *LHP III*, 204–5.

55. For Hegel's early yet lasting critiques of Kant's and Fichte's subjectivism derived from their confinement to the perspective of reflective understanding, see Hegel, *Faith and Knowledge*, 67–86, 153–87.

56. See *LHP III*, 85: "The exclusive concern is then to reconcile this opposition, to conceive the reconciliation at its ultimate extreme, to grasp the most abstract and the ultimate cleavage of being and thinking." In addition, as will be discussed in following chapters, for Hegel, modern subjectivism and dualism is not only a matter pertaining to the theoretical or epistemological sphere, but also that which leads to socio-political problems—for instance, the Reign of Terror in the French Revolution in his time.

To grasp a constant, gradual dialectic of subject (consciousness) and object (reality) toward its genuine, absolute unification, one that does not take place in the subject alone, Hegel holds that "conceptual thinking" (*begreifendes Denken*)⁵⁷ is absolutely needed. Simply put, the conceptual thinking of reason, as opposed to the representational or reflective thinking of the understanding that splits, fixes, and reifies things in their distinctive, particular determinateness, means conceiving things *concretely*,⁵⁸ which implies that every entity is seen not only in its own distinctiveness and particularity but also, and more importantly, in its internal, intrinsic, and constitutive relations to things other than itself. If different, distinctive things are internally related, then there must be a struggle or contradiction among them, which, in turn, demands reconciliation to overcome that contradiction. This whole process—*from* the immediate, undifferentiated unity or totality of different things in their implicit internal relationship *through* their differentiation with the struggle of contradiction *to* their mediated unity and reconciliation in accordance with their own intrinsic demand to overcome that contradiction—constantly repeats itself in such a way that things are becoming more enriched and closer to what they truly are, rather than in a circular way of simply reflecting back on themselves. Thus, for Hegel, thinking conceptually, which is also synonymous with thinking rationally, concretely, spiritually, dialectically, or speculatively,⁵⁹ denotes conceiving of things precisely as a spiraling *movement*, a teleological process to achieve an authentic identity in the middle of identity and difference.

By the same token, the human subject, according to Hegel, should be grasped in terms of the *concept*, namely, as *spirit*, as a dialectical and teleological movement, which other modern philosophers, including Descartes, Kant, and Fichte, fail to notice and thereby remain bound to philosophical subjectivism and dualism. Now then, let us turn to the basic conceptual structure of Hegelian spiritual subjectivity in its teleological, dialectical, socio-historical movement.

---

57. The "conceptual thinking" literally means grasping or holding together (*begreifen*) those elements that remain disparate in the representational thinking of the understanding.

58. "Concrete" (*concretus*) in its Latin origin literally means "growing together."

59. "Speculation" (from the Latin *speculum*, "mirror") for Hegel involves a relationship of double mirroring between consciousness (subject) and reality (object).

Hegel's Concept of Spiritual Subjectivity in Its Dialectical Structure

For Hegel, the "concept" of subjectivity precisely refers to "what the subject is and ought to be"[60] in its essential, that is, *dialectical* structure. In accordance with the logical moments of the concept *qua* concept, I would say, there are three moments of the Hegelian concept of *spiritual* subjectivity in its *self-explicating, dialectical movement*.[61] The first moment is that of being-in-itself (*An-sich-Sein*), i.e., the subject's abstract, immediate identity with itself in its indeterminate, undifferentiated, substantial unity with the object.[62] In the second moment, this abstract initial subjectivity is differentiated, in and through actualizing itself, into the relation of being-for-itself (*Für-sich-Sein*) and being-for-others (*Sein-für-Anderes*) as two distinct, separate, external oppositions. The third moment is that of being-in-and-for-itself (*An-und-für-sich-Sein*) or being-for-itself-in-others in which the external opposition or contradiction of the subject's identity with itself (being-for-itself) and its relation to others (being-for-others), the antithesis of subjectivity and objectivity, is reconciled or sublated, so that it becomes explicitly what it is implicitly in the first moment, i.e., the unification of subjectivity and objectivity. In this regard, according to Hegel, the human subject as *spirit* is not a simple identity of what it is—whether it be a self-sufficient, atomistic ego or a deistic creator and source of the objective world—but rather its identity is constitutively, intrinsically mediated by things other than itself; in other words, the human subject *is* a dialectical movement of the identity of identity and non-identity (otherness).[63]

To be a subject, therefore, the human being requires appropriate otherness or objectivity which can properly awaken her authentic subjectivity and in which she can truly find herself. In this respect, for Hegel, the journey of the human subject is, as it were, an odyssey searching for more universal and spiritual objectivity in relation to which it can

---

60. Along these lines, Beiser maintains that Hegel's "concept" is somewhat similar to the Aristotelian notion of "formal-final cause" of a thing; see Beiser, *Hegel*, 67, 81.

61. According to Hegel, the concept contains three moments: universality, particularity, and individuality (or singularity); see *SL*, 600–622. For Hegel's explanation about the three moments of spirit in its dialectical movement, see *EM*, 16; §382 Z and *LPR I*, 176–77.

62. Hegel likens this first moment to the seed; see *LPR I*, 182.

63. See Taylor, *Hegel and Modern Society*, 22–23, where he argues that the human subject models the Hegelian thesis of "the identity of identity and non-identity."

discipline and develop itself and thereby become more and more spiritual and universal. In this way, the human subject always calls for something determinate, but, at the same time, it goes beyond that determinacy as it stands in its immediacy and constantly looks for something *more* mediated and universal. That is, the subject has the capacity to reflect on and take a distanced view of the world (including both itself and others). It is in this specific sense that Hegel considers subjectivity a movement of *absolute negativity*.[64] The most ultimate, encompassing, and universal horizon and actuality that the subject is to search for is what Hegel calls the Absolute, or Absolute Spirit, in and through which the totality of the world, both subjectivity and objectivity, appears precisely as self-expressive moments of this encompassing whole. In this regard, Hegel insists, the human subject *is* a teleological movement toward the Absolute, absolute universality per se, as the unification of subjectivity and objectivity.

In short, Hegel *conceives* of the subject as a dialectical and teleological movement, that is, as a "spirit." As such the Hegelian spiritual subjectivity, devised as the corrective to the subjectivism and dualism of modern philosophy, is the dialectical, teleological process or becoming (*Werden*) whereby the subject develops its true subjectivity as it relentlessly moves from particularity to greater and greater universality through a series of mediations of the object in its greater and greater universality too. This is the fundamental structure of the human subject as *spiritual* subjectivity that Hegel *conceptually* grasps, which is what most sets him apart from the entire tradition of modern philosophy, though he shares its basic aspirations.

Now that the concept as such is "what is still enveloped, and the determinations or moments are contained within it but not yet spread out,"[65] the concept of Hegelian spiritual subjectivity should become determinate, actual, concrete, and explicit. Therefore, Hegel examines how the concept of the subject becomes the *idea* (in the Hegelian sense of the realization of the concept), in quest of its adequate form of subjectivity beyond all the alienating forms of immediacy and limitations which do not correspond to the concept; in other words, he shows how the human subject *actually* develops or universalizes itself toward the Absolute in the process of its internal and thus dialectical relations to objects/others in the concrete, socio-historical world. This actualizing process, I would

64. I will deal with the Hegelian concept of "absolute negativity" in more detail later in chapter 5, section 2.

65. *LPR I*, 181.

argue, is precisely what Hegel tries to philosophize about in his *Phenomenology of Spirit*.⁶⁶

---

66. Joseph L. Navickas's *Consciousness and Reality* is, among others, a lesser-known but very insightful work in this respect. Arguing that Hegel's *Phenomenology of Spirit* "contains the principles of his philosophy of subjectivity," Navickas attempts "to make intelligible the gradual constitution of Hegel's notion of subjectivity" in the way of reconstructing the sequence of different forms of consciousness described in the *Phenomenology* from the perspective of the development of human subjectivity (Navickas, *Consciousness and Reality*, viii).

CHAPTER 3

Hegel's Philosophy of Spiritual Subjectivity in the *Phenomenology of Spirit* (I)

As DISCUSSED IN THE preceding chapter, one of the distinctive marks of modern philosophy in general is its turn to the subject, that is, its preoccupation with the centrality of subjectivity, especially with reference to the epistemological capacity to know truth—starting from Descartes's thinking substance through Kant's transcendental self to Fichte's absolute ego. In this way, the human subject becomes construed for the modern mind as the constituting power and source of all objective knowledge and values. It is against this background that Hegel's philosophy in general and his view of subjectivity *as* "spiritual subjectivity" in particular should be seen, that is, as his critical response to such modern attempts. Hegel carries out an examination of the human subject in line with the tradition of post-Cartesian modern philosophy; yet, in opposition to its general tendency to characterize subjectivity as something fixed and given once and for all that is "already complete before its appearing," he instead advances a developmental and dialectical view of the subject that is "truly actual only through the determinate forms of its necessary self-revelation" in relation to the object.[1] Furthermore, Hegel maintains that such a view can overcome or transcend the sheer dichotomy of subjectivity and objectivity operative in the modern project. In short, for Hegel, the subject must be conceived not just as a substance but essentially as a "spirit," i.e., as the dialectical and teleological *movement* of self-transcendence toward the Absolute, absolute unification of subjectivity and objectivity, through a series of relations to, or mediations of, objects (otherness) in history.

1. *EM*, 5; §378 Z.

In fact, Hegel does not clearly define and theorize his view on the subject in the way that, for instance, Descartes, Kant, and Fichte do.[2] Yet, as indicated earlier, I argue that it is Hegel's *Phenomenology of Spirit* that truly unfolds the above-described teleological/dialectical nature and structure of "spiritual subjectivity," in terms not only of its concept but also of the very "process" of its concretization or explication in actuality. Accordingly, in investigating Hegel's philosophy of spiritual subjectivity in this chapter and the next, I take his *Phenomenology of Spirit* as the main text.[3] The sequence of different stages and forms of consciousness[4] described in the *Phenomenology* will be read and discussed as the journey of the human being to find her authentic subjectivity in the process of development or maturity, with a series of sublations (*Aufhebungen*) in dialectical relations to objects in the concrete world.[5] Thus, as we will observe, there is a logically and immanently "necessary progression and interconnection" of the forms of consciousness or subjectivity.[6] Starting from one position, the subject comes to find itself confronted with a certain predicament, i.e., the inner contradiction between what it claims

---

2. Lumsden, *Self-Consciousness*, 66.

3. When citing Hegel's *Phenomenology of Spirit* in this book, I occasionally correct Miller's translations that do not sufficiently reflect the emphasis and nuance of the original German text, *Phänomenologie des Geistes*, for which I sometimes consult two recent translations: one by Terry Pinkard and the other by Michael Inwood. For instance, I consistently change Miller's "notion" as a translation of *Begriff* to "concept." Concerning textual references, I provide both the page number(s) and the paragraph number(s) of the English translation (Miller's text)—e.g., *PS*, 58; §90.

4. In this book, I distinguish the terms "stage" and "form" in such a way, for instance, that in the *stage* of "Consciousness" there are three *forms* of "Sense-certainty," "Perception," and "Understanding."

5. In this sense, Hegel's *Phenomenology of Spirit* can also be read as a sort of coming-of-age novel (*Bildungsroman*) of humanity in general; see Pinkard's editorial introduction to *Phenomenology of Spirit*, xvii. It may also be seen as redefining the Greek notion of *pathei mathos* ("learning through suffering") in the sense that the human being searches for his true subjectivity (true self) in the process of going through a variety of obstacles and challenges.

6. *PS*, 50; §79. Forster succinctly characterizes this necessary progression and interconnection as follows: "The 'necessity' of a transition from a shape of consciousness A to a shape of consciousness B just consists in the complex fact that while shape A proves to be implicitly self-contradictory, shape B preserves shape A's constitutive conceptions/concepts but in a way which modifies them so as to eliminate the self-contradiction, and moreover does so while departing less from the meanings of A's constitutive conceptions/concepts than any other known shape which performs that function" (Forster, *Hegel's Idea*, 186).

to be true and what it experiences to be true in actuality, which is not resolvable from that existing position due to its one-sided and, more precisely, less-dialectical view of the world (including itself and others), and therefore falls into doubt and despair.[7] However, the subject cannot remain content with this frustration, for, essentially *as spirit* with the primordial demand (*Forderung*), drive (*Drang*), or urge (*Trieb*) for the Absolute, its immanent necessity to overcome the contradiction always "disturbs its inertia."[8] It must thereby move to another higher, more mature and inclusive form of subjectivity, where it adopts a new position, by *sublating*—i.e., *negating* and *transcending* but at the same time *preserving*—the assumptions of the position from which it began. In this way, the later forms do not merely supplant the previous ones but incorporate them as their *sublated moments*. This pattern of movement, for Hegel, is bound to continue until the subject arrives at its ultimate destination (telos), that is, the Absolute (Absolute Spirit or Absolute Knowing), absolute universality as such in the sense of the unification of universal subjectivity and universal objectivity, where the subject can be *fully* present to itself (*bei-sich-selbst-sein*).[9] For Hegel, as stated above, the Absolute is indeed always and already present as the implicit telos, immanent drive, or a priori condition for all developmental forms of the human subject as spirit, as a dialectical movement.

Additionally—and this is crucial—note that our purpose and intention must be clear: in discussing and unpacking Hegel's view on the human subject in this chapter and the next as we proceed to read the *Phenomenology*, we will become convinced that a Hegelian subjectivity is one that should be revitalized in the current context of globalization as an important source for the anthropology of globalization proper. In other words, we will find out in Hegel's philosophy of spiritual subjectivity the authentic vision of humanity adequate and necessary for a globalizing world, namely, a sort of cosmopolitan citizens who can constantly drive themselves toward a greater universality (*self-transcending drive toward universality*) through their self-determined ethico-political

---

7. Hegel observes in this regard that the journey of the human subject as spirit can be characterized as "the pathway of *doubt*, or more precisely as the way of despair" (*PS*, 49; §78).

8. *PS*, 51; §80.

9. See *PS*, 56–57; §89: "[C]onsciousness will reach a point at which it gets rid of its semblance of being burdened with something alien, that is, what is only for it and as an other."

actions (*self-determined or autonomous action*) in essential relations to others in history (*solidary relationship with others*). Indeed, as will be seen throughout these chapters, the paradigmatic structure of such human beings is embedded in Hegel's phenomenology of spiritual subjectivity in the form of a *dialectical* movement of being-for-itself (identity with itself) and being-for-others (relation to others) toward the Absolute (absolute universality).

This chapter, as the first part of the whole story, is divided into two sections. In the first section, "Subjectivity in the Womb," I will deal with the implicit context or horizon out of which subjectivity begins to emerge, which is an interpretation of the first chapter of the *Phenomenology*, Consciousness; and in the second section, "The Birth of Subjectivity," I will examine the emergence process of self-conscious subjectivity, which is an exposition of its second chapter, Self-Consciousness.

Subjectivity in the Womb: "Consciousness"

Insofar as subjectivity is construed generally as "the movement of positing itself" or "the mediation of itself and its becoming-other-to-itself" as stated in the Preface to the *Phenomenology*,[10] we may have to say that Hegelian subjectivity begins to emerge in the stage of self-consciousness, which will be examined in the next section. Nevertheless, in terms of our investigation into the process of development of human subjectivity in the *Phenomenology*, it is not a Hegelian move at all that we focus our attention solely on the reality (*res*) of subjectivity and thereby begin our study simply from the stage of self-consciousness, as Kant and Fichte seem to do; in other words, that is not a *dialectical* way of dealing with the subject matter. At the heart of the Hegelian dialectic is the comprehension of *internal* relations of actuality in its teleological and historical *movement*, which ultimately makes it possible to declare that "The true is the whole" (*Das Wahre ist das Ganze*).[11] In the same vein, as pointed out earlier, the forms of the human subject in the *Phenomenology* are internally related, each one necessarily appearing from the one before and leading to the one after. In this regard, it is crucial to first look into the preceding stage, Consciousness, which I would call "subjectivity-in-itself" (*Subjektivität-an-sich*), as the context which engenders its inner

10. *PS*, 10; §18.
11. *PS*, 11; §20.

necessity to sublate itself to a higher stage, Self-Consciousness,[12] which I would call "subjectivity-for-itself" (*Subjektivität-für-sich*).

In Hegel's *Phenomenology*, "consciousness" refers specifically to the consciousness *of* the object (object-consciousness; *Gegenstandsbewußtsein*), which is only possible when the subject stands *against* the object.[13] To be more specific, for Hegel, consciousness denotes a cognitive subject immersed in, and preoccupied with, the immediacy, or the in-itself, of an object without being aware of its own constitutive and mediating role or self-conscious reflective activity in the very cognition of the object.[14] The key claim of consciousness as object-consciousness is as follows. Since the object, not the conscious subject itself, should be posited as the essence (*Wesen*) because "the object *is* . . . regardless of whether it is known or not" by the subject—that is to say, the object remains even when it is not known, but "there is no knowledge if the object does not exist"[15]—and therefore the true object is the object in its immediacy, unmediated by and external to the conscious subject, we must refrain from "comprehending" (*Begreifen*) the object in our "apprehending" (*Auffassen*) of it.[16]

For Hegel, there are three forms of consciousness in their logically necessary sequence: sense-certainty, perception, and the understanding, each claiming to be the surest and truest way of grasping the object in its immediacy. The transition from one form to another is a dialectical process and development driven by the internal or structural necessity in its own movement to transcend itself to a more adequate form. As will

12. Hyppolite also states in this light that "Self-consciousness will thus appear as a result and not as a presupposition" (Hyppolite, *Genesis and Structure*, 77).

13. *Gegenstand*, the German term of "object," literally means "that which stands against."

14. Hegel characterizes as "ordinary" or "natural" this object-oriented feature that consciousness inherently assumes. In this respect, for Hegel, "consciousness," "object-consciousness," "ordinary consciousness," and "natural consciousness" are all interchangeable with one another.

15. *PS*, 59; §93. Similarly, in the pre-modern, classical tradition, "being" enjoyed a certain transcendence in relation to "consciousness" or the *Cogito*, in that being is in no way affected by the fact that it is known by us humans; our knowledge of the object is always inadequate because of the transcendent nature of the object in its being. However, as will be revealed throughout the journey of the *Phenomenology*, for Hegel, being or the object is always being enriched by the very process of being known by consciousness or the subject. As being-in-itself it is merely abstract; but as being-for-consciousness it is concrete.

16. *PS*, 58; §90. In this book, I employ the terms, "comprehend" and "conceive" interchangeably as a translation of the German word *begreifen*.

be shown, in knowing the object each form of consciousness involves a distinct contradiction within itself between its *immediately-claimed/ intended* object as the in-itself (what consciousness initially takes the object to be in itself) and its *actually-experienced* object as a being-for-consciousness of the in-itself (what consciousness comes to know that object to be). Importantly, according to Hegel, this contradiction is of necessity disclosed in cogni*tion*, i.e., the cognitive "action"[17] of the subject, which in turn requires a sublation into a higher form of consciousness adequate for the new object—the actually-experienced object.[18] Hegel clearly explains this process in his Introduction to the *Phenomenology* as follows:

> [S]ince what first appeared as the object sinks for consciousness to the level of its way of knowing it, and since the *in-itself* becomes a *being-for-consciousness of the in-itself*, this latter is now the new object. Herewith a new shape of consciousness comes on the scene as well, for which the essence is something different from what it was at the preceding shape. It is this circumstance that guides the entire series of the shapes of consciousness in their necessary sequence.[19]

Most importantly, it is gradually revealed in this process that "The truth of consciousness is *self-consciousness* and the latter is the ground of the former,"[20] namely, that "in the knowledge of its object it is in fact self-consciousness, knowledge of itself."[21] In this sense, I claim, in the stage of consciousness human subjectivity is gradually yet *implicitly* growing *in the womb*. Put another way, the developmental process of object-oriented consciousness is indeed structurally mediated by its own subjective conceptual activity, which enables it to constantly move and transcend itself. As we will be seen in each form of consciousness, the subject plays a more active role, though implicitly, than it did in the preceding form.

---

17. For Hegel, "action" always constitutes a dialectical turning point, in the sense that action activates contradiction between subjectivity (inner intention) and objectivity (outer consequence) which at the same time demands its sublation. For an in-depth interpretation and exploration of the *Phenomenology* from the perspective of this Hegelian concept of action, see Hwang, "Spiritual Action."

18. Note that what Hegel means by the "object" here is not an empirical object but a *form* of object.

19. *PS*, 56; §87.

20. *EM*, 152; §424.

21. Hyppolite, *Genesis and Structure*, 77.

Subjectivity-In-Itself in the Form of Sense-Certainty

According to Hegel, the first form of consciousness as object-consciousness should be "sense-certainty" (*sinnliche Gewißheit*)[22] or sense-certain consciousness, for its non-conceptual, purely sensuous approach to the object certainly seems to be most natural, direct, immediate, intuitive, and utterly receptive to what the object is in itself.[23] It claims to achieve the richest and truest knowledge of the object in its *immediacy* without any conceptual mediation, or subjective involvement, of adding to or subtracting from the object—that is, the object taken in its sheer givenness as an irreducible, particular *individual* or singular present to our senses. Sense-certain consciousness, therefore, refers to the object simply as "this" (*Dieses*) whose "truth contains nothing but the sheer *being* of the thing" qua a purely specific individual,[24] not by its concept or name such as "tree," "house," "salt," etc.; for any concept or name already involves certain mediations—for instance, "salt" is always understood in *distinction from*, or in contrast with, something else such as "sugar"—and the object would thus not be known immediately.

Having presented the basic claim or intention of sense-certainty about what it initially takes the object to be in itself, Hegel sets out to show through his phenomenological analysis a dialectic intrinsically involved in it by examining "whether in sense-certainty itself the object is in fact the kind of essence that sense-certainty proclaims it to be; whether this concept of it as the essence corresponds to the way it is present in sense-certainty."[25] With respect to the object, in fact, what sense-certain

---

22. J. M. Fritzman remarks that Hegel's sense-certainty is similar to Kant's *non-conceptual representation* produced by the forms of sensibility/intuition or Russel's *knowledge by acquaintance* which is distinct from knowledge by description; see Fritzman, *Hegel*, 52–53.

23. This first form of consciousness is intrinsically related to the question of "With what must philosophy or science (*Wissenshaft*) begin?" As the "hermeneutical circle" implies, there is no absolute, transcendent starting point in doing philosophy. Aware of this, what Hegel proposes is to begin with the most immediate kind of knowledge, i.e., sense-certainty, the certainty of the object in its pure being at the level of sense-experience. In the same vein, in his *Logic*, too, Hegel begins with the concept of "pure being" with no determination at all. For Hegel's detailed treatment of this matter, see *SL*, 67–78.

24. *PS*, 58; §91. It could be an interesting topic to compare the pure "this" of Hegel's sense-certainty with the "thisness" (*haecceitas*) of John Duns Scotus (1266–1308) as a non-qualitative property of a substance or thing.

25. *PS*, 59; §94.

consciousness *actually* experiences in the process of its cognitive *action* is far removed from what it has claimed at the beginning. The "*this*," along with its two constitutive spatio-temporal aspects of "here" and "now," is indeed not its intended purely-immediate, simple, particular individual, but rather a mediated *universal*, a property that can belong to many individuals, precisely because not only a specific object but *any* given particular objects can be referred to, or pointed to, immediately as "this."[26] After all, what sense-certain consciousness means (*meinen*) is *this* specific now or *this* specific here, i.e., "a sensuous This"[27] in its immediate being of particular individuality without further qualification, without invoking any universal; however, what it actually expresses and communicates by means of action related to cognition, such as "write down," "point to," and especially "say,"[28] is an indifferent plurality of now*s* or here*s*, i.e., "the *universal This*"[29] in its being in general "to which negation and mediation are essential."[30] In this way, the truth of sense-certainty turns out to be the very opposite of what it has claimed, namely, the abstract *universal* and not *this* particular individual.

For Hegel, this dialectic of sense-certainty, a movement from particular individuality to abstract universality, is made possible fundamentally because any knowledge of an object[31]—in this case, the cognitive content that appears to be immediately given in sensation—has always and already been "*mediated*" by the subject's cognitive or conceptual activity, "which is inherently universal," particularly in its linguistic expression,[32] although sense-certain consciousness itself is not as yet explicitly aware of it.

26. For Hegel's detailed explanation about the dialectic of the object in the form of self-certainty, see *PS*, 59–61; §95–99.

27. *PS*, 65; §109.

28. *PS*, 60; §95, 63; §105, and 66; §110, respectively.

29. *PS*, 60; §97.

30. *PS*, 61; §99. Incidentally, Hegel's argument for the inadequacy of *Meinen* here, in a sense, seems to preempt Wittgenstein's argument against the possibility of a private language.

31. For Hegel, "knowledge" ought to be expressible in language to be communicated to others.

32. *PS*, 59; §92, 66; §110. For Hegel, language is a medium in which the nature of consciousness, i.e., universality, is manifested. In addition, Hegel insists elsewhere that language exists only "*as the language of a people* [*Volk*]." Hegel, *System of Ethical Life*, 244.

Consequently, there emerges an inner discrepancy within sense-certainty, that is, the *structural* contradiction between what it means or intends for the object (the in-itself), *the pure "this" in its immediacy, simplicity, and singularity*, and what it actually says or expresses about it as the knowledge of the object (a being-for-consciousness of the in-itself), *the universal in its complexity*, or "a *simple* entity which, in its otherness, remains what it is."[33] This predicament or contradiction necessarily demands a sublation of itself into a transition to a new form of consciousness, viz., "perception" that is adequate to this new emerging object.[34]

Subjectivity-In-Itself in the Form of Perception

"Perception" (*Wahrnehmung*) or perceiving consciousness, a new form of object-consciousness as the *sublation* of sense-certainty,[35] takes as the object that which has turned out to be the truth of sense-certainty, i.e., the universal. More exactly, the object of perception is a universal of a specific kind, namely, a universal in its immediacy[36] or a "sensuous universal" in the sense that "its particularizations consist in the manifold material provided by sense-certainty."[37] According to Hegel, this new object, which is immediately apprehended as the sensuous universal, is taken up more precisely as *"the thing with many properties."*[38] Thus,

---

33. *PS*, 64; §107.

34. As Lauer aptly points out, Hegel's phenomenological analysis on the dialectic of sense-certainty with its transition to perception constitutes a paradigmatic model "not only for the subsequent dialectics to be described but also for the overall movement of the *Phenomenology*" (Lauer, *Reading of Hegel's Phenomenology*, 54).

35. "Perception" is at once *negating* and *preserving* sense-certainty as its *transcending* form: it negates the indeterminate and incommunicable sheer individuality or singularity of the object which is merely "meant" by sense-certainty, while preserving its simple sensuous immediacy in the form of sensible properties of the thing; see *PS*, 68; §113.

36. "A universal in its immediacy" means that particulars (sensuous properties) which are the components of the universal exist merely one after another (*aufeinander*) and side by side (*nebeneinander*) without any intrinsic connections or internal mediations.

37. Winfield, *Hegel's Phenomenology of Spirit*, 42. Winfield also characterizes this sensuous universal of perception as a "conditioned universal," in contrast with the unconditioned supersensible universal of the understanding, the next and final form of consciousness, in that the universal of perception contains within itself sensuous particular instances as extrinsic givens.

38. *PS*, 67; §112. From the epistemological point of view, three paradigmatic

perceiving consciousness, whose point of view also represents ordinary empiricism,[39] claims that the essence of the object lies in self-identical thing-for-itself or thinghood possessing sensuous givens, manifold particular qualities immediately sensed, each of which is connected with other qualities "only by the indifferent *Also*."[40] For instance, this grain of "salt" is a self-identical thing in which mutually indifferent and distinct sensible properties exist merely side by side without affecting each other, in such a way that "it is white and *also* tart, *also* cubical in shape, *also* of a particular weight, etc."[41]

In the process of *actual* perceiving, however, perceiving consciousness discloses that its claim is untenable as it experiences the contradiction of the thing, particularly in terms of the relationship between the identity or unity of the thing itself (*One*) and the diversity of its sensuous properties (*Also*). In other words, perceiving consciousness soon notices that the diversity of properties conflicts with the unity of one single, self-identical thing, and furthermore that the properties of the thing are themselves universal and so extend beyond the confines of this particular thing to other things, i.e., turn into free, independent sensuous "matters."[42] According to its claim, as said above, the truth of the object is meant to consist in the thing with many sensible properties as being-for-itself or self-identical sensuous universality which exists on its own account without any relation to others, "for in this relation rather its connection with others is posited, and the connection with others is the cessation of being-for-itself."[43] Yet what perceiving consciousness actually grasps in its actual experience is not only the thing as one separate, self-identical, independent being-for-itself, but also the thing whose "essence" lies "in an other,"[44] i.e., the thing as being-for-others in the sense that the essential or absolute character of a thing, which determines it as

---

relations are involved here: (1) What is the relationship among the properties of a thing?; (2) What is the relationship between a thing itself and properties?; (3) What is the relationship between a thing and other things?

39. Hyppolite, *Genesis and Structure*, 100.

40. *PS*, 69; §113.

41. *PS*, 68; §113. For example, in the constitution of salt the property of being white is independent of, distinct from, and thus unaffected by other properties such as being tart, cubical, etc.

42. *PS*, 74; §121.

43. *PS*, 75; §125.

44. *PS*, 76; §126.

this or *that* self-identical thing, always involves distinguishing itself from other things and so standing in "relation" to them.[45] After all, the thing is now perceived to be self-contradictory, which contains within itself its truth opposed to itself: "the object is *in one and the same respect the opposite of itself; it is for itself, insofar as it is for others*, and *it is for others, insofar as it is for itself*."[46]

As in the case of sense-certainty, the reason behind this contradictory consequence is that, though perceiving consciousness itself does not explicitly recognize, the object perceived is in its essential structure the same as the movement of consciousness in its cognitive *action* of *perceiving*, which is always mediated by the conscious subject's own reflective and conceptual activity of looking at a thing in all its constitutive, internal relations to its properties and other things.

Hence, once again, there emerges the inner gap within perception between what perceiving consciousness intends for the true essence of the object (the in-itself), that is, "conditioned sensuous universality" as an immediate, pure being-for-itself and what it actually grasps in its action of perceiving (a being-for-consciousness of the in-itself), that is, "unconditioned supersensible universality" in which the moments of being-for-itself and being-for-others are essentially related. This new object is, however, ungraspable within the capacity of perception and thereby demands a sublation of itself into a necessary transition to a new form of consciousness, namely, the "understanding."[47]

Subjectivity-In-Itself in the Form of the Understanding

The "understanding" (*Verstand*) or understanding-consciousness as the last form of object-consciousness, which also represents the scientific worldview, has as its object the "unconditioned universal,"[48] or the

---

45. As Spinoza observes, every distinction or determination involves negation: A is something that is *not* B and/or C, and so on. And this determinate negation always supposes the "relation" of A to B, C, etc.

46. PS, 76; §128. This internal split into "being-for-itself" and "being-for-others" in the Hegelian dialectic presented in the form of perception will appear as *the* crucial moment at every stage and form of human subjectivity in the *Phenomenology*.

47. PS, 77; §129.

48. PS, 79; §132. According to its German etymology, "unconditioned" (*unbedingt*) denotes "not-a-thing" (*un-be-dingt*); see Hyppolite, *Genesis and Structure*, 119.

"concept *in-itself*,"⁴⁹ in which the unity of being-for-itself and being-for-others, of the thing's self-identity and its other-relatedness, is posited, whose character is thus no longer purely sensuous. Unlike perception that would try to keep separate these two aspects of the thing, i.e., being-for-itself and being-for-others, the understanding affirms the passing over of each aspect into its opposite and indeed takes this transition into each other to be the true essence of its object. For the understanding, therefore, the object is not just a self-identical thing with properties, but a dynamic movement of the thing's self-identity and its other-relatedness.

According to Hegel, this new object of consciousness, the unconditioned universal, at first appears to understanding-consciousness as "force" (*Kraft*) animating perceivable things, which has two moments in their dialectical—that is, both differentiating and unifying—movement: force proper or force driven back into itself (being-for-itself) and force expressed or externalized (being-for-others).⁵⁰ These two constitutive moments of force are initially apprehended as the play of two distinctive forces, that is, the active or soliciting force and the passive or solicited force; however, it is shortly revealed that each ends up being "*on its own account* an absolute reversal and interchange [of the determinateness]"⁵¹ and thus appears only as a disappearing moment. Just as force is force proper only insofar as it expresses itself, so the soliciting force is made possible only insofar as the other force is solicited, and thus the solicited force turns out to be its opposite, i.e., the soliciting one that enables the initially-posited soliciting force to solicit. In this way, understanding-consciousness experiences that all the distinctions or differences of particular forces in their interplay, which were perceived to be present in this "absolute flux of appearance" (*Erscheinung*), are indeed only "*difference as*

---

49. Hyppolite, *Genesis and Structure*, 102. Emphasis mine. Hegel himself describes this in the following way: "This unconditioned universal, which is now the true object of consciousness, is still an *object* of consciousness; consciousness has not yet grasped its *concept* as *concept* (*Begriff*).... To consciousness, the object has returned into itself from its relation to an other and has thus become concept *in itself*; but consciousness is not yet for itself the concept, and consequently does not recognize itself in that reflected object" (*PS*, 79; §132).

50. *PS*, 81; §136. "First... the force driven back into itself *must* express itself; and, secondly, it is still force remaining *within itself* in the expression, just as much as it is expression in this being-within-itself." The fact that the necessity of force's expression lies in *itself* makes force an *unconditioned* universal in the sense that its expression is not conditioned by something extraneous to itself as in the case of the sensuous universal of perception.

51. *PS*, 90; §148.

universal difference" governing all sensuous, particular differences, which is expressed in the "*law of force*," i.e., the tranquil kingdom of law as "the *supersensible* world" (*übersinnliche Welt*).[52] Hence, understanding-consciousness now claims that its true object is "the *inner* of things qua *inner*"[53] which refers to the supersensible, intelligible realm of law that posits and determines the flux of forces in the sensible world of appearance as its manifestations.

However, understanding-consciousness, particularly in its cognitive *action* of "*explanation*" (*Erklären*),[54] soon notices that what its object actually turns out to be does not correspond to what it has claimed, namely, that ultimately "the understanding experiences only *itself*."[55] To be more specific, in "explaining" the supersensible world of law as the essence of the sensible world, and particularly the source and necessity of law *qua* law in its determinacy and differentiation, understanding-consciousness has to reintroduce force "as the essence of the law,"[56] in the sense that, for instance, the law of gravitational attraction is grounded upon the force of gravity, that the law of electricity is grounded upon electrical force, and so on; yet, at the same time, force, as defined earlier, is nothing other than the posited operation of law as its expression. Consequently, the explanation of law by appealing to force as its ground presents nothing but an empty tautology, finding itself just going around in a circle, just as there is no way to separate force proper from its expression or the soliciting force from the solicited force.

Through this tautological movement that understanding-consciousness experiences in its action of explaining, the supersensible world of law is transformed into the "*second supersensible world*" or the "*inverted world*" (*verkehrte Welt*).[57] Unlike the first supersensible world as the immediate elevation of the sensuous into a universal abstraction and thus standing only in an *external* relation to the sensible world, this second supersensible world draws *within itself* its opposite, the constant flux of sensible appearances: "it is itself and its opposite in one unity."[58] In this

---

52. *PS*, 90–91; §148–49.
53. *PS*, 86; §142.
54. *PS*, 94; §154.
55. *PS*, 103; §165.
56. *PS*, 94; §154.
57. *PS*, 96; §157.
58. *PS*, 99; §160.

way, understanding-consciousness now confronts its object as a movement of distinguishing and overcoming what is distinguished, for which then difference is "*inner* difference" or "difference as *infinity*,"[59] that is, the object that generates and contains finite, determinate otherness *within* itself and thereby has nothing external to itself without yet losing its determinacy and differentiation. According to Hegel, this new object, whose essence is "infinity, or the absolute concept," is characterized by "life": infinity, inner difference, or the absolute concept is "the simple essence of life, the soul of the world, the universal blood, whose omnipresence is neither disturbed nor interrupted by any difference, but rather is itself every difference, as also their sublation; so it pulsates within itself but does not move, vibrates within itself, yet is at rest."[60]

The object of consciousness, then, turns out to be "life," the autonomous process of *self*-movement, as infinity, which consciousness experiences to be no different from itself since what understanding-consciousness does in and through *its* "explanation" is, as discussed above, precisely making infinity emerge as its object. In other words, the sensible realm of appearance, or the play of forces, and the supersensible realm of law cannot be necessarily related to each other on their own, but their relation must be *mediated* by consciousness' own conceptual activity of relating, i.e., *explaining*. Thus, Hegel states, "the understanding's *explanation* is primarily only the description of what self-consciousness is," in the sense that what understanding-consciousness encounters in its attempt to discover something truly objective lying behind the veil of appearance is none other than its own movement, i.e., its own action of explaining.[61] This means that consciousness has reached the point at which it has itself for its object or it can reflect upon itself.

This is a decisive moment where the inner contradiction or discrepancy between what understanding-consciousness intends for the object (the in-itself), that is, "the law of force" as the supersensible world and what it actually grasps as the knowledge of the object (a being-for-consciousness of the in-itself), that is, "life and consciousness itself" as

---

59. *PS*, 99; §160. Hegel also calls this "absolute difference" (*PS*, 96; §156).

60. *PS*, 100; §162. What Hegel argues here is that life is a higher and more comprehensive truth than law. Viewing this from a standpoint of the critique of scientism, Gadamer thinks highly of this insight; see Gadamer, *Hegel's Dialectic*, 35–53.

61. *PS*, 101; §163. In the process of explanation, "consciousness is, so to speak, communing directly with itself, enjoying only itself; although it seems to be busy with something else, it is in fact occupied only with itself."

the second supersensible or inverted world is disclosed and at the same time demands its sublation. What is crucial at this moment is that consciousness' sublation of itself here is not just a transition to its new form of consciousness as object-consciousness which posits the object as the essence, as is the case with the transition from sense-certainty to perception to the understanding. Since consciousness is confronted with a great crisis where it begins to be aware that the essence lies not in the object as something *other* than itself—i.e., a mere "this" in sense-certainty, a "thing with many properties" in perception, and "the law of force" in the understanding—but in the very consciousness itself, a sort of radical, qualitative transformation ensues, which necessitates the transition of the stage of consciousness to *self-consciousness*, that is, from consciousness of the object to consciousness *of itself*:

> It is true that consciousness of an other, of an object in general, is indeed itself necessarily *self-consciousness*, reflectedness into itself, consciousness of itself in its otherness. The *necessary advance* from the previous shapes of consciousness for which their truth was a thing, something other than themselves, expresses just this, that not only is consciousness of a thing possible only for a self-consciousness, but that self-consciousness alone is the truth of those shapes.[62]

As we have observed in each form of consciousness, the seed of self-consciousness or subjectivity is always and already present in its movement or process. That is, the experience of consciousness of the object—sense-certain consciousness of the simple being of *this*, perceiving consciousness of the self-identical thing-for-itself with many sensible properties, and understanding-consciousness of the supersensible law of force—is implicitly, structurally, or unconsciously mediated by its own subjective conceptual activity in the form of the cognitive actions of saying, perceiving, and explaining, which enables consciousness to constantly move and transcend itself. In terms of human subjectivity, to analogize, we may say that in the stage of consciousness it remains *implicit* or latent as potentiality "in the womb," and it is in the stage of self-consciousness that it becomes *explicit* in the process of its "birth" out of the womb.

---

62. *PS*, 102; §164.

The Birth of Subjectivity: "Self-Consciousness"

For Hegel, as explicated in the preceding section, every human being is a subject-in-itself; that is, all human beings have the *intrinsic* structure, or the in-itself, of self-consciousness. Yet this does not necessarily mean that they are by default the subject-for-itself who is explicitly aware of itself as the subject. Indeed, the human being is to be awakened into self-conscious subjectivity or subjectivity-for-itself only in and through the process of a series of stimulations or mediations of the object, i.e., the process of returning to himself through his relations to others. The point Hegel is trying to make in his philosophy of subjectivity in general, as discussed earlier, is that the subject cannot exist merely by and for itself, in isolation; rather, its very being is constituted by its relationship to the object. In other words, it cannot achieve its true, genuine identity with itself without the mediation of otherness. Since being without otherness simply means being without content, the human subject without being mediated by things other than itself would be merely an empty subject, i.e., "the motionless tautology of: 'I am I.'"[63] Its filling comes from the outside, objective world, and thus it needs otherness or, rather, its relations to the object, yet in such a way that this otherness or relation does not destruct the unity of the subject with itself but rather promotes and enriches its identity with itself. This is, according to Hegel, made possible fundamentally because "the I is the content of the relation and the relating itself," in and through which the object as being-in-itself and the object as being-for-consciousness become identical—that is to say, in relating itself to an other, "the I is its own self, and at the same time it overreaches this other which, for the 'I,' is equally only the I itself."[64]

In short, for the human being to be a subject-for-itself, she should be confronted with objects which can awaken her to the consciousness of herself. In this respect, Hegel insists that the stage of consciousness as *object*-consciousness is a necessary moment in the process toward self-consciousness or subjectivity-for-itself in which the human being becomes explicitly conscious of himself. However, in the stage of consciousness, as we have discussed, subjectivity was not fully awakened

---

63. PS, 105; §167.

64. PS, 104; §166. In the same vein, Hegel states elsewhere that "The I . . . is implicitly identity in otherness; the I is itself and extends over the object as an object *implicitly* sublated, the I is *one* side of the relationship and the *whole* relationship—the *light*, that manifests itself and an Other too" (*EM*, 142; §413).

because the relationship between subject and object remained purely *theoretical*. In other words, consciousness as a sheer object-oriented *cognitive* consciousness could not yet fully recognize itself in the lifeless, theoretical objects which are apprehended as existing independently of the conscious subject, such as a "this" as a simple individual, a "thing" as a self-identical sensuous universal, and "the law of force" as an unconditioned supersensible universal.

According to Hegel, subjectivity begins to be *explicitly* awakened and emerge in the stage of self-consciousness in its relations to living, *practical* objects that are at the same level as the subject itself; for only in the practical relation or confrontation with the concrete, real otherness of the world the human subject is compelled to be driven into itself and becomes conscious of itself as an authentic self-consciousness. In this regard, the subject as self-consciousness at this stage, though it is not yet aware of the fact that the human subject is all reality in the sense of the unity of subjectivity and objectivity, does achieve a transformative moment, which I would call "the birth of subjectivity." In this section, I will examine the gradual, developmental, and dialectical process of this birth of subjectivity expressed by Hegel in different forms of self-consciousness in their logically necessary sequence: master vs. slave, stoicism, skepticism, and the unhappy consciousness.

The Desiring Subject vs. the Laboring Subject: The Master-Slave Dialectic

As mentioned above, self-consciousness or subjectivity-for-itself must always be mediated by practical objects or real others that challenge the subject and thereby make it driven into itself. In this way, the birth of self-conscious subjectivity requires several forms of *practical* mediation and action in terms of its relations to objects or others. According to Hegel, self-consciousness exists in its first form only as being immediately immersed in itself, namely, as pure self-certainty (*Gewißheit seiner selbst*), the immediate "unity of self-consciousness with itself"[65] in its purely *negative* relation to the object—the object that is now regarded not merely as a sensuous *this*, a thing with many properties, or a lawful force, but as a "*living thing.*"[66] It asserts its self-certainty by removing the independent

---

65. *PS*, 105; §167.
66. *PS*, 106; §168. Remember that the actual object emerging through the dialectic

otherness of the object in such a practical way that it consumes or assimilates the object into itself: "Certain of the nothingness of this other, it posits *for itself* this nothingness as the truth of the other; it destroys the independent object and thereby gives itself the certainty of itself as *true* certainty."[67] This first form of self-consciousness is what Hegel calls "*desire*" (*Begierde*).[68] Desire may be construed either as the lowest, the least developed and the most natural form of self-consciousness or the intermediate stage between consciousness and self-consciousness.[69]

However, in its immediate action of greedy consumption to satisfy its desire of self-certainty only by abolishing or destroying the object in its independence, self-consciousness as the desiring subject gets caught up in its own self-contradiction. It soon reveals that its self-certainty is rather "conditioned by the object," for it exists only from simply negating the object in its otherness; in other words, "in order that this sublation can take place, there must be this *other*."[70] Therefore, inversely, the essence of desire shifts from the subject to the object, and in this sense desire is "characterized by a necessary otherness."[71] After all, the desiring subject "cannot sublate the object by its *negative* relation to it; it is really because of that relation that it generates the object again, and the desire

---

of the last form of consciousness, i.e., the understanding, was "life" as infinity which consciousness experiences to be no different from itself. Yet, as Hegel points out later, there is the difference between what is merely living and a self-consciousness in that "life is the *natural* setting of consciousness, independence without absolute negativity" (*PS*, 114; § 188). For Hegel's detailed description of the dialectic of life as a prefiguration of *spirit* in the sense of self-differentiating, self-developing totality, see *PS*, 106–9; §168–72.

67. *PS*, 109; §174.

68. *PS*, 105; §167. It should be noted that the aspect of self-certainty in the sense of the identity of self-consciousness with itself by overcoming otherness becomes explicit for the first time in "desire," which will be *preserved* all the way to the end of the journey, though its aspect of immediacy, i.e., its purely negative relation to the object will be *negated*. In this regard, Hegel states that "self-consciousness is desire in general." Thus, as Taylor puts it, "desire reflects not just the factual need for an object, but also the fundamental drive for integrity" (Taylor, *Hegel*, 151).

69. This characterization of desire as the intermediate stage is based upon the fact that desire is confronted with a twofold object: one is the immediate object inherited from the stage of consciousness, i.e., the object of consciousness, and the other is consciousness itself.

70. *PS*, 109; §175. Emphasis mine.

71. Hyppolite, *Genesis and Structure*, 162.

as well."⁷² Through the action of consumption, i.e., desiring in its immediacy, therefore, the subject has learned that "it can achieve satisfaction only when the object itself effects the negation *within* itself."⁷³ That is to say, so as to satisfy my desire of self-certainty, I as a self-consciousness demand as the object not merely an external living thing but a being that is identical to, yet equally independent of, myself. That being considers life to be *its* genus (*Gattung*), conscious of itself as one instance of a kind, and has the capacity to negate itself *voluntarily* and thereby to be "just as independent in this negativity of itself."⁷⁴ In this way, the object of self-consciousness becomes another living consciousness⁷⁵ that can recognize me and thereby make me driven into myself: "*Self-consciousness achieves its satisfaction only in another self-consciousness.*"⁷⁶

In my view, this is a crucial moment in which self-consciousness as the desiring subject moves itself from desiring its self-certainty "by immediately negating the other in its total being in the form of consumption" (the *immediate* desiring subject as life; a physical/material desire for survival and self-preservation) to "by mediately negating the other only in its independent otherness in the form of recognition" (the *mediated* desiring subject; a spiritual/social desire for recognition). In this way, the desiring subject now realizes that only through the other's recognition (*Anerkennung*) can its authentic self-consciousness be attained: "Self-consciousness is *in* and *for itself* when, and by the fact that, it is in and for itself for another self-consciousness; that is, it is only as a recognized being."⁷⁷

However, Hegel points out, this process of recognition in the concrete, real world is at first a far cry from a free exchange of mutual recognition among equal individuals in their reciprocal relationship standing on

---

72. *PS*, 109; §175. Emphasis mine.

73. *PS*, 109; §175. Emphasis mine.

74. *PS*, 110; §176. For Hegel, "life" *per se* is not yet a self-consciousness in that it is not a *self-related* genus as absolute negativity; see *PS*, 108–9; §172.

75. "Since the object is the negation in its own self, and in being so is at the same time independent, it is consciousness" (*PS*, 109–10; §175).

76. *PS*, 110; §175.

77. *PS*, 111; §178. Hegel also indicates that the concept of "spirit" (*Geist*) is already present here: "we already have before us the concept *of spirit*. What still lies ahead for consciousness is the experience of what spirit is—this absolute substance which constitutes the unity of its oppositions in their perfect freedom and independence, namely, the oppositions of diverse self-consciousnesses existing for themselves: the *I* that is We and the We that is *I*" (*PS*, 110; §177).

the same footing. Rather, it begins with one that is characterized by what Hegel terms a "life and death struggle" (*Kampf auf Leben und Tod*).[78] This is primarily due to the fact that with its roots in *desire*, each individual subject seeks for pure self-certainty or "pure *being-for-itself*"[79] by immediately obliterating the independence of the other, to wit, only by asking for the other's recognition without itself willing to recognize the other. Such a life-and-death struggle for recognition among individual desiring subjects is bound to end up in their one-sided and unequal relation, that is, the relationship of "master and slave" (*Herr und Knecht*) which is occasioned by one of them in this struggle not willing to stake its life and thus giving up its desire for recognition.[80] Hence, the winner of this struggle, the master as "the independent consciousness," gets the desired recognition from the loser, the slave as "the dependent consciousness," who recognizes the other without himself being recognized in return.[81] In this sense, I would contend, the master could count as the epitome of the desiring subject in its *mediated*, not immediate, sense, i.e., not simply negating the other in its being but overcoming otherness while the other remains in being.

According to the Hegelian master-slave dialectic,[82] however, this initial picture of the relation turns out to be an inverted one. At first, it seems as though the master enjoys self-certainty in and through the slave's

---

78. *PS*, 114; §187. This struggle is not the Hobbesian "war of all against all," in that the dominating drive behind this struggle is, for Hobbes, a natural desire for self-preservation, whereas, for Hegel, it is a rational demand for the other's recognition. Furthermore, as will be described, the outcome of this life and death struggle is not, as Hobbes would have it, a sort of contract between parties but the unequal relation of domination (the master) and servitude (the servant).

79. *PS*, 114; §187.

80. This implies that, for Hegel, one of the fundamental conditions for the possibility of genuine self-conscious subjectivity lies in the subject's willingness to stake its life, which demonstrates its rational status beyond the realm of mere biological life, realizing that "its essence is not *being*, not the *immediate* form in which it emerges, not its submergence in the expanse of life" (*PS*, 114; §187). Much later on, Lacan and Žižek further accentuate this condition for subjectivity as absolute negativity, particularly by connecting it with the Freudian notion of "death drive" (*Todestrieb*).

81. *PS*, 115; §189.

82. The master-slave dialectic in the *Phenomenology* has been characterized as the most famous, well-known, and crucial theme in Hegel's philosophy as a whole, and there are, *ipso facto*, plenty of comments on it in Hegel scholarship. Among them, Alexander Kojève's has counted as most influential; see Kojève, *Introduction to the Reading of Hegel*.

recognition without himself being forced to recognize the slave, and thus feels completely independent[83]—that is to say, the master appears to be the essence for both himself and the slave. Yet the master indeed does not truly have his essence in himself because his self-certainty and independent subjectivity, in effect, *depend on* the slave's recognition and labor, in that the master is a master *only insofar as* he is served by the slave. Thus, deep down, the master's desire is bound, conditioned, or mediated by the slave, and thus the master turns out to be "the slave of the slave."[84] The slave, by contrast, whose essence has been believed to lie in the master is the inverse of what he immediately counts; in other words, the slave, in a sense, is revealed to be "the master of the master."[85] Hegel summarizes the outcome of the master-slave dialectic in the following way:

> The object in which the master has achieved his lordship has in reality turned out to be something quite different from an independent consciousness. What is for him is not an independent consciousness, but a dependent one. . . . The *truth* of the independent consciousness is accordingly the *servile consciousness*. . . . But just as lordship showed that its essence is the inverse of what it wants to be, so too servitude in its consummation will really turn into the opposite of what it immediately is; as a consciousness *forced back* into itself, it will withdraw into itself and be converted into true independence.[86]

Hegel enumerates three mediated moments, which force the slave back into himself and thereby bring about "the synthesis of being-in-itself and being-for-itself":[87] the fear of death, service to the master, and labor. For Hegel, it is "labor" (*Arbeit*) based on the initial fear of death and the discipline of service that enables the slave to become *explicitly* aware of himself as self-conscious subjectivity, albeit within the condition of ongoing subordination to the master: "the feeling of absolute power both in general [the fear of death], and in the particular form of service [to the master], is only dissolution *in itself* . . . Through labor, however, the slave

---

83. As discussed above, the master has attained this status by keeping his desire for recognition above his desire for life.

84. Hyppolite, *Genesis and Structure*, 172. Hegel seems to prove the wisdom behind Rousseau's famous dictum that "There are some who may believe themselves masters of others, and are no less enslaved than they" (Rousseau, *Social Contract*, 45).

85. Hyppolite, *Genesis and Structure*, 172.

86. PS, 116–17; §192–93.

87. Hyppolite, *Genesis and Structure*, 174.

becomes conscious of what he truly is."[88] According to Hegel, the slave's action of laboring is called the "formative *activity*,"[89] giving a new form to things simply given or imprinting his own image upon things, which makes his implicit subjectivity explicit, externalized, objectified, and concretized. Instead of simply consuming and enjoying the object provided by the slave as the master does, the slave works on and transforms the object to make it consumable and enjoyable by the master, and, in so doing, he is able to negate the object while at the same time preserving it—the slave must keep it for the master's satisfaction of desire. In this way, the laboring slave now "comes to the intuition of independent being *as its own self*,"[90] putting himself as the essence which determines the being of the object; that is, the slave's labor "attains the authentic realization of being-for-itself in being-in-itself."[91] What the master was unable to attain, the slave attains now. In this regard, I would claim that in and through the slave's own experience the desiring subject *sublates* itself to "the laboring subject" that overcomes the contradiction of desire:

> Desire has reserved to itself the pure negating of the object and thereby its unalloyed feeling of self. But, for that reason, this satisfaction is itself only a fleeting one, for it lacks the *objective* side or *permanence*. Labor, by contrast, is desire *held in check*, fleetingness *staved off*, or labor *cultivates*.[92]

However, the laboring subject is soon confronted with a new contradiction. Since the laboring subject still in its servile consciousness bound by life (the fear of death) cannot dare to free itself from its submission to the master, its formative activity continues to be restricted by the master's needs and desires, and thus it does not as yet *explicitly* know that the form it imposes upon things belongs to itself as much as to the object. Yet the more it acts or labors—though at this stage its formative activity remains a particular "skill which is master over some things, but not over the universal power and the whole objective essence"[93]—the more grow-

---

88. *PS*, 117–18; §195. In a sense, since the master, too, has already experienced and conquered the fear of death in the process of the initial life-and-death struggle, it seems reasonable to take "labor" to be the decisive factor that distinguishes the slave from the master.

89. *PS*, 118; §195.

90. *PS*, 118; §195.

91. Hyppolite, *Genesis and Structure*, 176.

92. *PS*, 118; §195.

93. *PS*, 119; §196.

ing sense of independence and freedom it has, which is contradictory to the milieu wherein it is situated. Hence, in its dialectical necessity, the laboring subject demands its transcendence into another form of labor, namely, the labor of the concept as the thinking subject.

The Thinking Subject: Stoicism and Skepticism

Beginning to be aware of the importance of its own self as free subjectivity, particularly in its formative activity on things (laboring), but at the same time recognizing a confrontation with its real situation in the concrete world which does not fit in with its growing self-consciousness, the subject now withdraws from the external, real world into its interiority of *thought*, i.e., the labor of the concept or "the infinity or the pure movement of consciousness,"[94] where any actual and external conditions imposed on the subject have no bearing on the confirmation that what it confronts is nothing else than *itself* and therefore that it is truly free. I would call this free self-consciousness "the thinking subject."

According to Hegel, the first moment of the thinking subject in its self-developing dialectical movement is "stoic consciousness." Stoicism as a form of self-consciousness that knows itself insofar as and to the extent that it reduces the object to the form of thought, which, as Hegel observes, represents the "freedom of self-consciousness."[95] In thinking, regardless of my actual dependence on, or bondage to, the other, "I *am free*, because I am not in an other, but remain simply present to myself, and the object, which is for me the essence, is in undivided unity my being-for-myself."[96] To think means ultimately to have the "concept" (*Begriff*) which is the product of my own immanent activity, as opposed to representation (*Vorstellung*) which is given or presented to my consciousness from without and thus external to, or distinct from, me: "in the case

---

94. *PS*, 120; §197.

95. *PS*, 121; §198. Many commentators say that Hegel refers here to Stoicism as a philosophy popular in the Greek world and the Roman Empire. However, as Hyppolite aptly suggests, it would be more appropriate at this stage to regard it as "the name not merely of one particular philosophy but of a universal philosophy that is a part of the education of every self-consciousness" (Hyppolite, *Genesis and Structure*, 179).

96. *PS*, 120; §197. Hegel elsewhere calls this kind of freedom "*negative* freedom," "the freedom of the understanding," or "the freedom of the void," in the sense that freedom here is secured only through "the flight from every content as a limitation" (*PR*, 38; §5 A).

of representation . . . consciousness still has especially to remind itself that this is *its* representation; on the contrary, the concept is for me immediately *my* concept."[97] In other words, the object for the stoic thinking subject is a sort of *sublated* otherness, i.e., "the otherness within itself"[98] as "the *immediate* unity of *being-in-itself* and *being-for-itself*."[99] In this way, for stoic consciousness, *my* pure thought is the only proper essence positing the truth, value, and even difference of the other, and everything else is a matter of indifference:

> Its principle is that consciousness is the thinking essence, and that something only has essentiality for consciousness, or is true and good for it, insofar as it thinks it to be such. . . . What alone has more essentiality is the difference posited by *thought*, or the difference which is not immediately distinct from me. This consciousness accordingly has a negative attitude toward the master and slave relationship . . . whether on the throne or in chains . . . its aim is to be free, and to maintain the lifeless indifference which consistently *withdraws* from the movement of existence . . . into *the simple essentiality of thought.*[100]

Hence, the subject as stoic consciousness claims that it can achieve the freedom of self-consciousness by means of its thinking.

As expected, however, this purely stoic thinking subject cannot but disclose its inherent contradiction in its actual experience. Recognizing that there is a discrepancy between the world that it molds in thinking by reducing everything into the pure form of thought and the world filled with the determinations of real life in which it must live and act, it realizes that what it has achieved in the midst of life is "not living freedom itself"[101] but merely the contentless, empty, formal concept of freedom.

---

97. *PS*, 120; §197.

98. *PS*, 121; §200.

99. *PS*, 120–21; §197. It must be noted, as Hegel points out by emphasizing the term "*immediate*," that conceptual thinking (*begreifendes Denken*) here in this form of stoic subjectivity should not be identified with that which is to be reached at the end of the entire journey, that is, philosophical thinking or Absolute Knowing, but considered only as a *moment* in the process toward that end. The concept (*Begriff*) at this stage is still mired in the perspective of self-consciousness, aware of itself as "*thinking* consciousness *in general*" and hence as a "universal mode of being in general"; in other words, the concept in stoicism is not yet something *absolute* penetrating all "the development and process of its manifold being."

100. *PS*, 121; §198–99.

101. *PS*, 122; §200. For Hegel, "freedom" essentially means being present to oneself

In other words, the stoic thinking subject's returning into "the *pure universality* of thought"[102] and thus its *indifferent* attitude or lifeless impassiveness toward all differences and particularities of the real, living world leads only to the subjectivity of abstract freedom that has no applicability to the realm of actuality. No matter how hard stoic consciousness affirms itself and universalizes itself in thought, the otherness of life remains inasmuch as it cannot not *act* as a living being in the real world.

Consequently, Hegel argues, the stoic thinking subject in the form of abstract freedom, retreating from reality into itself and thus lacking the actuality of life, does not achieve "itself as absolute negation," but remains only as "the incomplete negation of otherness,"[103] i.e., abstract negation. It is *abstract* in the sense that the world is negated only in a way that is apathetic and indifferent to the subject, which yet leaves the otherness of reality as it is. Thus, in order to make reality truly its own in thought and thereby attain unconditioned, unrestricted freedom, the thinking subject should now abandon the attitude of indifference toward the content of the world full of particularities, multiplicities, and contingencies, and this necessarily leads to the next moment of its dialectical movement toward a higher form of thinking subjectivity, namely, from the stoic thinking subject to "the skeptic thinking subject."

Forsaking its merely formal, abstract notion of freedom and its indifference toward the determinate, particular content of the world, the thinking subject now enters the realm of skepticism, with the hope that its action of universal doubt and rigorous negation of all alien contents it confronts in the domain of thought could effectively dissolve all otherness, not only "the objective [reality] as such" but also "its own relationship to it, in which it counts as objective and is established as such."[104] Along these lines, Hegel defines skepticism as "the realization of that of which stoicism was only the concept."[105] In this sense, the emergence of

---

in one's other or object (*bei sich selbst im anderen*). However, the stoic thinking subject cannot be *bei sich* in relation to the reality of the objective world, for the real world is so foreign to itself that it withdraws from reality; see Taylor, *Hegel*, 159.

102. *PS*, 121; §199.

103. *PS*, 122; §201.

104. *PS*, 124; §204. Hyppolite remarks that what Hegel has in mind here is not a modern Humean skepticism but an ancient Pyrrhonian skepticism. While the former negates universal knowledge by means of sense experience and common sense based thereupon, the latter negates the validity of sensibility and common sense as such; see Hyppolite, *Genesis and Structure*, 185.

105. *PS*, 123; §202.

skeptic consciousness indicates the subject's capacity to regard everything as succumbing to its own infinity of negation in thought. Explicitly aware that thought involves essentially the power of negation, the skeptic thinking subject now wages war on the external world and wholly annihilates all particular, contingent, and determinate otherness as unessential. It is through this self-conscious negation that the thinking subject as skeptic consciousness expects to secure "*the certainty of its freedom,*" to engender "the experience of that freedom," and hence to elevate it "to *truth.*"[106]

However, this expectation soon turns out to be an unachievable pure intention. The subject realizes in its experience that to act consistently upon the principle of skepticism is neither simple nor feasible: "It lets the unessential content in its thinking vanish, but in this very act it is the consciousness of something unessential. . . . It pronounces the nullity of seeing, hearing, etc., yet it *itself sees, hears,* etc."[107] Something very similar to the predicament experienced by the desiring subject and master consciousness happens to skeptic consciousness. The skeptic thinking subject claims that it absolutely justifies itself as completely free, self-identical subjectivity only insofar as it acts upon the principle of negation, but the act of negation itself depends solely on the very particular, contingent otherness in a changing, external world which it should negate. In effect, what is regarded as unessential to the skeptic thinking subject turns out to be so much essential to itself. Here again, what it intends *in thought* and what it actually experiences *in life* constantly contradict each other: "Its acts and its words always contradict each other, and equally it itself has the doubled contradictory consciousness of unchangeableness and sameness, and of utter contingency and non-identity with itself."[108]

In short, the skeptic thinking subject in its action of radical doubt and negation experiences itself as a contradictory, restless movement which "passes back and forth from the one extreme of self-identical self-consciousness to the other extreme of the contingent consciousness" without being able to reconcile these two into itself.[109] This experience of the inner contradiction between unchangeable self-identity and changeable contingency or particularity impels the skeptic thinking subject to transcend itself into a new form of self-consciousness which brings

---

106. *PS*, 124; §204.
107. *PS*, 125; §205.
108. *PS*, 125; §205.
109. *PS*, 125; §205.

together *within* itself these two contradicting aspects that the skeptic consciousness keeps apart. Subjectivity is revealed in this new form as *essentially* dual-natured and contradictory, which I would term "the split subject." Hegel calls this new form of self-consciousness "the unhappy consciousness" that, according to Hyppolite, represents in principle human consciousness as such in the sense that "it has not yet reached the concrete identity of certainty and truth, and therefore it aims at something beyond itself."[110]

The Split Subject: The Unhappy Consciousness

It is "the unhappy consciousness" in which the birth of subjectivity culminates through the experience of self-alienation as a divided being that has been implicit in the skeptic thinking subject. In short, the unhappy consciousness is essentially the consciousness of itself *as* the split subject, conscious of the division (*Entzweiung*) between unchangeable self-identity and changeable particularity or contingency *within* itself. Unlike the skeptic thinking subject, therefore, the unhappy split subject looks upon the contradiction, bifurcation, or split of the two as *constitutive* of its very nature: "The unhappy consciousness itself *is* the gazing of one self-consciousness into another, and it itself *is* both, and, to itself, the unity of both is also the essence."[111]

However, "since it is at first only the *immediate unity* of the two" without being as yet explicitly aware that it *is* the unity of the two *in and for itself*, the subject considers them to be "not the same, but opposites" and takes the unchangeable consciousness to be essential and the changeable consciousness to be unessential.[112] For Hegel, as always, the subject fundamentally as spirit in its restless, dialectical movement toward the Absolute—the unification of subjectivity and objectivity, of being-for-itself and being-for-others—cannot simply stand this contradiction within itself, but must address itself to a serious task of reconciling its inner split of the unchangeable, essential consciousness and the changeable, unessential consciousness. For the split subject in its *immediacy*, i.e., the immediate togetherness of the opposing two within itself, the only plausible way of reconciling these two is to negate one of them.

110. Hyppolite, *Genesis and Structure*, 190.
111. *PS*, 126; §207.
112. *PS*, 126–27; §208.

It is natural, as Hegel observes, that the split subject identifies itself with the changeable consciousness "because it is *itself the consciousness of this contradiction*," and therefore that it seeks to overcome the contradiction by negating itself taken to be changeable and unessential, while searching for the unchangeable and essential from without, "something alien."[113] This is in fact something that the human subject projects its aspect of unchangeable self-identity into a beyond (*Jenseitige*).[114] In this way, the split subject's pursuit for the unchangeable and essential leads to a sort of religious consciousness, identifying a transcendent, divine reality as the unchangeable and essential and hence seeking to be united with it.

To this end, however, one important thing must first be given and experienced. For the subject to overcome the contradiction between the unchangeable/essential and the changeable/inessential within itself by raising itself to union with a divine being, the divine as the unchangeable/essential should not simply remain the wholly transcendent, faceless Beyond (as in the case of Judaism), but take the form of individual personality with which the subject can identify (as in the case of Christianity). Only then can the unity not just be thought but also be actualized,[115] and thus the split subject can gain "the ground of hope"[116] to have its unity. Historically, for Hegel, this ground of hope appeared as an individuality of the unchangeable, the incarnation of God, that is, Jesus Christ in whom the substantial union between divine (unchangeable/essential) and human (changeable/inessential) is believed to have been accomplished.[117]

---

113. *PS*, 127; §208. Emphasis mine.

114. As Taylor observes, we may be able to see here "the origin of the Feuerbachian and Marxian conception of religious consciousness as alienated" (Taylor, *Hegel*, 160n).

115. See *PS*, 127–28; §210, where Hegel implies that the development from Jewish consciousness (the consciousness of separation between divine and human) to Christian consciousness (the consciousness of their union) would be necessary for this actual unity. It must be noted, however, that although Hegel alludes to Judaism and Christianity here, what he says of them at this stage also applies to every form of religious consciousness and life in general.

116. *PS*, 129; §212.

117. At this level, however, the incarnation of God is *apprehended* as something immediately posited, as a merely contingent, historical event without *comprehending* its conceptual necessity. The true, speculative meaning of the Incarnation in its universal significance will be unfolded later in the stages of Religion and Absolute Knowing. Along the same lines, it is premature to think that Hegel intends to define the essence of Christianity here in the Unhappy Consciousness. If we want to know what he truly thinks of Christianity *as* religion, we must see "The Revealed Religion" (*PS*, 453–78; §748–87) or "The Consummate Religion" (*LPR III*, 61–347).

According to Hegel, the split subject's efforts to overcome its inner split by unifying itself as unessential consciousness with the incarnate God as essential consciousness involve three moments in the forms of religious attitude and practice: "first, as *pure consciousness*; second, as a *singular essence* that, as desire and work, relates itself to *actuality*; and third, as *consciousness of its being-for-itself*."[118] As will be seen, none of these three religious moments leads to reconciliation; rather, all three consequently accentuate the unhappiness of split subjectivity. With respect to the first moment, the split subject as pure consciousness claims that the way of assuring its communion with the incarnate God is to have an attitude of "*devotion*."[119] However, devotion (*Andacht*), in the sense of "movement *toward* thinking," does not reach the level of thought (*Denken*) proper, thereby failing to conceive (*begreifen*) or internalize the spiritual meaning of the Incarnation and just remaining an "infinite, pure inner feeling" or an "infinite *yearning*" toward something external, unapproachable, and vanishing, i.e., the "unattainable *Beyond*."[120] The split subject as devotional consciousness, therefore, cannot overcome the split that is characteristic of the unhappy consciousness, but only encounters itself in its devotion as "the inward movement of the *pure* heart which painfully *feels* itself as estranged."[121] In other words, the unchangeable is supposed to be found through the subject's feeling of devotion, but all that is known is *its own self*, i.e., changeable consciousness, because feeling is not "the knowing of something else" but "just one's own internal modification, a state of oneself."[122] The first experience of the unhappy split subject thus simply reinforces the sense of itself.

As the subject as pure consciousness in its inner feeling of pious devotion experiences its inability to unify itself with the unchangeable and thus remains unhappy, it now moves to the next moment in which, instead of yearning toward the unchangeable (the incarnate God) through devotion, it begins to pay attention to the real, concrete world and take a more active approach to the unchangeable. The split subject now immerses itself in actual transformations of "the world of actuality," whose

---

118. *PS*, 130; §214; see also *LPR I*, 445–47. Historically speaking, Hegel seems to say, these were practiced in the Christianity of the Middle Ages.

119. *PS*, 131; §217. Hegel takes up the Crusades as a notable example of this pious devotion. See also *LPWH*, 492–93.

120. *PS*, 131; §217.

121. *PS*, 131; §217.

122. Winfield, *Hegel's Phenomenology of Spirit*, 113.

meaning and value have already been changed by the Incarnation into a "sanctified world" as a "form of the unchangeable," and seeks to achieve its unity with the unchangeable through its "desire and work" in the sanctified world of actuality.[123] According to Hegel, this sense of unity would be made possible through the "two moments of *reciprocal self-surrender* of both parties": on the part of the unchangeable, it "*surrenders* its embodied form" and yields it to the subject, while, on the part of the changeable, the subject "*gives thanks* [for the gift]" to the unchangeable, that is, "*denies* itself the satisfaction of the consciousness of its *independence*, and assigns the essence of its action not to itself but to the beyond."[124]

Although the split subject claims that it is committed to denying the satisfaction of its independent individuality in desire, work, and enjoyment and rather attributing everything to the grace of God, this claim turns out to be an impossible intention contradicted by its own experience in *action*. For, though it "*makes a show* of renouncing the satisfaction of its own self-feeling, it obtains the *actual* satisfaction of it,"[125] in that it is the subject *itself* that posits and recognizes God in its willing, laboring, and enjoying. Even its action of thanksgiving to God in which the subject supposedly relinquishes itself to the unchangeable is no less "*its own* activity."[126] Through this experience, therefore, the split subject *in and through* its action "feels itself therein as this particular individual consciousness, and does not let itself be deceived by its own show of renunciation, for the truth of the matter is that it has not renounced itself," and the outcome is again "the renewed division into the opposed consciousness of the *unchangeable*" and "the consciousness of *independent individuality* as such."[127] Unfortunately, however, the split subject does not know how to sublate this *structural* division and contradiction caused by the very nature of its action, so it cannot help remaining "unhappy." Insofar as the subject *acts*, it can never be free from the contradictory division within itself and thus is doomed to remain the *unhappy* split subject.

---

123. *PS*, 132–33; §219.

124. *PS*, 134; §222. Put differently, the subject in its self-surrender believes that "I appear to desire and work myself, but in fact I am directed by the power and grace of God."

125. *PS*, 134; §222.

126. *PS*, 134; §222.

127. *PS*, 134–35; §222.

Realizing the inadequacy of the strategy of self-negation in the spheres of desire, work, and enjoyment in the service of, with gratitude to, the unchangeable, the unhappy split subject should transcend itself to another moment, at which its dialectical movement toward the unity of the unchangeable/essential and the changeable/inessential within itself as an individual self-consciousness reaches its end. The essence of the final moment of the unhappy split subject is the complete renunciation or nullification of the independent, autonomous individuality *per se* by declaring itself to be the enemy (*Feind*) and freeing itself from the authority and responsibility for *its own action*, which was not successfully suppressed in the preceding moment. The unhappy split subject thus attempts to make this self-renunciation or self-abnegation complete by giving up its authority and responsibility of three sorts in particular through the *mediating action* of the "mediator," i.e., the church or the priest that represents the unchangeable and essential: first, "its autonomous will" through engaging in strange rituals and prayers which are meaningless to itself; second, "the fruit of its labor or external possessions" through giving alms of what it has acquired; third, "its enjoyment" through fasting, penance, and mortifications.[128] By giving these up, the unhappy split subject renounces its independence altogether and makes its being-for-itself into a "*thing*,"[129] wholly determined by the unchangeable, that is, "nothingness" in relation to God, and thereby tries to divest itself of its dividedness and unhappiness.

According to Hegel, however, this reduction of subjectivity and individuality to thinghood cannot last forever. When the subject seems to succeed in renouncing itself, its own action in particular, by giving up everything in obedience to the clerical authority, it indeed only finds *itself* in its self-renunciation precisely because, in effect, "its giving up everything is *its own doing*."[130] In other words, self-affirmation or the sense of the "I" as being-for-itself is the presupposition of all (religious) experiences even including self-renunciation, i.e., the very act of nullifying "the *action* as its own."[131] In this way, as we expect in the Hegelian dialectic where a negative moment is at the same time positive in itself,

---

128. See PS, 136–37; §228, and Lauer, *Reading of Hegel's Phenomenology*, 147. These correspond to the three evangelical counsels (religious vows) of Christianity: "obedience," "poverty," and "chastity," respectively.

129. PS, 137; §229.

130. Lauer, *Reading of Hegel's Phenomenology*, 147. Emphasis mine.

131. PS, 137; §230.

the subject rather gains *a sense of its own subjectivity, individuality, and actuality*, experiencing "itself as actual and effective" and knowing that "it is *true* that it is *in and for itself.*"[132] What is more, in its seeking to be united with the unchangeable (God) who is the source of all reality, the subject acquires *a sense of universality and totality* through the religious acts or practices of surrendering its own will as a "particular individual will" and of positing the will of God, though mediated by the actions of the clerical authority, as a "universal will."[133]

Consequently, the subject—though at this stage ultimately unsuccessful in *explicitly* realizing "the *unity* of objectivity and being-for-itself which lies in the *concept* of action"[134]—does achieve a genuine ground for transformation that serves to effect the transition to "Reason"[135] as the *explicit* affirmation of the self-consciousness' implicit unity of individuality and universality and of subjectivity and objectivity. What must be emphasized here, in my view, is Hegel's deep conviction that the entire process of self-consciousness as the birth process of subjectivity is the dialectical movement toward rationality, i.e., self-conscious universality in the sense of "the unity of consciousness (the in-self) and self-consciousness" (the for-itself).[136] In this respect, for Hegel, the dialectical negation, or *determinate* negation, of individual subjectivity in the unhappy consciousness is an absolutely *necessary* moment in its movement toward universal rational subjectivity and ultimately toward absolute spiritual subjectivity.[137] Importantly, as we have seen, it is in and through its *action* that the subject necessarily proceeds on that journey.

---

132. *PS*, 135; §223.

133. *PS*, 138; §230.

134. *PS*, 138; §230.

135. It is necessary to understand "reason" in the *Phenomenology of Spirit* from two perspectives: one in its narrow sense as a specific stage of spirit, a form of natural consciousness toward the Absolute, which comes after the stages of "consciousness" and "self-consciousness"; and the other in its broad sense as equivalent to spirit (*Geist*).

136. Hyppolite, *Genesis and Structure*, 215.

137. The entire process that the unhappy consciousness has experienced as a sort of religious consciousness seems reminiscent of Matt 16:25: "For whoever would save his life will lose it, but whoever loses his life for my sake will find it."

CHAPTER 4

Hegel's Philosophy of Spiritual Subjectivity in the *Phenomenology of Spirit* (II)

The Growth of Subjectivity

FOR HEGEL, AS STATED previously, the human subject is not simply a self-identical, self-sufficient, self-contained "substance" in the modern sense of the term—something that is only relating itself to itself, which is the simple identity of what it is as an unchanging identity. Rather, in fact, its identity is always and already pervaded by its relations to things other than itself. The subject *is*, so to speak, a dialectical movement of "the identity of identity and non-identity," of the unity of being-for-itself (identity with itself) and being-for-others (relations with otherness). That is, the subject's relations to objects are *constitutive* of its very subjectivity not only in the birth process of its being awakened to self-conscious subjectivity that is conscious of itself as itself (subjectivity-for-itself), but also in the growth process, or *Bildung*, of its being driven into rational, universal subjectivity that is conscious of itself in relation to all reality in its otherness (subjectivity-in-and-for-itself).

Unlike the human subject at the preceding stage of self-consciousness where its relations to otherness have been a negative one, "concerned only with its independence and freedom"[1] and thereby struggling to remove the otherness of the object, it now enters into a *positive* relation to otherness and constantly searches for *more appropriate* objects in

---

1. *PS*, 139; §232.

which it can truly find its truth and essence as spiritual subjectivity. In this way, for Hegel, the growth of subjectivity is made possible in virtue of its movement of absolute negativity or infinity in the sense of not accepting the object simply given as it is in its immediacy, but instead finding mediation involved in it and so transcending its status quo. Thus, the human subject is *always* asking for something determinate as its object and, at the same time, sublating that determinateness in its immediacy and particularity, which is an ongoing process or movement toward something more absolute, infinite, rational, spiritual, and universal. It is in and through this process that human subjectivity becomes more and more absolute, infinite, rational, spiritual, and universal as well.

Only when the subject is fully universal, going beyond its parochial subjectivism and trying to be as objective as possible, and thereby its one-sidedness or sheer finitude disappears,[2] can it then do better justice to the object in its otherness. The truly mature and hence universal subject is, therefore, one that has the capacity to look upon objects as what they *truly* are. This also means that the object can fully reveal itself to the subject only insofar as the subject is truly universal and objective. Ultimately, Hegel argues, it is only in the Concept (*Begriff*), the concept-in-and-for-itself,[3] or the absolute concept, that truly universal (objective) subjectivity and truly universal (subjective) objectivity meet. In the concept as the absolute,[4] which is the absolute unification of subject and object, of consciousness and reality, the totality of the world is seen precisely as the expression of Absolute Spirit in its dialectical movement. In this sense, for Hegel, the human subject will not be a truly authentic, mature subject

---

2. For Hegel, the one-sidedness, which makes things finite, is due largely to our remaining at the level of the understanding (*Verstand*) that looks at things as self-contained, fixed, or reified without any internal, constitutive relatedness to others.

3. When we read Hegel's works including the *Phenomenology*, we need to pay attention to the usage of the word "concept," which is one of the most important terminologies in comprehending his philosophy. There seems to be largely three distinctive yet interrelated senses in its usage: first, as "the mere concept" that is purely subjective in character; second, as "the concept-in-itself" that contains the entire nature of a thing, i.e., what it truly is and ought to be in its intelligible, essential, dialectical structure, but has not yet been realized in actuality; and third, as "the concept-in-and-for-itself" that is the realization of the concept in its second sense above through the developmental process of its self-determination and self-reconciliation.

4. For Hegel's own exposition of the "concept" in its absoluteness, see *SL*, 577–95.

until it can *conceive* (*begreifen*) of the whole world, including itself, as the self-manifestation of Absolute Spirit that is in religion called "God."[5]

According to Hegel, this universalizing or spiritualizing movement of the human subject as the growth of subjectivity begins with "rational subjectivity" (Reason) which claims that it *as the individual* is all reality. Yet the rational individual soon realizes that it cannot be the measure of all reality unless in some way its claim is acceptable to other individuals in a communal setting. Therefore, rational subjectivity as individuality needs to grow into "social/communal subjectivity" (Spirit) that is, as it were, socialized reason, where the human subject is no longer merely an individual but a *member* of society that involves the shared context of life such as customs, traditions, values, laws, and so forth. The human subject as social subjectivity first lives simply in the midst of all the given customs and laws of society which it takes for granted. It then moves to a more self-critical spirit, where it goes through some different moments until it comes to moral subjectivity in its peculiarly modern, particularly Kantian, sense. Here the human subject runs into a great crisis again, for it sees that what it thinks as moral truth is not always acceptable and prevalent in the actual society. To resolve this contradiction, i.e., to reconcile the actuality of the world and the certainty of personal morality, it moves to "absolute subjectivity," that is, absolutely spiritual and universal subjectivity, where it becomes explicitly aware that all reality is the expression of Absolute Spirit (God) which is first presented to it in the form of *Vorstellung* (Religion) and then in the form of *Begriff* (Absolute Knowing). It is in this stage of absolute subjectivity that the human subject as spiritual subjectivity is to come to reach the fulfillment of its immanent telos, where the human subject *as* spirit is fully present to itself in all others equally *as* spirit.

In this relatively long chapter, I will investigate in some detail this whole process toward absolute subjectivity, where the human subject develops itself into becoming more and more spiritual and universal, which is a comprehensive reading of the remaining chapters of the *Phenomenology* from the viewpoint of "the growth of subjectivity."

---

5. For Hegel's identifying Absolut Spirit with God, see, to mention but a few, *LPR I*, 164, 370–71, 431–32; *LPWH*, 151.

Individual-Rational Subjectivity: "Reason"

As self-consciousness is becoming "reason" (*Vernunft*), i.e., *universal* self-consciousness,[6] the subject is not afraid of otherness, but instead expresses itself *positively* toward the object. At the stage of self-consciousness, the subject, whose concern was only to "save and maintain itself for itself," took a negative stance toward the objective world, that is to say, only "desired it" (the desiring subject), "worked on it" (the laboring subject), "withdrew from it into itself" (the stoic thinking subject), "abolished it as an existence on its own account" (the skeptic thinking subject), and "demolished its own self as consciousness—both as consciousness of the world as the essence and as consciousness of its nullity" (the unhappy split subject).[7] At the stage of reason, however, the subject, who seeks *in* this world its infinity, the unity of self-consciousness and the object, has a positive relationship to what it confronts and thus accepts both itself and the world, recognizing that the distinction between the world, the object, or external reality "as in itself" and "as for consciousness" is indeed made by the subject itself: the *I* as the subject is the one who makes this distinction.[8]

Certain of itself as all reality, the rational subject as the *individual* thus takes the world as its own construct: "the *existence* of the world becomes for self-consciousness its own *truth* and *presence*; it is certain of experiencing only itself therein."[9] In this sense, for Hegel, reason is a synthesis of "consciousness" (object-consciousness) and "self-consciousness"; in other words, in reason "what *is*, or the *in-itself*, only is insofar as it is *for* consciousness, and what is *for consciousness* is also what is *in itself*."[10] Hence, it is in this individual-rational subjectivity that the essential and ultimate truth of the identity of subjectivity and objectivity

---

6. When reason is called *universal* self-consciousness, it contains two distinctive aspects. First, it implies that *every human individual*—irrespective of empirical, cultural, or historical differences, regardless of being a master or slave—is essentially a rational self-consciousness. Second, it also indicates the universal nature of its claim, namely, that reason claims itself to be *all reality*.

7. *PS*, 139–40; §232.

8. This can be understood along the same lines as what Kant means by saying that "The *I think* must *be able* to accompany all my representations" (*CPR*, B131).

9. *PS*, 140; §232.

10. *PS*, 140–41; §233. This is something that fundamentally differentiates Hegel from Kant: for Hegel, there is no Kantian thing-in-itself (*Ding an sich*) beyond, or behind, phenomena.

begins to emerge for the first time. In short, according to Hegel, reason proceeds from "the certainty of consciousness that it *is* all reality."[11] For the rational subject, all reality is reducible to itself: the world is what I consider it to be. In other words, the rational subject as the individual takes itself to be the normative, constitutive source and criterion of all objectivity, which, Hegel observes, is the typical modern sense of reason that also corresponds to "idealism" in its most general sense of the term: "'I am I'"[12] in the sense that "'The I is all of reality' and 'All reality is the I.'"[13]

At first, however, the *certainty* of reason in its *immediacy* is merely a subjective and abstract claim which has not as yet been objectified and concretized into the *truth* of reason.[14] Hegel argues that such a purely subjective, abstract notion of reason is bound to issue in a self-contradiction, the contradiction *between* "empty idealism" in the sense of emptily proclaiming the pure form of reason, i.e., the mind's categories, to be all reality *and* "absolute empiricism" in the sense of absolutely requiring the content of reality as an external impulse which triggers and gives filling to this pure reason. In this way, Hegel observes, similar to the predicament of skepticism, "this reason remains a restless searching, which in its very searching declares that the satisfaction of finding is utterly impossible."[15]

---

11. *PS*, 140; §233. Emphasis mine.

12. *PS*, 140; §233.

13. Hyppolite, *Genesis and Structure*, 225. See also Winfield, *Hegel's Phenomenology of Spirit*, 128, where he succinctly explains what Hegel means by idealism here, particularly in contrast to solipsism: "He [Hegel] is not talking about solipsism, but idealism. We would have solipsism if all we were left with was self-consciousness that is merely subjective . . . Here, however, we have an idealism, where knowing is at one with all reality without reality losing its independent, essential being."

14. *PS*, 141; §233: "this reason which comes immediately on the scene appears only as the *certainty* of that truth. Thus, it merely *asserts* that it is all reality, but does not itself comprehend this . . ." Particularly, Hegel seems to have the subjective idealism of Kant and Fichte in mind here. Simply put, as alluded to in the second chapter (section 2) of this book, Hegel's critique is that although Kant and Fichte understood the principle of idealism that the rational subject is all reality, they just remained at the level of *immediate certainty* as to this principle, without raising it into the level of *mediated truth*. To put it another way, Kant and Fichte might not recognize the distinction between the initial claim or certainty of reason and the complete truth of reason. See also *PS*, 142–45; §235–39, where Hegel specifically presents his critique of Kant's transcendental idealism on this score.

15. *PS*, 145; §239.

For Hegel, therefore, reason must "become" (*Werden*) all reality *in process* or in history. That is, true rationality is destined to go through various forms of mediation of otherness and to sublate them into itself in its self-determining, self-transforming, and self-transcending movement. The rational subject *is*[16] all reality, Hegel writes, "not merely *for itself* but also *in itself*, only through *becoming* this reality, or rather through *demonstrating* itself to be such."[17] According to Hegel, to prove itself to be all reality, i.e., to give concrete filling to pure reason, the subject is now impelled to proceed to become, firstly, observing reason (the theoretical rational subject), secondly, active reason (the practical rational subject), and finally, self-actualizing reason (the universal-individual rational subject).

The Theoretical Rational Subject: Observing Reason

The subject must now embark on its journey to true subjectivity in earnest through raising its abstract, formal certainty of being all reality to actual, concrete truth, that is, through itself validating the unity of subjectivity and objectivity. To do this, the rational subject engages first in discovering itself in the content of the *given*: "Reason is dimly aware of itself as a deeper essence than the pure I *is*, and must demand that difference, *diverse being*, become its very own, that it behold itself as *actuality* and find itself present as both a shape and a thing."[18] This undertaking is, according to Hegel, characterized as the activity of "observing reason" (*Beobachtende Vernunft*), i.e., the subject's observation or theorization[19]

---

16. For Hegel, the "is" here must be taken in a dialectical term. That is, the dialectical sense of *is* refers not simply to an immediate, static, or reified identity but to a "mediated" identity in its dialectical movement, i.e., the identity of identity and non-identity/otherness.

17. *PS*, 140; §233.

18. *PS*, 146; §241. Emphasis mine. The whole section of "Observing Reason" in the *Phenomenology* could be read as a sort of Hegel's critique of modern scientific positivism which claims that something is true simply because it is *given* as fact according to the criteria of scientific experimentations. In this section, Hegel provides a very prolonged dialectical critique of the positivistic scientific procedure relying on so-called *observation*—particularly, in the fields of physics (observation of inorganic nature), biology (observation of organic nature), and psychology (observation of the human being).

19. The word "theory" comes from the Greek *theoria*, and its verb *theorein* means "to see, to observe."

about the object as given, which begins with the observation of things out there in nature, followed by that of the being which has interiority or self-consciousness, that is, the human being.

Before moving into details of the itinerary which the subject goes through as observing reason, it should be noted, as Hegel points out, that although the subject appears to revert to the stage of "consciousness" (object-consciousness) in that it has great interest in the world of objects, it is, at this stage, not conscious of the world as pure otherness, but certain of itself *as* this other. It thus "*itself* makes the observations and engages the experience," rather than merely being immersed in the object given in its immediacy without being conscious of its own constitutive and determining role as in the case of object-consciousness.[20] Hence, what the subject now seeks to find in the object is not pure sensuous thinghood given to itself as brute otherness, but "*its* other" as *sublated* otherness, that is, a "*concept*," which is at once subjective and objective, "knowing that therein it possesses nothing else but itself."[21]

However, as will be seen repeatedly in its observations of inorganic nature, organic nature, and the human being, the subject always finds itself in a self-contradictory predicament, namely, the discrepancy between what it *as* reason essentially intends to achieve (i.e., itself as the *concept*, or conceptual determinacy, of reality in its universality and necessity) and what it actually encounters in its observation (i.e., the extrinsic essence of reality in its particularity and contingency). This is, Hegel insists, due fundamentally to the *inherent* limitation of observing reason in its immediate *action of observation*.[22] "Observation" *per se* involves congealing, fixating, or reifying objects as given in the form of thinghood, thereby necessarily finding itself (the observing subject) therein, too, as reason in the form of being in its immediacy and not yet as reason in its mediated, conceptual movement:

> Consciousness *observes*; i.e., reason wants to find and to have itself as existent object, as an *actual, sensuously-present* mode. The consciousness that observes in this way opines and indeed says that it wants to learn from experience *not about itself* but, on the contrary, *about the essence of things qua things*. That

20. *PS*, 145; §240. In other words, unlike object-consciousness, reason is not simply passive vis-à-vis the world of objects.

21. *PS*, 145–46; §240. Emphasis mine.

22. This is also characterized, in Hegel's phrase, by "the instinct of reason" (*PS*, 149–57; §246–58).

this consciousness means and says this, is implied in the fact that it *is* reason; but reason as such is not as yet object for this consciousness.[23]

According to Hegel, the movement of the theoretical rational subject "in its observational activity" passes through some different dialectical phases, which gradually makes *explicit* the belief that "it is only as concepts that things have truth" or that the essence of things and the essence of the subject are one and the same.[24] These phases are largely, first, the observation of nature (*Beobachtung der Natur*) and secondly, the observation of self-consciousness (*Beobachtung des Selbstbewußtseins*).

Observation of Nature

The theoretical rational subject begins with its observation of inorganic things in nature,[25] for which the essence of things is at stake, i.e., "a *universal*," and not simply the sensuous apprehension of them such as "tasting, smelling, feeling, hearing, and seeing."[26] Hegel distinguishes here three dialectical moments in observing nature to discover what is universal in the given, each also corresponding to the tripartite of object-consciousness (sense-certainty, perception, and the understanding): description (*Beschreiben*), differentia (*Merkmal*), and law (*Gesetz*).

The theoretical rational subject's first way of observing things in nature to discover their universal essence takes the form of "description," which is the lowest level of observing reason. The description of natural things means, simply put, observing them *sensuously* and describing some regularities repeatedly found in these sensuous givens.[27] Hegel

---

23. *PS*, 146; §242. Hegel continues to argue in this paragraph that: "If it [consciousness] knew that *reason* is equally the essence of things and of consciousness itself, and that it is only in consciousness that reason can be present in its own proper shape, it would descend into its own depths, and seek reason there rather than in things. If it were to find reason within, it would be directed from there outside to actuality again, in order to behold therein its sensuous expression, but at the same time to take it essentially as *concept*."

24. *PS*, 147; §242–43.

25. In this section of "Observation of Nature," Hegel takes on the examination of the Schellingian philosophy of nature rather than the investigation of empirical science in general since Bacon; see Hyppolite, *Genesis and Structure*, 233–34.

26. *PS*, 147; §244.

27. Winfield, *Hegel's Phenomenology of Spirit*, 135.

regards this as the "superficial raising out of singularity, and the equally superficial form of universality into which the sensuous object is merely taken up, without having in itself become a universal," which "does not yet have the movement in the object itself; the movement is really only in the describing."[28] In this way, description is not to enter into the interiority of things, but merely to state their appearance in universal terms from the extrinsic point of view. Since it does not engage in the intrinsic essence of things, description is soon faced with its limits. That is, there is no end to the activity of describing things because "if one object has been described, then another must be dealt with, and continually looked for"; furthermore, observing reason cannot discern whether this or that statistical regularity as described is essentially universal and necessary or merely contingent.[29] Therefore, the theoretical subject that wants to observe in nature its rationality (i.e., universality and necessity) can no longer remain satisfied with merely describing things in their sensuous regularities. It must move to a higher moment of observing things in nature, namely, seeking out their distinguishing features, *differentiae*.

The theoretical rational subject now undertakes the task of distinguishing the essential and necessary properties of things in nature from their inessential and accidental ones, through which "the things themselves *break loose* from the universal continuity of being as such, *separate* themselves from others, and are explicitly *for themselves*."[30] For example, in the case of animals, "claws and teeth" are observed as their differentiae, universal determinacies, whereby each animal is itself distinguished and separated from others, and in that way "it maintains itself *for itself* and keeps itself detached from the universal."[31] However, observing reason soon finds such features subject to change; animals, for instance, can lose their claws or teeth. Thus, these differentiae are no longer seen as stable, necessary, universal determinacies but as "vanishing *moments*."[32] Put another way, the theoretical rational subject that looks for what is universal and necessary in the differentiae of things confronts what is particular and contingent instead. As such, Hegel observes, the differentia as the *fixed* universal determinacy necessarily involves the opposition between

28. PS, 147–48; §245.
29. PS, 148; §245.
30. PS, 149; §246.
31. PS, 149; §246.
32. PS, 150; §248.

universality and particularity within itself, for it is in essence "the unity of opposites, of what is determinate and what is in itself universal; it must therefore split up into this opposition."³³ It is the *law* that unifies this opposition in terms of *relation*, and therefore observing reason moves from searching for the differentiae, the fixed distinguishing marks of natural things, to the laws that govern what it confronts, the changing of determinacies.

The observing subject now seeks after the laws of nature, which are believed to provide a way of finding itself in nature, in place of differentiae. According to Hegel, as already pointed out in our discussions about the understanding as a form of object-consciousness, the law is "*in itself* a concept,"³⁴ for "if the law does not have its truth in the concept, then it is a contingency, not a necessity, or not in fact a law."³⁵ Through the law, the subject as observing reason thus deals with things experienced in nature not merely as sensuous givens like "bodies" or "properties," but as concepts or, more precisely, as what Hegel calls "*matters*" (*Materien*), that is, "being in the form of a *universal*, or being in the mode of a concept."³⁶ However, the law that is discovered through observing inorganic nature in an experiential framework by means of experimentation and inference relying on analogy leads to no more than a probability,³⁷ for it is still conditioned by objective being in its externality and thus cannot get away from contingent empirical instances.³⁸ What the observing subject experiences through this is that the law cannot be truly universal and

33. *PS*, 150; §247.
34. *PS*, 152; §251.
35. *PS*, 151; §249.
36. *PS*, 153–54; §251–52. This reminds us again about the meaning of the principle of idealism mentioned earlier that "reason is all reality." In virtue of the law, the subject secures its reality or objectivity, and the object acquires universality. In this way, the subject and the object, or the I and the world, proceed to a more internal relation one step further through the law. It must be noted, however, that to the observing subject, "the *truth of the law* is in *experience*, in the same way that *sensuous being* is *for it*; it is not in and for itself. . . . In other words, the concept presents itself in the mode of thinghood and sensuous being" (*PS*, 151; §249).

37. See *PS*, 152; §250, where Hegel explains the law of gravitation as an example: "The assertion that stones fall when raised above the ground and dropped certainly does not at all require this experiment to be made with every stone; it does perhaps say that the experiment must have been made with at least a great number, and from this we can then *by analogy* draw an inference about the rest with the greatest probability or with perfect right."

38. We can easily notice that Hegel points out the problem of induction here.

necessary *insofar as* it remains caught in the sensuous, contingent events of inorganic nature. This limitation experienced in the observation of things in nature prompts the theoretical rational subject to turn its activity of observation to a new sort of object, namely, living being or the "organism."

According to Hegel, the organism as life is an object that "in itself contains the process in the *simplicity* of the concept" and the "absolute fluidity in which the determinateness, through which it would be only *for others*, is dissolved"; in other words, the organism "maintains itself in its relation," within which being-for-itself and being-for-others are *internally* related, while an inorganic thing exists only as being-for-others without reflecting on itself in relation to other things.[39] In this sense, unlike inorganic things, the organism exists as "*necessity realized*,"[40] and not merely as the necessity of relation for consciousness.[41]

The theoretical rational subject as observing reason, first, proceeds to discover the laws governing organisms that define the relations of individual organisms to the environmental elements of inorganic nature such as air, water, earth, zones, climate, etc.[42] In other words, the observing subject tries to discover the law that demonstrates "the connection of an element with the formation of the organism."[43] Yet such a relation— for instance, a lawful connection between air and the nature of birds or between water and the nature of fish—cannot be called law; for, "firstly, such a relation in its content . . . does not exhaust the range of the organisms concerned, and secondly, the moments of the relation themselves remain mutually indifferent and express no necessity."[44] Hence, the relation of inorganic environment to the organism is not a lawful necessity but merely a matter of influence: "the expression of the necessity of the

39. *PS*, 154; §254.

40. Hyppolite, *Genesis and Structure*, 241.

41. Particularly, according to Hegel, the animal organism alone, as opposed to the vegetable organism, is most suitable one for the essence of organism; see *PS*, 161; §265.

42. The contemporary term for this relation could be called "adaptation."

43. *PS*, 155; §255.

44. *PS*, 155; §255. As shown in this quoted passage, the relation of the organism to inorganic nature is not one of internal relation but merely external and contingent one. Here the law means that which governs the relations between the environmental elemental factors of inorganic nature and the particular features of the organism; in fact, however, there is no necessary connection between them. For example, no matter how hard observing reason tries to analyze the nature of water, it cannot draw the shape of a fish therefrom.

laws cannot be other than superficial and amounts to no more than the *great influence* of environment."[45]

As it encounters an arbitrary, contingent, external relation, rather than a lawful, necessary, internal relation, between the organism and the environmental elemental factors of inorganic nature, the observing subject, who searches for the essence of the organism, now turns to "teleological" explanation according to which, instead of external causes (the environmental elemental factors of inorganic nature) producing determinate effects (the features of the organism), the organism possesses an end or purpose. However, at this level, the observing subject in its still instinctive immediacy never rises above the purview of *external* or extrinsic teleology in the sense that it regards the telos of the organism as something objective, belonging to some supernatural intelligence *external* to the organism itself. The truth is, however, that the organism is the real end itself, or the realized purpose, in which the activity of the organism and its purpose are not to be separated out; that is, it must be the product of *internal* or immanent teleological process:

> The organism shows itself to be something that *preserves* itself, that *returns* and *has returned* into itself. But this observing consciousness does not recognize in this being the concept of purpose, or the fact that the concept of purpose exists just here and as a thing, and not elsewhere in some other intelligence.[46]

As expected, however, this kind of external teleological explanation does not lead the theoretical rational subject to what it has originally intended to observe in the organism, i.e., itself *as* lawful, conceptual rationality in its universality and necessity. In external teleology there is always an element of contingency lurking in the relation of the action of the organism as instrumental means and the realization of its purpose. It is because the organism (being) is itself *observed* as different from, and external to, its purpose (concept), and therefore the action of the organism cannot guarantee that it would fully fulfill its instrumental role for that purpose.[47]

45. *PS*, 155; §255.
46. *PS*, 158; §259.
47. As Hyppolite points out, this whole discussion on external teleology may be seen as a critique of Kant's philosophy set forth particularly in his *Critique of Judgment*, where Kant recognizes teleology in nature, but separates the telos from nature and makes it conceivable only for an intuitive understanding that is not ours; see Hyppolite, *Genesis and Structure*, 248.

To overcome this separation of the concept of purpose from the actual being or reality of the organism, which is based on external teleological explanation, the theoretical rational subject now seeks to observe a new kind of lawful relation that goes beyond merely pointing to their external connection. In this way, the organism now appears to observing reason—though it does not as yet recognize the intrinsic unity of the universal conceptual purpose and the particular activity of the organism—as "a relation of two *fixed* moments in the form of *immediate being*," i.e., a relation of the organism's two *observable* realities of "the *inner*" (the concept of purpose) and "the *outer*" (actuality), which then produces "the law *that the outer is the expression of the inner*."[48]

In accordance with this law, the observing subject claims that the inner of the organism has its corresponding outer expression in a way that links the organic functions of the organism with its anatomical organs. For example, the nerve system is the expression of sensibility, the muscular system is that of irritability, and the visceral system is that of reproduction.[49] There is certainly a connection between these inner and outer aspects of the organism, but observing reason soon finds this claim untenable. In fact, one inner organic function, be it sensibility, irritability, or reproduction, is neither strictly distinct from other functions nor exhaustively delimited by one particular system; instead, the organic functions are the "moments" of the movement of the organism as a whole (unity) and therefore go beyond their particular systems. Hegel writes in this regard:

> Since the *being* of the organism is essentially universality or reflection-into-self, the *being* of its totality, like its moments, cannot consist in an anatomical system; on the contrary, the actual expression of the whole, and the externalization of its moments, are really present only as a movement which runs its

---

48. *PS*, 159–60; §262.

49. Hegel defines these three inner organic functions in the following manner: "*Sensibility* expresses in general the simple concept of organic reflection-into-itself, or the universal fluidity of the concept. *Irritability*, though, expresses organic elasticity, the capacity of the organism to behave *reactively* at the same time within that reflection, and the actualization which is opposed to the initial quiescent *being-within-itself*, an actualization in which that abstract being-for-itself is a being-*for-others*. *Reproduction*, however, is the action of this *whole* organism reflected into itself, its activity as a purpose in itself, or as *genus*, in which the individual thus repels itself from itself, and in procreative act reproduces either its organic parts or the whole individual" (*PS*, 161; §266; see also Hegel, *Philosophy of Nature*, 359–60; §354).

course through the various parts of the structure, a movement in which what is forcibly detached and fixed as an individual system essentially displays itself as a fluid moment.[50]

In short, if both inner functions and outer organs are not regarded as aspects of the *totality* of the organism in its *movement*, i.e., as the moments of the concept of the organism, it would be tantamount to considering the organism a *thing*, which is completely contradictory to the very nature of the *organic* as the life process. Consequently, the observing subject reveals that the law that it has claimed to discover in the life of organic nature must be sublated—the law proposed on the basis of the separation of the inner of the organism and the outer as its expression, in which both the inner and the outer and their relation are viewed as something observable and thereby displayed only quantitatively taking on the mode of a fixed determinateness. Such a quantitative law, Hegel observes, cannot be properly applied to the organism, for "each aspect of the organism is in its own self just this: to be simple universality in which all determinations are dissolved, and to be the movement of this dissolution."[51] After all, the theoretical rational subject, which, in its instinctive immediacy, has attempted to observe the law of the organism in a way that reifies the inner and outer aspects of the organism in their fixation and separation and thus abstracts the relational process of its moments quantitatively and mechanistically, fails to find itself as a *concept* in the organism.[52]

Observation of Self-Consciousness

The theoretical/observational rational subject was unsuccessful in finding itself in nature. Particularly, it failed to discover necessity and universality—in terms of the law—in the relation of the inner and outer of the organism. Once again, this failure is due fundamentally to the inherent inadequacy of *observation* as such: observing the organism in its immediate givenness and so seeing the relation of its inner and outer as something observable, i.e., something congealed, fixed, or reified, without any movement or process. With this failure, the theoretical rational subject now claims that the necessary connection between the

50. PS, 166; §276. See also Hegel, *Philosophy of Nature*, 360–72; §354 Z.
51. PS, 167; §278.
52. PS, 169; §281.

inner and the outer, in which the unity of universality and individuality can be grasped, is to be found not outside the subject itself but *within* itself. That is, the essence, truth, or concept of the object is captured not in the individual organism that is out there as observed, but in the human mind that observes it. Thus, the observing subject now moves from the observation of nature to the observation of itself, i.e., the observation of human self-consciousness, where it again searches for the universal laws that govern all reality as given.[53]

What observing reason turning in upon itself first seeks to find is the "*laws of thought*," viz., logical laws, understood as "the abstract movement of the negative, a movement wholly retracted into simplicity ... outside of reality."[54] In other words, in the first moment of the observation of self-consciousness the theoretical rational subject focuses on discovering the laws that regulate the process of thinking consciousness in its purely immediate givenness, independently of its relation to any external reality even including its own body. Yet these purely formal laws of thought without any internal relatedness to reality is merely *contentless* abstraction.[55] Confronted with the invalidity of logical laws given to observation merely as a formal, fixed, reified collection of lawful determinations, observing reason now proceeds to the observation of self-consciousness in its actuality as "*active consciousness*"[56] in relation to external reality, yet without itself being aware of the internal, intrinsic connection between thinking consciousness and active consciousness. Hence, "psychological laws" are now the new object for observation.

The psychological laws concern some causal necessity of the individual's ways of relating itself to external reality as given. Observing reason thus attempts to discover some lawful determinations that account for the influence of the given circumstances, habits, and customs of universal reality on the psychological faculties, inclinations, and passions of individuals. However, psychological observation's claim that there is a lawful necessity found in this relationship turns out to be an empty

---

53. It would be interesting to take a close look at a parallel between this move and the previous transition from the stage of consciousness to self-consciousness.

54. *PS*, 180; §299.

55. According to Hegel, no content can be obtained without the *internal* division of subject and object: "what is purely formal without reality is a mere figment of thought, or an empty abstraction without that internal division which would be nothing else but the content" (*PS*, 180; §299).

56. *PS*, 181; §301.

assertion, for there is always an inherent contingency lurking in *how* individuals act in face of the way of the world as given. In other words, the significance of the influence that the actual world exerts on individuality varies from individual to individual according to each individual's preferences in their particularity and contingency: "the individual either lets the stream of actuality with its flowing influence *have its way* in him, or else breaks it off and inverts it."[57] Consequently, observing reason reveals, through this experience, that it cannot find any laws which *universally* and *necessarily* regulate self-consciousness in its relation to actuality, or the way of the world, and that it is rather the individual itself as independent, free actuality that truly counts.[58]

With that realization, the theoretical rational subject as observing reason now turns its observational activity *from* discovering psychological laws, which govern the relation of self-consciousness to the world it confronts outside itself, *to* finding the laws that determine self-consciousness, taken now as actual individuality in its own right, in relation to its own immediate actuality, namely, *its own body*. Observing reason, with its instinct, immediate nature of fixation or reification, turns its eyes on the visible *being* (body) of invisible individuality (spirit, mind, or consciousness), in accordance with the law that the exteriority is the manifestation of interiority. For observing reason, the body, as the external manifestation of inner individuality, refers to *both* an "*intrinsic* being" or "*original* determinate being" of individuality as given, or inherited, *and* an expressive "*sign*" of individuality as produced, or acquired, by its own activity.[59] In this respect, Hegel states, the body is "the unity of the natural (*ungebildet*) being and the cultured (*gebildet*) being," i.e., the being in its totality that "contains within it the determinate original fixed parts and the traits arising solely from the activity," and in that way it is the

---

57. PS, 184; §307. As Hegel writes in PS 182; §302, there are, to be specific, two basic ways in which the individual can act in relation to the way of the world it confronts: *either* conforming to it *or* opposing it in which then there are two different modes as well, namely, violating it as a criminal and transforming it as a reformer or revolutionary.

58. See PS, 185; §308: "Individuality is what *its* world is, the world that is its *own*. Individuality is itself the cycle of its doing, in which it has exhibited itself as actuality, and as simply and solely the unity of *being present* and *being made*; a unity whose sides do not fall apart, as in the representation of psychological law, into a world present *in itself* and an individuality existing *for itself*. Or, if those sides are thus considered each for itself, then there is no necessity and no law of their relation to each other."

59. PS, 185–86; §310.

actuality (being-in-itself) of inner individuality (being-for-itself), "the *expression* of the inner, of the individual posited as consciousness and as movement."[60] From this point of view, the theoretical rational subject as observing reason now seeks to validate its claim that the individual's body is the true and necessary expression of its interiority.

Particularly, Hegel points out two pseudo-sciences that are in line with this undertaking of observing reason: physiognomy (*Physiognomik*) and phrenology (*Schädellehre*).[61] Physiognomy is a science that studies about the necessary causal relationship between one's inner character and the form and movement of one's countenance, to the extent that it claims to detect the individual's inner intention by observing facial traits and expressions. Following Lichtenberg's trenchant criticism against physiognomy, Hegel characterizes it as a "science of mere subjective opinion,"[62] in the sense that the laws governing the relations between one's inner character and outer countenance it claims to discover is nothing more than "idle chatter, or merely the voicing of *one's own opinion*," which is tantamount to saying: "'It always rains when we have our annual fair,' says the dealer; 'and every time, too,' says the housewife, 'when I am drying my washing.'"[63] In short, one's countenance not only possibly expresses his true intention but also falsely disguises it, and, in this respect, not lawful necessity but merely arbitrary contingency is to be found in physiognomy.

To avoid such contingency in the correspondence between the inner and outer of individuality in physiognomy, observing reason now seeks to find in phrenology the true and necessary outer expression of the inner, which is neither an organ of action, e.g., the speaking mouth, the laboring hand, etc., nor an expressive sign such as countenance. Unlike physiognomy in which the outer is a sort of "speaking sign," a "mediated being" for the self-conscious individual in its movement, in phrenology the outer is a "wholly *immobile* actuality" as the *immediate* actuality of self-conscious movement, independently of any signifying visible activity, that is to say, a "mere thing."[64] To be more specific, phrenology says

60. PS, 186; §311.

61. These two sciences drew lots of attention in Hegel's time. The then leading exponents of physiognomy and phrenology were Johann Kaspar Lavater and Franz Josef Gall, respectively.

62. PS, 193; §322.

63. PS, 193; §321.

64. PS, 195; §323.

that one's dispositions are exhaustively expressed in the shape and size of her skull with its bumps and hollows. This is based on the belief that it seems commonsensical that among the indifferent, natural thing-like, inert parts of the human body is the skull-bone, which takes its shape directly from the brain perceived as the most plausible organ of self-consciousness, "the proper location of spirit's outer existence."[65] In this way, it insists, the self-conscious individual's spirit is broken down into the localized faculties of the brain, each of which in turn *causally* corresponds to an adjacent particular cranial area.

Following phrenology, the theoretical rational subject as observing reason claims to discover the true observable manifestation of the individual's self-conscious interiority in the skull-bone as a purely immediate thing, and it presents its final peak in the form of infinite judgment (*das unendliche Urteil*): "*The being of spirit is a bone.*"[66] In order to justify a "necessary reciprocal relation" between the skull-bone and spirit, observing reason even advances a "pre-established harmony of the corresponding determination of the two aspects."[67] Yet, for phrenological observation, as is the case with physiognomy, there is no lawful necessity which can be discovered in this relation; rather, "there remains for observation the entire *contingency* of their relation."[68] No matter how many observations confirm the correlations among a particular disposition of the individual, a particular area of the brain, and its corresponding bump or hollow of the skull-bone, there is no guarantee both that observations will be able to exhaust those relations and that new observations will not contradict them:

> If the children of Israel, who were likened in number to the sands of the sea-shore, should each take unto himself the grain of sand which stood for him, the indifference and arbitrariness of such a procedure would be no more glaring than that which assigns to every capacity of soul, to every passion . . . its particular area of skull and shape of skull-bone.[69]

Just as the fact that it rains has nothing to do with the fact that a particular housewife does the laundry or that a particular man eats roast

---

65. *PS*, 197; §328.
66. *PS*, 208; §343.
67. *PS*, 202; §335.
68. *PS*, 202; §335. Emphasis mine.
69. *PS*, 202; §335.

beef, so a particular disposition of the individual as spirit is indifferent to a particular shape of the skull. In this way, observing reason comes to reveal that contrary to its claim, there is indeed no internal, necessary relation at all between self-consciousness and the skull-bone, since free and active spirit that constantly differentiates itself from itself in the movement of negativity cannot be expressed in what merely *is*, i.e., an inert, reified, fixed reality or a thing.

With this despairing experience of phrenological observation, which is the culmination of the whole dialectical process of observing reason, the rational subject runs into a great crisis, which then, as expected, constitutes a dialectical turning point. The subject "no longer aims to *find* itself *immediately*" by means of its action of *observing* objects as simply *given*, starting from inorganic things in nature to the organism, even to human individuality (self-consciousness), but it now attempts to "produce itself by its own activity."[70] How, indeed, is this transition possible, the transition of the rational subject from "observing reason" (*the theoretical I*) to "active reason" (*the practical I*)? Hegel explains it in connection with the ways to read an infinite judgment. As mentioned above, the theoretical rational subject in its phrenological observation formulates its final claim in the form of infinite judgment that "The spirit is a bone."[71] At first glance, this infinite judgment appears as a sheer paradox with some categorical mistake, in that it combines two completely incommensurable terms in an immediate manner. However, Hegel argues, there is another way of reading this infinite judgment which negates this initial *representational* reading that reduces self-conscious individuality immediately to a thing. It is the speculative, dialectical, or *conceptual* reading that allows the subject to get at the truth of the identity of the I (spirit) and being (bone), the identity not as a simple, immediate sameness but as the identity of identity and non-identity. Since the infinite judgment in its conceptual reading allows the subject to see a greater contradiction involved in the phrenological idea and *at the same time* the demand of its sublation, it leads to a greater transformation. More specifically, confronting the real contradiction and crisis of itself turning into a mere thing, a bone, the rational subject is compelled to be driven into itself, through which it confirms that "the object that is present or

---

70. PS, 209; §344.

71. Among Hegel scholars, Žižek studies more in depth the meaning and implication of Hegelian infinite judgment, with special emphasis on negativity. For this, see Žižek, *Sublime Object of Ideology*, 234–41.

given is consequently determined as a negative object; consciousness, however, is determined as *self*-consciousness over against it."[72]

In this way, the rational subject finds "the thing as itself, and itself as a thing," not in the sense of the immediate, representational unity between them, but in the sense of the mediated, conceptual unity; in other words, "*it is aware* that it is *in itself* objective actuality" as its true essence.[73] Hence, the object is now seen only as the appearance of the subject's inner essence as reason, and thus the unity of reason into reality requires the activity of the rational subject which transforms the world as given into something that can be at one with itself. Therefore, instead of merely seeking to discover itself as a being, i.e., as the category in the object that is already given and thus ready to be observed, the rational subject now decides to find itself *in its very own activity*; that is to say, it attempts to construct and transform the world through its own activity.

The Practical Rational Subject: Active Reason

As having just examined above, the rational subject as observing reason has gone through various dialectical moments in its journey of raising its certainty of being all reality to truth, not least in the way that it seeks to find in the object as given the category or law which exhibits the unity of subjectivity and objectivity. However, the experience of all the modes of observing reason—which began with the observation of inorganic nature, moved to that of organic nature, and then finally to that of self-consciousness in its pure interiority (logical laws), in its relation to external reality, i.e., the environing natural and social circumstances (psychological laws), and in its relation to its immediate actuality, i.e., its own body (physiognomy and phrenology)—disclosed that its intention to discover itself universally and necessarily in the object in the form of the category would never be able to be fulfilled. This insurmountable gap between its claim and the actuality it experiences reached its peak in phrenological observation, where, though observing reason at first glance, or at the level of representation, seemed to achieve its goal by finding itself as a thing, as the most immediate form of the category, "the unity of the I and being,"[74]

---

72. *PS*, 209; §344.
73. *PS*, 211; §347.
74. *PS*, 208; §344.

it came to realize that the I as reason, as a self-differentiating movement, cannot be reduced to a mere inanimate, inert thing.

Negating the limitation of the theoretical subject inherent in its very action of observation—that is, congealing or fixating what it confronts as already given and so finding itself merely in the reified given—but, at the same time, preserving the awareness of observing reason particularly in its final moment of crisis in the pursuit of proving itself to be all reality, namely, the awareness that the subject is the inner essence of the object, the rational subject now develops into "active reason" that produces itself by acting on the given, the world. The practical rational subject as active reason claims that it can explicitly bring the unity of reason into reality by actualizing itself in the object or, in other words, by transforming the world it confronts. It intends to confirm the world *as* the work (*Werk*) of its own activity, thereby validating its certainty that all reality is rational. As Hegel points out, the *ultimate* end of the practical rational subject's own activity lies in "the *realm of ethical life*" (*das Reich der Sittlichkeit*) or the "ethical *substance*," in which the dialectical, mediated unity of being-for-itself and being-for-others, namely, "the absolute spiritual *unity* of the essence of individuals in their independent *actuality*" is to be accomplished.[75] To attain this realm of ethical life (*Sittlichkeit*), the subject as the practical individual must raise itself into "universal reason"[76] or socialized reason that achieves mutual recognition (*Anerkennung*) *in and for itself*—finding itself in other self-conscious individuals while at the same time finding in its own individuality all other free, independent self-conscious individuals. In short, Hegel argues, in the realm of ethical life as the spiritual essence I am present to myself in all other individuals: "I intuit them as myself and myself as them,"[77] that is, "the *I* that is *We* and the *We* that is *I*."[78]

Yet, as stated above, this "*happy state*" of the unity of the I and the We in and through the ethical, spiritual, universal substance is not a reality

---

75. PS, 212; §349. Specifically, Hegel presents a "people or nation" (*Volk*) as the primary place in which the concept of *Sittlichkeit* is to be actualized.

76. For Hegel, reason is, in and of itself, universal. However, "reason" as discussed in this stage, be it observing or active reason, is still the reason of individuality or subjectively-universal reason. In this sense, "universal reason" here as the goal of active reason refers to reason that knows itself as objectively universal, namely, as "*spirit* that has the certainty of having its unity with itself in the duplication of its self-consciousness and in the independence of both*" (*PS*, 211; §347).

77. *PS*, 214; §351.

78. *PS*, 110; §177.

as something already given, but an implicit goal (*in-itself*) as something to attain explicitly (*for-itself*) through a series of practical mediations.[79] Therefore, the rational subject as active reason, as the practical individual, must now step into the world to actualize this goal of happiness. As we will see, however, what the rational subject aims to achieve will not be realized by this form of active reason, which will in turn lead to the last section of Reason in the *Phenomenology*, entitled "Individuality which takes itself to be real in and for itself" (*Die Individualität, welches sich an und für sich reell ist*).

According to Hegel, there are three dialectical moments in the practical rational subject's voyage toward universal reason and *Sittlichkeit*:[80] pleasure (*Lust*), the law of the heart (*das Gesetz seines Herzens*), and virtue (*Tugend*).[81] Hegel sketches out the whole process of these three moments as follows:

> Its initial end . . . is its *immediate* abstract *being-for-itself* [pleasure]; in other words, intuiting itself as *this singular individual* in another, or intuiting another self-consciousness as itself. The experience of what the truth of this end is raises self-consciousness to a higher level, and from now on it is itself its own end, insofar as it is at the same time *universal* and has the *law immediately* within it. In carrying out this *law* of its *heart*, however, it learns from experience that the *singularly individual* being, in doing so, cannot preserve himself, but rather that the good can only be accomplished through the sacrifice of the singularly individual being, and self-consciousness becomes *virtue*. What virtue learns from experience can only be this, that its end is already attained in itself, that happiness is found immediately in the action itself, and that action itself is the good.[82]

Let us briefly consider these three moments of active reason in the order.

---

79. *PS*, 215; §356.

80. See *PS*, 211; §348, where Hegel says that just as observing reason repeated, by the mediation of the category, the movement of Consciousness, i.e., sense certainty, perception, and the understanding, so will active reason repeat at a higher level the movement of Self-Consciousness.

81. All these moments correspond to the different forms of modern individualism; see Hyppolite, *Genesis and Structure*, 274–75. In this respect, this whole section can be read as Hegel's critique of modern individualism and its concomitant divisions of modern society in the light of *Sittlichkeit*—such as divisions of individual and society, individual will and general will, inclination and morality, etc.

82. *PS*, 216–17; §359.

Pleasure

To begin with, as always, the practical rational subject as active reason in its *immediacy*, which has just come to intuit itself as the essence of the world through the process of various experiences in the form of observing reason, aims "to become conscious of itself as an *individual* essence in the other self-consciousness, or to make this other into itself."[83] Immediately certain that all others are essentially itself, the subject attempts to actualize its pure, given individuality by taking or enjoying, rather than making, *pleasure* without regard to all sorts of the social context in which it is situated.[84] According to Hegel, "pleasure" (*Lust*) is, on the one hand, similar to "desire" (*Begierde*), the first and most immediate, natural form of self-consciousness, in that both intend to enjoy its pure being-for-itself in relation to the otherness of objects it confronts. Yet, on the other hand, they are different in that, unlike desire that strives to abolish the object in its total being because it appears to oppose self-consciousness, pleasure aims to negate the object only in its *form* of otherness because the subject at this level (i.e., as reason) is already certain that it is in principle the inner essence of the object and thus that the otherness of the object is fundamentally nothing more than a mere appearance (*Schein*) of itself. In this sense, active reason's enjoyment of pleasure means its "consciousness of its actualization in a *consciousness* which appears as independent," or its "intuition of the unity of the two independent *self-consciousnesses*."[85]

However, the practical rational subject as pleasure, the first moment of active reason, which seeks only its enjoyment of pure individuality, soon confronts itself with a self-contradictory predicament. That is, the *realization* of its pretension or intention to actualize itself as a pure being-for-itself, as a singular individual by intuiting its own self in the seemingly independent other is indeed rather the *cancellation* of this aim, i.e., the death of pure individuality.[86] It is because in this very action of pleasure, which is in itself something not unilateral but reciprocal, the subject no

---

83. PS, 217; §360. Emphasis mine.

84. Hegel uses Goethe's story of *Faust* to illustrate what he means by "pleasure." For a detailed description of this illustration, see Pinkard, *Hegel's Phenomenology*, 93–98.

85. PS, 218; §362. Emphasis mine. Some exegetists interpret this dialectic of pleasure in terms of Faustian eroticism. For instance, see Hyppolite, *Genesis and Structure*, 280–84; Winfield, *Hegel's Phenomenology of Spirit*, 179–84; Taylor, *Hegel*, 163; Bisticas-Cocoves, "Path of Reason," 175–76.

86. PS, 220; §364: "It experiences the double meaning which lies in what it did. When it *took hold* of its *life*, it possessed it, but in doing so it really laid hold of death."

longer remains a *singular individual* at all, but rather "the *unity* of itself and the other self-consciousness, hence as a sublated singular individual, or a *universal*."[87] In this way, the practical rational subject in its immediate action of pursuing pleasure in the world experiences that the negation of the alterity of the object for the sake of enjoying its pure individuality leads of necessity to the negation of its ipseity and, in turn, to the rise to universality.

This *necessity* experienced in the subject's enjoyment of pleasure appears, at first, to be an alien, blind, external, irresistible fate or an empty, incomprehensible negative power of abstract universality whereby individuality is doomed to perish.[88] Now the practical rational subject, faced with this self-contradictory crisis, is impelled to be reflected into itself, and becomes aware that this fateful necessity or abstract universality is produced by its own search for pleasure and so indeed belongs to itself as its own essence. This awareness leads active reason to the next moment which Hegel calls "the law of the heart."[89]

The Law of the Heart

Recognizing that the unity of its own individuality and necessity, or universality, is immanent *within* itself, the practical rational subject as active reason moves to its second moment, in which, rather than pursuing the egoistic hedonism of pure individuality in relation to the world full of other individuals, it seeks to actualize itself *as* a universal law that governs the world. Since the subject construes this law, necessary and universal, no longer to be an inexorable fate outside of itself but to be *immediately* present within itself, Hegel calls it "the *law of the heart*."[90]

87. PS, 218; §362.

88. PS, 219; §363: "[N]ecessity, *fate*, and the like, is just that about which we cannot say *what* it does, what its determinate laws and positive content are, because it is the absolute pure concept itself intuited as *being*, the *relation* that is simple and empty, but also irresistible and imperturbable, whose work is merely the nothingness of singular individuality."

89. According to Hyppolite, just as Hegel explains "pleasure and necessity" by referring to Goethe's work of *Faust*, Schiller's *The Robbers* (*Die Räuber*) is helpful in understanding the section of the law of the heart; see Hyppolite, *Genesis and Structure*, 285.

90. The law of the heart implies that the subject at this moment still takes itself as individuality in its immediate, natural singularity to be the essence just like the previous moment, viz., the subject as pleasure, even though the law of the heart transcends

Hence, the rational subject as the practical individual now intends to actualize its *own* law, the law of the heart, which is considered to be *immediately* in accord with the universal law that governs all individuals in the real world, thereby at once "displaying the *excellence* of its own essence" and "promoting the *welfare of mankind*."[91]

However, as active reason seeks to make its own law of the heart universally effective, dilemmas arise at several levels. Above all, just as seen in the previous dialectic of pleasure and necessity, the practical rational subject as the law of the heart gets caught up in a similar self-contradiction. As soon as the subject *acts* to realize the law of the heart as a way of preserving, actualizing, and universalizing its own individuality, the law of the heart "ceases to be a law of the *heart*" that is valid only insofar as it remains a particular heart without a fixed universal form. In other words, by means of the very action of the subject, the law of its heart turns into the law of actuality, the order of the real world, taking "the form of *being*," as "a *universal* power for which *this* particular heart is a matter of indifference."[92]

Furthermore, and more importantly, since it is universal only in *form* and not in content, where the content still remains the *particular* content of this or that individual's heart, yet this particular content is imposed upon other individuals as universally binding, "others do not find in this content the fulfillment of the law of *their* hearts, but rather

---

purely contingent, particular being-for-itself in the sense that it has "the character of necessity or universality" within itself (*PS*, 221; §367). In any case, "the law of the heart" as such is apparently an oxymoron because the *law* is something universal, whereas the *heart* is something particular.

91. *PS*, 222; §370. This belief already presupposes that the nature of human individuality is inherently good. Hyppolite says that Hegel has Rousseau in mind in this regard; see Hyppolite, *Genesis and Structure*, 85–86.

92. *PS*, 223; §372, where Hegel also, for the first time in the *Phenomenology*, explicitly presents his dialectical concept of "action" as at once the unifier of dualisms or bifurcations and the source of contradiction, since one's action is both internal and external to himself: "By his act the individual posits himself *in*, or rather *as*, the universal element of existent actuality . . . But he has thereby *set* himself *free* from himself; he goes on growing as universality for himself and purges himself of singularity. The individual who wants to recognize universality only in the form of his immediate being-for-itself does not therefore recognize himself in this free universality, while at the same time he belongs to it, for it is his doing. This doing, therefore, has the reverse significance of contradicting the universal order, for the individual's act is supposed to be the act of *his* particular heart, not some free universal actuality; and at the same time he has in fact *recognized* the latter, for his action has the significance of positing his essence as free actuality, i.e., of acknowledging the actuality as his essence."

the law of another's heart."⁹³ On top of that, this universalizing of the law of the heart is to be carried out by each and every individual. Admittedly, the universal actuality that the subject confronts now as the social order is no longer "dead necessity" alien to itself as in the case of pleasure, nor purely a law of *my* particular heart, but it is rather "necessity animated by the universal individuality" and "the law of all hearts."⁹⁴ Nonetheless, as stated above, this is a universality only in form, a universality *in-itself*, or merely a fancied universality; in effect, it makes for a sort of a Hobbesian "universal resistance and struggle of all against one another"⁹⁵ due to the contingency and particularity of the content of their hearts for which each claims validity with the frenzy of self-conceit (*der Wahnsinn des Eigendünkels*).

After all, the practical rational subject as active reason experiences that the actualization of the law of the heart turns out to be the opposite of what it intends. It finds itself in a state of contradiction, derangement, madness, or inner perversion, where the law of its own heart, regarded as the essence, is immediately inverted into something inessential, while at the same time the universal actuality, envisaged as its own essence and reality, is immediately turned into something alien, oppressive, and unreal to itself:

> [C]onsciousness, in its law, is aware of *itself* as this actuality, and, at the same time, since the very same essentiality, the same actuality, is *alienated* from it, it is, as self-consciousness, as absolute actuality, aware of its own non-actuality; or the two sides in their contradiction are immediately valid to it as *its essence*, which is thus in its inmost being distraught.⁹⁶

Through this whole experience, Hegel observes, the practical rational subject as active reason has learned that it cannot validate its certainty of being all reality by actualizing the law of the heart as the *immediate* unity of individuality (heart) and universality (law) within itself. To actualize universality not only in form but also in content, to make the

---

93. PS, 224; §373. Emphasis mine.
94. PS, 224–25; §374.
95. PS, 227; §379.
96. PS, 225–26; §376. Hegel goes on to say in the next paragraph (§377) that in an effort to save itself from destruction, the subject tries to escape this inner perversion by turning it into the perversion of some bad guys, such as priests and despots, who have introduced it into humanity that is meant to be good by nature. Hegel calls this endeavor "the ravings of an insane self-conceit."

world truly rational and find itself therein, the subject comes to realize, it should rather sacrifice its own undisciplined individuality that is the source of perversion. Therefore, instead of imposing its own individuality (the law of the heart) on the world, the rational subject as the practical individual now develops into its third moment, "virtue," hoping that it as virtuous consciousness could save the world, i.e., bring rationality into the world against what Hegel calls "the *way of the world* (*Weltlauf*), the semblance of an unchanging course that is only a *meant universality*, and whose content is rather the essenceless play of establishing and dissolving singular individualities."[97]

Virtue

After failing in its attempt to actualize itself in the world—firstly, by enjoying its own pleasure of pure individuality, and secondly, by realizing its own law of the heart—the practical rational subject as active reason now begins to walk its third path for finding itself in the world. Especially, the outcome that the subject has reached at the end of the preceding moment, that is, the awareness that "undisciplined individuality" (individualism) is the source of the problem, the principle of perversion, whereby the way of the world comprises, leads to a new moment of active reason that Hegel calls "virtue." The subject now believes that the law within itself can be actualized without perversion only if individuality is sacrificed in such a way that it subordinates its individual self-interest to "the discipline of the universal, what is in itself true and good."[98] To be more specific, the practical rational subject, which pursues virtue in face

---

97. *PS*, 227–28; §379.

98. *PS*, 228; §381. According to Hyppolite, "virtue" emerging in this phase of reason represents the character of a modern romantic ideologue who attempts to reform the world only in his noble mind, which reminds us of Don Quixote in a novel by Miguel de Cervantes; see Hyppolite, *Genesis and Structure*, 290. In *PS*, 234; §390, Hegel satirically depicts this kind of quixotic, utopian virtue devoid of reality as follows: "Ideal essences and purposes of this kind are empty, ineffectual words which lift up the heart but leave reason empty, which edify, but raise no edifice; declamations which specifically declare merely this: that the individual who professes to act for such noble ends and who deals in such fine phrases is in his own eyes an excellent creature—a puffing-up which inflates him with a sense of importance in his own eyes and in the eyes of others, whereas he is, in fact, inflated with his own conceit." In this respect, modern virtue in question here has nothing to do with virtue in the ancient Greece or Rome that is concerned with living in accordance with the mores of one's people or nation (*Volk*) considered as the actual good.

of the way of the world and has *faith* in its ultimate victory over the way of the world, first distinguishes between the ideal order of the world (the universal-in-itself as having not yet been realized) and the actual way of the world (the universal as having been realized in a perverted way). Since this perversion of the actual world stems from individuality, it then contraposes the universal *in-itself* as good and individuality *for-itself* as evil. In this way, by nullifying its own individuality that is regarded as perverted and perverting, the subject as the knight of virtue intends to actualize the true and good universal, the absolute order, which is present immanently or implicitly as an *inner essence* of the world, *against* the actual way of the world perverted by undisciplined individuality.

In pursuing virtue, however, the subject soon finds that the stark opposition it has set up between individuality perverting the actual way of the world and the universal-in-itself as the ideal order of the world is untenable. For one thing, inasmuch as the in-itself of the universal, the good, *inheres in* the world as its inner essence, what the way of the world actually manifests in virtue of individuality should not be something that is as perverted as it has been construed, but rather should be, to some extent, the actual existence of the ideal order itself, i.e., "*the actual good*."[99] For another thing, insofar as the in-itself of the universal is actualized in and against the way of the world *only through* the self-sacrifice of individuality, the ideal order is indeed to be realized, paradoxically, only by the very *action* of *individuality*, i.e., one's own action of sacrificing oneself, which is, however, precisely what has to be suppressed or nullified. Through these experiences—both that the way of the world cannot be so evil as it presumes and that virtue cannot be realized in the way of the world if it requires the self-sacrifice of individuality—the practical rational subject as active reason now becomes aware that, in truth, the in-itself of the universal is, by virtue of individuality in its action, "inextricably interwoven in every appearance of the way of the world."[100] Hyppolite succinctly puts the true nature of action of individuality, which the subject has learned in this dialectical experience, in the following way:

> When I act, even if I subtly explain my action by egoistic considerations, I transcend myself, and I actualize potentialities of which I was unaware. Thanks to my act, what was in-itself becomes actual. I imagine myself to be limited to my own

99. *PS*, 232; §386.
100. *PS*, 232; §386.

individuality, but in fact I more or less embody a universal that transcends me. I am not only for-itself; I am also in-itself.[101]

Consequently, the practical rational subject realizes that the *virtuous* undertaking to bring the true universal into the actual world by opposing the universal-in-itself as the ideal order to individuality as the source of perverting the way of the world and thus suppressing its own individuality is doomed to fail; for "individuality is precisely the *actualization* of what is-in-itself," that is, "the movement of individuality is the reality of the universal."[102] It is in this sense that Hegel famously calls individuality in its action "the principle of *actuality*" (*das Prinzip der Wirklichkeit*).[103] Recognizing that individuality is the principle of actuality in and through which alone the universal becomes actual, the subject now considers the activity of individuality as an end in itself, not as a means for realizing something other than itself as in the case of the three preceding moments of active reason, namely, pleasure, the law of the heart, and virtue. In this regard, Hegel observes, the practical rational subject as active reason needs to be sublated into a new form of reason in which, against self-denying virtue, it becomes "self-actualizing reason," taking the movement of individuality in its action (for-itself) to be true actuality (in-itself)—that is, individuality is posited as *in-and-for-itself*.

The Universal-Individual Rational Subject: Self-Actualizing Reason

Not just abstractly certain of itself in imagination, thought, or rhetoric, the rational subject now *knows* itself to be all reality. It recognizes through experiences in the preceding form of reason (i.e., active reason as the practical individual) that the movement of actualizing individuality is *itself* what makes the universal truly actual, since "the universal cannot find real expression (*Wirklichkeit*) except through the lives and actions of particular individuals."[104] Hence, rather than, as in active reason, seeking "only to realize itself as *end* in *opposition* to immediately existent actuality," the rational subject now considers the *action* of expressing its own

---

101. Hyppolite, *Genesis and Structure*, 294.
102. *PS*, 235; §391.
103. *PS*, 233; §389.
104. Taylor, *Hegel*, 167.

individuality *per se* to be "the end in and for itself."[105] In this way, the rational subject's certainty that "it is all reality" rises into truth at this stage. I would call this last form of the rational subject "the universal-individual rational subject" as *self-actualizing* reason, not only in the sense that into it the two previous forms of reason (i.e., observing reason and active reason) are synthesized, but also in the sense that "the interfusion of *being-in-itself* and *being-for-itself*, of the universal and individuality" is realized in and through its "action" which is now taken to be *the* essence of individuality.[106]

As expected, however, Hegel argues that to grow into such self-actualizing reason in its full sense, namely, individuality in-and-for-itself, the subject must go through three dialectical moments, and these are what he terms "the spiritual animal kingdom and deceit, or the Thing itself" (*das geistige Tierreich and der Betrug oder die Sache selbst*), "reason as lawgiver" (*die gesetzgebende Vernunft*), and "reason as testing laws" (*die gesetzprüfende Vernunft*). It must be noted again that the ultimate but still implicit term or end of the rational subject consists in the ethical substance, and thus that the truth of the action of individuality taking itself to be real in and for itself lies in the *Sittlichkeit* beyond the individual level.[107] In this respect, self-actualizing reason in its full-grown form could be also called "socialized reason."

The Spiritual Animal Kingdom

The universal rational subject as individuality that knows itself to be all reality is, to begin with, posited "*immediately* as simple *being-in-itself*," the individual whose "original determinate nature" is a "simple principle, a transparent universal element," in which its activity begins and ends with itself; that is to say, it "remains free and self-identical as it is unimpeded in unfolding its differences, and in its actualization is in pure

---

105. *PS*, 236; §394.

106. *PS*, 236; §394. According to Hegel, it is in *action* that what is implicit becomes explicit, what is internal becomes external, what is potential becomes actual, what is subjective becomes objective, what is invisible becomes visible, and so forth. In this regard, action is at once the essence of individuality and of actuality: "Action is in its own self its truth and actuality, and the *exhibition* or *expression* of *individuality* is, for this action, the end in and for itself."

107. In this sense, in Hegel's *Phenomenology of Spirit* this part, the last section of Reason, serves as a transitional moment between Reason and Spirit.

reciprocity with itself."[108] Hegel calls this first moment of self-actualizing reason "the spiritual animal kingdom," in the sense that one, despite a variety of constraints imposed by things other than itself, remains equal to itself within the limit of its intrinsically-given, original determinate nature and thereby cannot think of going beyond its own sphere.[109] For the rational subject as the universal individual in its *immediacy* that identifies itself with the spiritual animal kingdom, the sole task is to actualize or express its own original determinate nature, potentiality, or capacity in and through its *action*.[110] The subject *believes* the immediate identity of its implicitly determinate essence, or original natural potentiality, and actuality as its explicit expression. In the same vein, it claims the simple unity among the three moments of action, viz., its intended object or end, means, and achieved reality or the work (*Werk*) produced; that is to say, action is simply the pure translation of the form of not yet exhibited (implicit) being into that of exhibited (explicit) being.[111] Since there is

---

108. PS, 237–38; §398.

109. Hegel employs this term by likening it to the natural animal kingdom. Particularly, according to Hyppolite echoing Emile Brehier, Hegel points to "specialists, teachers, and artists, who ascribe absolute value to their work" (Hyppolite, *Genesis and Structure*, 297).

110. PS, 238; §399, where Hegel also explains in advance the dialectic of action in relation to the original determinate nature. In brief, the action of individuality both preserves (*is*) and negates (*is not*) its original determinate nature: "as regards action, that determinateness is, on the one hand, not a limitation it would want to overcome, for, regarded as an existent quality, it is the simple color of the element in which it moves itself; on the other hand, however, negativity is *determinateness* only in being, but *action* is itself nothing else but negativity. Therefore, in the acting individuality determinateness is dissolved into the general process of negativity or into the inclusive concept of all determinateness."

111. See PS, 239–40; §401. Incidentally, when Hegel explains here about the identity of the original determinate nature (the in-itself; potentiality) and the work produced (the for-itself; actuality) in and through action, it seems to me that he has in mind the Aristotelian distinction between the order of explanation and the order of existence. The original determinate nature as potentiality is first in the order of explanation, but not first in the order of existence. With this framework in mind, I believe, we could understand more properly—meaning *dialectically*—the following sentences in the same paragraph: "True, this original content is only explicit *for* consciousness *as consciousness has actualized the content*"; "Accordingly, the individual cannot know what *he is* until he has brought himself to actuality through action." In my view, as Beiser maintains, this kind of Aristotelian distinction is truly crucial in grasping the dialectical character of the whole system of Hegel's philosophy without falling into a trap of *either-or*: either universalism or historicism, either rationalism or empiricism, either subjectivism or objectivism, either realism or nominalism, either theism

no comparison with something outside itself, the subject does not have "feelings of *exaltation*, or *lamentation*, or repentance," but instead "knows that in his actuality he can find nothing else but its unity with himself, or only the certainty of himself in its truth" and thereby "*can experience only joy in himself*."[112]

However, the rational subject as the spiritual animal kingdom is soon bound to run into the fundamental contradiction inherent in the work or, more precisely, the opposition between action and being in the work. The work produced by the subject through its action has been meant to be the true expression of its individuality, the actuality with which it immediately identifies and in which it fully makes explicit what is already implicit within itself; for example, an artist fully manifests her own original character or worldview in her work of art. Yet what the subject actually experiences is that its work does express its own intrinsic essence, *but never completely*. It is because, first of all, there is an internal disparity between the subject as the universal process of action and the work as something determinate or particular: the subject as self-transcending movement, as "*absolute negativity*" in its action of self-actualization always "goes beyond itself as it is in the work, and is itself the indefinite space which is left unfilled by its work."[113] Furthermore, the work exists not only for the subject itself that has produced it, but also for other individuals who also believe the unity of the self and actuality and thus want to find in it themselves, "*their* original nature," by means of their own action of interpretation, either appreciating or criticizing it; however, their interest in the work is "different from this work's *own* peculiar interest," and the work is thereby "converted into something different."[114] Consequently, the work turns into "something transitory, which is obliterated by the counter-action of other forces and interests, and exhibits the reality of individuality as vanishing rather than as achieved."[115]

---

or pantheism (or atheism), and the like. See Beiser, *Hegel*, 56–57, 138–39, 212–13; see also *LPR III*, 290–91.

112. *PS*, 242; §404.

113. *PS*, 243; §405. As Hegel does in this section, we must distinguish two modes of "negativity": negativity in the Spinozistic sense as a static determination in the in-itself and negativity as action *qua* action, the very movement or becoming of the for-itself.

114. *PS*, 243; §405.

115. *PS*, 243–44; §405.

Experiencing both that the work in its determinacy and particularity does not exhaustively express its own true individuality as action or absolute negativity and that the work is not only its own action but also always pervaded by the actions of others, the rational subject comes to discover that individuality (subjectivity) and actuality (objectivity) are indeed opposed. To be more exact, it is in the work in its *contingency* that the subject as individuality opposes not only itself but also other individualities. In order to overcome this opposition and attain a new form of synthesis or reconciliation, therefore, the subject must go beyond the contingency of the work in its particularity and rise to a new concept of actuality or objectivity in which it feels at home regardless of the particular contents or determinations of its own action and the contingencies of the work thereupon in question. Hegel calls this new, sublated concept of actuality "the Thing itself" (*die Sache selbst*)[116] as the true work, that which the subject now takes to be its self-actualization:

> In this way, then, consciousness is reflected out of its transitory work into itself, and affirms its concept and certainty as what *is* and *endures* in the face of the experience of the contingency of action. . . . actuality therefore counts for consciousness only as *being* as such, whose universality is the same as its action. This unity is the true work; it is the *Thing itself* which completely affirms itself and is experienced as that which endures, independently of the *contingency* of the individual's action, the contingency of circumstances, means, and actuality.[117]

In this respect, for Hegel, the Thing itself as the true work is not a mere collection of all particular, physical works, but fundamentally something in complete indifference to their contingent character. In other words, it is the "*spiritual* essentiality"[118] as the higher unity of individuality (the universal subject) and actuality (the universal object) in and through the universal process of action, into which each particular work is sublated as its vanishing moment—its contingency *negated* and at the same time its necessity based on the necessity of action *preserved*.

---

116. The German expression "*die Sache Selbst*" is translated to various terms, such as "the thing itself," "the 'matter in hand' itself," "the crux of the matter," "the heart of the matter," "the real fact," "the main thing," "what really matters," and so on.

117. *PS*, 246; §409.

118. *PS*, 246; §410. For Hyppolite, it is also called "spiritual objectivity" (*l'objectivité spirituelle*); see Hyppolite, *Genesis and Structure*, 308.

At this stage, however, "the Thing itself" in its immediacy appears in the *form* of "*abstract* universal" without having a distinctive content of its own, i.e., in the form of a universal "*predicate*" that the subject can attach to anything it does, not as yet developed into a concrete *subject* in its own right.[119] Hence, the subject seeks to actualize itself in "the Thing itself" that is free of and indifferent to the content of its action, work, and original nature in all its particularity and contingency. Hegel characterizes as "honest" (*ehrlich*)[120] the subject that is concerned with this abstract Thing itself, the formal and indeterminate actualization of its equally abstract character of individuality. Since the subject honestly thinks that the Thing itself is the universal formal predicate or genus always applicable to any of its own determinate activities as the particular, concrete moments or species of the Thing itself, it now enjoys satisfaction and fulfilment in whatever it is doing, though its goal may or may not be realized. In other words, it attempts to justify all its own particular activities according to the abstract Thing itself as the universal predicate. In this way, the subject even claims that what is essential for its self-actualization in the end is not whether it does *realize* its end or purpose in and through action, but rather the very fact that it at least does *will, intend, or have interest in* that purpose.

However, the self-actualizing subject as honest consciousness soon cannot but find a contradiction lodged within its claim and reveal its honesty as rather *deceitful*.[121] Although it holds fast to the pure honesty of its own intention while it acts, and thus equates the abstract Thing itself immediately or indiscriminately with its honorable intention, it can never be free from the *dialectic of action*, the dialectic of being-for-itself and being-for-others in action, as long as it lives and so *ought to* act. Insofar as action is to express one's own intention or interiority, it is, to be sure, *for itself*; yet, insofar as action is to externalize itself in the actual world, it is, at the same time, *for others*. Thus, the Thing itself as the consequence or actuality of action is, too, not only the work of one individual alone but also the work of other individuals, in principle, the work of

---

119. *PS*, 247; §411.

120. *PS*, 247; §412. According to Hegel, individuality can go beyond the spiritual animal kingdom and rise to the ethical realm (*Sittlichkeit*) by way of the form of universality called *honesty* (*Ehrlichkeit*), which is somewhat similar to the Kantian morality.

121. Hegel remarks, "The truth of this honesty, however, is that it is not as honest as it seems" (*PS*, 248–49; §418).

all individuals. As soon as an individual posits a work, as Hegel puts it figuratively, other individuals flock to it "like flies to freshly poured milk" and want to find and enjoy themselves in it.[122] After all, the subject's claim that action is only its *own* action which is completely at one with its pure intention and that the Thing itself is its *own* thing turns out to be self-contradictory and untenable:

> [I]n doing something, and thus presenting and exposing themselves to the light of day, they immediately contradict by their deed their pretense of wanting to exclude the light of day itself, universal consciousness, and everyone else's participation. Actualization is, on the contrary, a display of what is one's own in the universal element whereby it becomes, and should become, the *fact of matter at issue* for everyone.[123]

Through this experience, the rational subject has learned that the seemingly contradictory but essentially unifying moments of *being-for-itself* and *being-for-others* inherent in the dialectic of action (subjectivity) are constitutive moments of the Thing itself (objectivity), and that in this respect, the true nature of the Thing itself is neither merely a work of a single individual's action nor a work of others' actions, but a common work whose being consists in "the *action* of *each* and *everyone*."[124] Thus, the Thing itself now rises from being a universal predicate or an abstract, formal universal to being a universal subject, concrete universality, or "*spiritual essence*" as consisting of the "action of each and all," in which, in turn, each and every individual achieves self-actualization as universal reason and finds itself as the universal subject—that is, "being that is the I or the I that is being"[125] and "the *I* that is *We* and the *We* that is *I*."[126] However, this "*absolute Thing* which no longer suffers from the opposition of certainty and its truth, of the universal and the individual, of purpose and its reality"[127] is still, at this stage, "in the form of *thought*."[128] In other words, it is not as yet the ethical substance *as* subject or spirit,

---

122. PS, 251; §418.
123. PS, 251; §417.
124. PS, 252; §418.
125. PS, 252; §418.
126. PS, 110; §177.
127. PS, 253; §420.
128. PS, 252; §418.

which will come on the scene later in "Spirit" in the *Phenomenology*, but just the "thought" of it.

Law-Giving and Law-Testing Reason

Thinking that the Thing itself (*die Sache selbst*) as the object is in truth the ethical substance as the spiritual essence, in which the subject is present to itself as the universal subject, while, in reality, remaining an individual consciousness as distinct from such ethical substance, the rational subject now becomes "*ethical* consciousness,"[129] the consciousness *of* the ethical substance. In the first instance, the rational subject as ethical consciousness, which knows itself to be an intrinsic moment of the ethical substance in terms of constituting its content, particularly its "*determinate laws*,"[130] identifies itself as "law-giving reason" (*gesetzgebende Vernunft*) that Hegel also calls "*sound reason*" (*gesunde Vernunft*).[131] Law-giving reason, or sound reason, claims that it *immediately* knows the laws which are not unique to the single individual, but rather shared by all as the universal work of each and all.[132] In this vein, the law is presumed to be something already given, i.e., already accepted and followed as valid by everyone, and thus what law-giving reason precisely does is nothing else than affirming and expressing that this or that law is "right and good."[133]

However, as Hegel observes, the rational subject as law-giving reason soon experiences that it cannot validate its claim, for the law that law-giving reason might count immediately as *necessarily and universally* right and good—for example, "Everyone ought to speak the truth" or "Love your neighbor as yourself"—turns out to be a conditional or situational commandment, not an unconditional or categorical law; that is to say, it is rather *contingent* upon certain conditions or circumstances in their particularity.[134] The law "everyone ought to speak the truth" needs

129. *PS*, 253; §420.

130. *PS*, 253; §420.

131. *PS*, 253; §422. It can also be translated as "commonsense reason" or "healthy reason."

132. Remember that at the end of the preceding moment, the Thing itself turns out to be the common work of each and all.

133. *PS*, 253; §422.

134. Here Hegel, without doubt, problematizes Kant's "categorical imperative." Kant insists that the "categorical imperative" alone, which is universally valid as duty without regard to inclination, can and must be taken to be the moral law. But, Hegel

to be qualified by the proviso that *only if people know the truth*, which in fact depends on their individual conviction and the particular circumstances in which they are situated; likewise, the law "love your neighbor as yourself" needs to be qualified by the proviso that *only if people know what is good for their neighbor in specific circumstances*.[135] After all, it is revealed through the experience of the subject's law-giving activity that the immediately given and affirmed content, which is presumed to be already accepted and followed by each and all, cannot be justified *as* the law in its necessity and universality, because it can be always subject to various qualifications. In this way, the rational subject realizes that the source of universality and necessity must be found not in the *content* of laws but only in their *form*.

Confronted with the predicament of law-giving reason as it found particularity and contingency inherent in the content of laws, the rational subject, who wants to be present to itself in the universality and necessity of the ethical substance, particularly of the realm of law, now becomes a merely formal criterion by which to examine the validity or legitimacy (universality and necessity) of existing laws in their formal logicality:

> The ethical essence . . . is not itself immediately a content, but only a standard for deciding whether a content is capable of being a law or not, i.e., whether it is or is not self-contradictory. Law-giving reason is demoted to a reason which merely *tests* laws.[136]

Hegel calls this "law-testing reason" (*gesetzprüfende Vernuft*). The rational subject as law-testing reason is, therefore, no longer concerned with the content of a law, but only with its *formal universality*[137] on the basis of the principle of non-contradiction—that is, whether it is consistent or coherent with itself as a law, regardless of what content it may profess: "is there a contradiction in following a given maxim, or not?"[138] As

---

criticizes, even such a seemingly unconditional moral law cannot but always be conditioned by the qualifications already set.

135. For more detailed analyses on each of these two laws provided by Hegel, see *PS*, 254–56; §424–25.

136. *PS*, 256; §428.

137. This "formal universality" is similar to the "abstract Thing itself" discussed earlier in the spiritual animal kingdom. Yet the former differs from the latter in that "it is . . . no longer the unthinking, inert genus, but is related to the particular and counts as its power and truth" (*PS*, 257; §429).

138. Taylor, *Hegel*, 168.

Hyppolite says, "we come to Kant's rule, which proclaims nothing but the general condition in which a maxim can be established as a universal law."[139]

The rational subject, however, becomes aware in its activity of testing given laws that a merely formal standard, which is indifferent to its specific content and so only requires the absence of self-contradiction in its logical form, is indeed no criterion at all. Since it "fits every case equally well," and thus any law can be made formally self-consistent, it is nothing but a "tautology."[140] To illustrate this, Hegel employs an example: both property (*Eigentum*) and non-property, insofar as they are thought of as simple abstractions or in and of themselves, are equally justifiable without formal self-contradiction; though in the concrete world, where they are taken in relation to some other factors and considerations, both involve plenty of contradictions.[141] In this way, as Hegel concludes, a merely formal criterion, i.e., the principle of non-contradiction, is useless for the cognition of theoretical truth, let alone the cognition of practical truth.

Experiencing that its appeal to either an immediate affirmation of the given content of law (law-giving reason) or a purely logical examination of its form (law-testing reason) proves to be unsuccessful in validating the legitimacy of law as the ethical substance and thereby fails to find itself as universal reason therein, the rational subject as ethical consciousness becomes aware that the reason for this failure lies fundamentally in its *individual* immediacy in relation to the ethical substance. In the two moments of the rational subject as individual ethical consciousness, law-giving and law-testing, the law as the ethical substance has appeared "only a *willing* and *knowing* by this particular individual, or the *ought* of a non-actual command and a knowledge of formal universality."[142] Thus, the *rational* subject now must sublate itself qua *individual* consciousness, i.e., its giving and testing laws on the basis of its own particular will and knowledge, into the communal subject that identifies itself with the ethical substance, in which the ethical substance becomes the essence of the subject, and the subject becomes the actuality of the ethical substance. If this is the case, the law is no longer grounded in the arbitrary will

---

139. Hyppolite, *Genesis and Structure*, 317. See also Hegel, *Natural Law*, 75–76.
140. *PS*, 259; §431.
141. For Hegel's analysis in detail, see *PS*, 257–59; §430–31.
142. *PS*, 260; §435.

and knowledge of the individual, but rather is valid in and for itself as the spiritual essence of each and all. Furthermore, since the law is valid unconditionally as the universal work constituted by the activities of all members of the community, it is not a command which simply ought to be believed in and obeyed, whether it be a Jewish commandment as external compulsion or a Kantian moral law as internal compulsion, but the absolute, objective being immediately at one with the subjective essence of all individuals in the community: "They are."[143]

In short, the subject as individual-rational subjectivity that is certain of itself as all reality is now transcended into communal-spiritual subjectivity in which its certainty is raised to truth, negating the immediacy of individuality and, at the same time, preserving the passion and longing for universality. In other words, the subject is no longer an isolated individual who just claims to be abstract universality, but rather a member belonging to the community that constitutes and actualizes concrete universality. In this way, the subject grows into the stage of what Hegel identifies as "Spirit" (*Geist*).

Communal-Spiritual Subjectivity: "Spirit"

The rational subject as the *individual*, certain of itself as *universal* self-consciousness, has pursued in various and different ways the verification of its certainty. However, as we have discussed in the preceding section, in and through the dialectical process of reason the subject has come to know that its claim to universality remains only within individuality. In other words, the modern, particularly the Kantian, rational subject as universal self-consciousness could not move beyond the individual level of the "I" as merely subjective and formal universality, without attaining the "We" as truly objective and concrete universality.[144] Especially, in the last moment of the rational subject in its activities of law-giving and law-testing, where it as the individual has to confront crucial difficulties

---

143. *PS*, 260; §437.

144. While Kant is content to focus on the individual since reason is itself universal, irrespective of who that individual might be, Hegel thinks that attention must be paid to what counts as reason in a specific society. Consequently, Hegel insists that human reason cannot and should not remain at the level of the individual but must move to the social/communal level. Along the same lines, it is Hegel's original insight that reason has a *history* in its teleological sense, which is something that Kant never imagined.

in validating the universality and necessity of law on the basis of either its legislating the content of law or its examining the form of law, the subject has realized that it *constitutively* belongs to a community of law, in which its own activities for validating laws are intrinsically connected to the activities of all other members of the community.[145] In this way, the subject also became aware that the ethical substance as the community of law, each and every member of which is engaged in lawful interactions, is not merely external to but truly internal to the very realization of its individuality and rationality. Hence, the subject must now sublate its individual-rational subjectivity ("Reason") into communal-spiritual subjectivity ("Spirit"), spiritual or spirit in the sense of actualized reason *in* the community, where reason's "certainty of being all reality has been raised to truth, and it is conscious of itself as its own world, and of the world as itself."[146]

As expected, the subject as communal-spiritual subjectivity is to pass through a series of different forms as the intrinsic, necessary moments for its growth toward absolute subjectivity, which indeed correspond to different forms of the world as the forms of "spirit"—spirit here precisely in the sense of what Hegel elsewhere calls "objective spirit." These forms are: first, as the moment of immediacy or abstract identity (the in-itself), *the ethical (sittlich) subject* corresponding to the ethical world; second, as the moment of differentiation (the for-itself), *the self-alienated cultural subject* corresponding to the world of culture; third, as the moment of reconciliation or mediated unity (the in-and-for-itself), *the moral subject* corresponding to the world of morality.[147] These forms of subjectivity and objectivity, as will be observed, gradually move toward and develop into the realm of Absolute Spirit:

> The ethical world, the world rent asunder into this-worldly present and the other-worldly beyond, and the moral worldview, are thus the spirits whose movement and return into the simple

---

145. These activities of validating laws by all individuals as members of the community are no longer an activity of giving or testing laws, but rather an activity of *fulfilling* the legal order that is already enacted as something valid in the community.

146. PS, 263; §438.

147. These three moments also correspond to the three moments of the concept in Hegel's *Logic*, namely, universality, particularity, and individuality. Besides, according to Hegel, each moment was epitomized historically by the Greco-Roman world, the Middle Ages to the Enlightenment, and German idealism and romanticism, respectively.

self-subsisting self of spirit will develop, and as their goal and result, the actual self-consciousness of Absolute Spirit will arise.[148]

The Ethical Subject

The first form of communal-spiritual subjectivity is, as always, characterized by "immediacy." It is the subject taking itself to be a member of the community, having its essence in its given, or naturally determined, community as the actuality of spirit, and therefore identifying itself *immediately* with the laws and customs of that community. In this way, the subject is exhaustively defined by its communal roles, and those roles are unmistakably perceived as upholding the community to which it belongs. I would call this first form of communal-spiritual subjectivity the "*ethical* subject."[149]

Before proceeding to describe the specific movement of the ethical subject, it must be emphasized again that the subject at this stage is no longer conscious of itself simply as an individual, but rather as a member of the community. Therefore, the laws or customs of the community and the corresponding roles of membership, though these are naturally given, are not regarded by the subject as something alien and inessential to itself, but rather as something intrinsic and essential to itself. According to Hegel, there are two differentiated spheres in this ethical world in which the ethical subject finds itself immediately: the family and the nation or people (*Volk*). The former can be considered as the private sphere, whereas the latter as the public or, rather, political sphere. In particular, Hegel characterizes these communities by the laws which govern each distinctive sphere as ethical powers: the "divine law" that governs the family and the "human law" that governs the nation.[150] The divine law concerns the blood relationships of the family as the elementary, unconscious being of the ethical order, that is, the ethical relations of family members to their household community that are already embedded in their private

---

148. *PS*, 265–66; §443.

149. Hegel characterizes the spirit of ancient Greece as "ethical" (*sittlich*), which is particularly manifested in works of classical literatures; especially, when he presents the decline of the ethical community in Greece, he employs Greek tragedies such as *Antigone* and so on.

150. *PS*, 267–68; §448–49. According to Hegel, this distinction also corresponds to a distinction between woman (the guardian of the divine law) and man (the guardian of the human law).

life directed at the particular good of the family as a whole.[151] By contrast, the human law deals with the conventional relationships of the nation as a conscious ethico-political community freed from kinship, that is, the ethical relations of all citizens to their political community that are already embodied in their public life directed at the universal good of the nation.

At first, as stated above, the ethical subject, which identifies itself immediately with the ethical substance (or the law), claims that it feels at home in both given communities (family and nation) to which it already belongs. It believes that the divine law of the family and the human law of the nation complement each other and indeed constitute a beautiful harmony or a "stable equilibrium."[152] Put simply, the nation (human law) requires the family (divine law) for the provision of its people and the natural needs of their survival, whereas the family needs the nation for its protection:

> Just as the family in this way has in the polity [the nation] its universal substance and subsistence, so, conversely, the polity has in the family the formal element of its actuality . . . Neither of the two alone is in and for itself; human law proceeds in its living movement from the divine, the law valid on earth from that of the nether world, the conscious from the unconscious, mediation from immediacy, and equally returns whence it came.[153]

However, this initial picture of complementary and harmonious relation between these two spheres is soon shattered. For Hegel, as has been the case with the preceding stages and forms of subjectivity, it is "action" or, more precisely, *ethical action* that necessarily "disturbs the peaceful organization and movement of the ethical world."[154] A praiseworthy action vis-à-vis the divine law turns out to be a blameworthy action vis-à-vis the human law, and vice versa. Here Hegel draws on a tragic

---

151. PS, 268–75; §450–59, where Hegel observes that as an "ethical" community the family *ultimately* concerns something beyond the particularities and accidentalities of its individual members as sensuous, mortal existence whose bond is constituted by their kinship-based contingent feelings or love. Therefore, the *ethical* bond of the family in its full sense rather consists in their sheer duty, obligation, or commitment to the household as a whole.

152. PS, 277; §462.

153. PS, 276; §460.

154. PS, 279; §464.

story of Sophocles's Antigone, the necessity of her ethical action and its consequence, in describing the inherent possibility of conflict between the laws of two communities.[155] When Antigone, who as a woman identifies immediately with the divine law of the family, *acts* upon her natural duty and commitment, that is, buries her brother (Polyneices)[156] who has fought against the political authorities to which she belongs, she finds herself in opposition to the human law of the nation. The same predicament is true for those political authorities whose representative figure in this story is Creon, Antigone's uncle. His ethical action of prohibiting Antigone from burying her brother, in accordance with its natural, immediate yet conscious allegiance to the human law of the nation to which he belongs, equally violates the unconscious demands of the divine law. In short, one's ethical action of observing one of the laws—whether it be the divine law or the human law—leads inevitably to one's violation of the other.

Consequently, in and through ethical action the ethical substance is torn apart, and in turn the ethical subject, who identifies immediately with its particular ethical community as its own true reality and self-actualization, necessarily experiences itself as guilty (*Schuld*). The ethical subject feels guilty precisely because it believes that the breakup of the ethical world is due to the partiality and exclusiveness of its own ethical decision, commitment, and action. The ethical subject, thus, ends up abandoning "the determinateness of the ethical life" in its immediacy and instead positing "the separation of itself . . . as the active principle" and "the actuality over against it."[157] In this respect, Hegel observes, the ethical substance now appears to the subject as "destiny" in the sense that the conflict and destruction of the ethical community is inevitable, insofar as the subject as its member *acts ethically*. Once again, as Hegel emphasizes, it is the "action" of the subject that is "itself this splitting into two, this

---

155. Two centuries later John Rawls similarly points out, from the viewpoint of "justice," the possibility of an inherent irreconcilable conflict between family and state in his seminal book, *A Theory of Justice*.

156. For Hegel's view on the ethical nature of the family (divine law) in relation to "death," see *PS*, 270–72; §452–54, where he states that the preeminent ethical function of the family is to save death from nature, i.e., to sublate death into a spiritual meaning by burying the dead, through which the dead individual is raised to universality. In this regard, Hegel argues, the paradigmatic divine law of the family concerns how to deal with its deceased, not living, members, which is best exhibited and implemented in the relation between Antigone and her brother Polyneices.

157. *PS*, 282; §468.

positing of itself for itself and this positing of an alien external actuality over against itself."[158]

Finding itself in destiny as an alien actuality, i.e., in its necessary confrontation with the inevitable downfall of the ethical substance to which it naturally belongs, the subject is now withdrawn into itself and aware that its relation to the community must be purely formal and abstract. In this way, the ethical substance becomes a spiritless community or an abstract universality of separate, atomic, free, independent individuals, and by the same token the ethical subject now counts itself as a rights-bearing self or what Hegel calls a *person*. By the "person," as Winfield aptly points out, Hegel means here specifically a property owner, the owner of its own bodily self in particular, and not a Kantian moral subject who ought to will and act universally.[159] It is the *formal* universality of legal recognition, purged of natural determinations in their particularity, that underlies the freedom and equality of all persons in the community. In brief, the ethical subject in its beautiful, living bond with its natural substance—as a member of the family or as a citizen of the nation—is transformed into the *person* in its spiritless relation to an abstract, universal community that is based upon the legal recognition and formal equality of persons. As Hegel says, what was for stoicism only in the form of thought[160] now becomes an actual world:

> By its flight from *actuality* it attained only to the thought of independence; it is absolutely for *itself*, in that it does not attach its essence to anything that exists, but . . . posits its essence solely in the unity of pure thinking. In the same way, the right of the person is not tied to a richer or more powerful existence of the individual as such, nor again to a universal living spirit, but rather to the pure One of its abstract actuality . . .[161]

In this world of abstract persons who are no longer bound up with any natural givens or particular determinations and thus relate to each other only *formally* under the principle of legal equality, the subject considers the community an abstract lawful power that is completely indifferent to all the concrete, particular content of its members and therefore reigns

158. *PS*, 282; §468.

159. Winfield, *Hegel's Phenomenology of Spirit*, 239. See also *PS*, 291; §480, and *PR*, 67–69; §35.

160. For my explorations of the stoic thinking subject, see "The Thinking Subject: Stoicism and Skepticism" (chapter 3, section 2) of this book.

161. *PS*, 291; §479.

over them only in the formally universal way, i.e., in a way that recognizes their legal status as persons, irrespective of their natural differences, such as gender, race, ethnicity, etc., and of their particular needs and desires. It is a formally universal legal empire without boundaries, so to speak.

However, what the subject as legal personality actually experiences in this empire is far removed from what it has been certain of. Its claim to recognize one another as a free, independent person and thereby feel at home in this legal community as the abstract, formal universality turns out to be a mere illusion. Just as stoicism had to move to skepticism due to its inability to uphold the freedom of self-consciousness only by taking an indifferent, impassive attitude toward differences, particularities, and contingencies constituting the *real* world, so, too, the world of abstract persons, which is believed to operate only under the formally universal order of legal recognition that is common to all, is bound to give way to the destructive rule of the "lord of the world" (*Herr der Welt*), "the monstrous self-consciousness that knows itself as the actual God."[162] In the legal community there is no necessary connection between the subject as formal legal personality and the actual—particular and contingent—content that is also constitutive of the subject in other respects, and thus, in reality, the entire movement of content is gathered up in "an *autonomous power*, which is something other than the formal universal . . . a power which is arbitrary and capricious."[163] In this way, the presumed validity of persons in the legal community turns into the tyranny of an individual who wields universal sovereign power in the empire.[164] Under the sway of the lord of the world, the subject finds itself *subjected* to the arbitrariness and contingency of the despotic emperor who imposes upon all *his* subjects his *own* particular content as the source of unity and continuity for the empire of persons. Indeed, to the subject, this imposition of particular, arbitrary content is experienced as "the destructive violence," external, alien, and hostile to its very personality.[165]

---

162. PS, 292–93; §481. Hegel is thinking here of the Roman Emperors like Caligula and Nero.

163. PS, 292; §480. Hegel continues, "Consciousness of right, therefore, in its actual validity itself, experiences instead the loss of its reality and its complete inessentiality, and to designate an individual as a *person* is an expression of contempt."

164. For Hegel, as Min succinctly states, "the road of individualism also leads to totalitarianism" (Min, "Speculative Foundation of Religion," 175).

165. PS, 293; §482.

Analogous to skepticism that failed to realize the absolute freedom of self-consciousness in a way that succumbs all particularities of the world to the infinite destructive power of negation in thought and thus proceeded to the form of the unhappy consciousness, the ethical subject in its moment of legal personality, with its necessary subjection to the monstrous excesses of the lord of the world, has found itself alienated in an alienating community and thus now moves to a new form of communal-spiritual subjectivity. This new form is what I would call "the self-alienated cultural subject" that tries to overcome this ethical, communal predicament of alienation on its *own* initiative, that is, by *radicalizing* self-alienation—*voluntarily* alienating itself—under the slogan of culture or cultivation (*Bildung*).[166]

The Self-Alienated Cultural Subject

Finding itself situated in its explicit opposition to, or alienation from, the realty of the world, the subject is driven into itself and comes to realize that it must divest itself of its *immediate*, natural way of existence in relation to the social substance—either as the immediate embodiment of the ethical substance (the divine law of the family or the human law of the nation) or as the immediate validity of its abstract legal personality and natural rights. Therefore, the subject now becomes "the cultural subject" in its *mediating* movement of self-alienation, the movement of willfully alienating or renouncing its *natural* immediacy, through which it is in turn to acquire content and produce the social substance as *its* own work, thereby becoming "the *universal self*, the consciousness grasping

---

166. Similar to the difference between skepticism and the unhappy consciousness, the self-alienated cultural subject in the world of culture differs from the ethical subject as legal personality in the world of abstract persons ruled by the individual tyrant, in that the former posits the world outside itself by *voluntarily* alienating itself, while the latter still exists *immediately*. Through the voluntary alienation of itself, as having seen in the transition from the unhappy consciousness to reason, the subject will eventually make itself universal. In this respect, from the standpoint of Hegel's philosophy of history, the Roman empire serves as a necessary moment in the transition of spirit to the modern world, in other words, as a bridge between the ethical world of Greece and the modern world of culture. Meanwhile, it must be emphasized again that unlike the split subject as the unhappy consciousness in the stage of self-consciousness, the self-alienated cultural subject here operates in the stage of spirit, i.e., as the member of the community.

the *concept*."¹⁶⁷ In other words, in order to overcome the immediate opposition between itself and the actual world and thus find itself in the world *as* its own essence, the subject must cultivate (*bilden*) itself through the process of alienating itself from natural, immediate being, and in that way take "possession of this world."¹⁶⁸ In this sense, as Hegel states, the process or movement in which the subject cultivates itself counts as "at the same time its coming-to-be as the universal, objective essence, i.e., the coming-to-be of the actual world."¹⁶⁹

The actual world as the universal substance, at first, appears to the subject as something immediately alienated, "which has the form of a fixed and unshakeable actuality for it"; yet, at the same time, the cultural subject, who is "certain that this world is its substance," considers it essentially as *its* in-itself, as what it is to become *through cultivation*, i.e., through the process of self-alienation.¹⁷⁰ Just as in the ethical world substance as objective spirit differentiated itself into the moments of nation/people (the law of universality) and family (the law of individuality), so, too, in the cultural world those moments of substance appear in the objective forms of "*state power*" (political/public sphere) and "*wealth*" (economic/private sphere):

> As state power is the simple *substance*, so too is it the universal *work*—the absolute *Thing itself* in which individuals find their *essence* expressed, and where their singular individuality is only the very consciousness of their *universality*. . . . This *simple*, ethereal substance of their life is, in virtue of this determination of their unchangeable self-equality, [mere] *being* and, in addition, merely *being-for-others*. It is thus in itself the opposite of itself, *wealth*.¹⁷¹

---

167. *PS*, 296; §486. Different from abstract, spiritless legal universality in the previous form, the universality which counts as valid here is one that *has become* and is *ipso facto* concrete and actual. From the standpoint of Hegel's philosophy of history, this period of culture spans a long period of time from the Middle Ages to the eighteenth century.

168. *PS*, 297; §488.

169. *PS*, 299; §490.

170. *PS*, 299; §490. For Hegel, as we have observed all along, the gap between the in-itself (universality; objectivity) and the for-itself (individuality; subjectivity) is characteristic of the development of subjectivity as *spirit*.

171. *PS*, 301; §494. Hegel proceeds to argue that although "wealth" represents the moment of being-for-itself in the sense that each individual labors on his own behalf and enjoys himself with the fruits of his labor, it is at the same time a universal essence in that "it is equally the perpetually produced *result* of the *labor* and the doings *of all*,"

Standing in face of the spheres of state power and wealth as the two objective essences of the actual world, which yet remain alien to itself, the self-alienated subject in its cultivation begins to *judge*[172] them in terms of "good" and "bad." The subject considers to be good that in which it finds the "likeness" to itself and to be bad that in which it finds the "unlikeness" to itself. Therefore, according to Hegel, there are two possible judgments—the judgment essentially as a "power which *makes* them [state power and wealth] into what they are *in themselves*."[173] One is that state power is good, while wealth is bad, because the subject can find only in state power its being-in-itself or its intrinsic being (universality); and the other is that wealth is good, while state power is bad, because the subject can find only in wealth its being-for-itself (individuality). That is, when the subject focuses on the universality of work of one and all, the political sphere appears to be good and the economic sphere bad; on the contrary, when the subject focuses on its individuality, the economic sphere appears to be good and the political sphere bad. In judging the substance of the actual world (state power and wealth), therefore, the subject makes them transcend their *immediate* determination and validity. They are in fact what they truly are *only in relation to* the subject; in other words, they are good only insofar as and to the extent that the subject finds itself in them.

From the standpoint of the subject that has now become the essence in relation to state power and wealth, there are "two opposite modes of this relation: one is an attitude to state power and wealth as to something *like*, the other as to something *unlike*."[174] Hegel calls the former the "*noble (edelmütig)* consciousness" which is immediately judged to be good and the latter "*base (niederträchtig)* consciousness" which is immediately judged to be bad.[175] However, as is the case with the judgments of state power and wealth, the subject experiences that the distinction between noble consciousness and base consciousness is also subject to the same dialectic; that is to say, depending upon which moment is highlighted, universality or individuality, what the subject judges to be good ends up being bad, and vice versa.

---

and thereby "this enjoyment itself is the result of the universal doing."

172. To judge something is to overreach (*übergreifen*) it. In judgment, a thing is taken to be not just something as a given but as a being for consciousness.

173. *PS*, 303; §496.

174. *PS*, 305; §500.

175. *PS*, 305; §500-501.

Having experienced such contradictions and inversions in its political and economic activities in the process of cultivation, the subject discovers that there is no absolute ground for distinguishing good and bad or noble and base in its judgments. The subject finds itself remaining alienated from state power and wealth, insofar as its service and obedience to state power requires the suppression of individuality, and insofar as its pursuit of wealth leads to the subordination of universality to individual interest and enjoyment. After all, the self-alienated cultural subject expresses that all the various distinctions in the process of cultivation end up inverting themselves, so that all is vanity (*Eitelkeit*) in this world:

> What is experienced in this world is that neither the *actual essence* of power and wealth, nor their determinate *concepts*, good and bad, or the consciousness of good and bad (the noble and the base consciousness), possess truth; on the contrary, all these moments become inverted, one changing into the other, and each is the opposite of itself.[176]

With the experience of the inversions of all the distinctions that the subject has drawn to overcome its alienation and to establish its unity with the world (state power and wealth), which consequently made it aware of the vanity of all external reality, the self-alienated cultural subject now returns to itself and seeks to find its genuine self-actualization, the unity of itself (individuality) and the world (universality), not in this actual world, the world of culture and alienation, but in the *beyond* of this world, "the unactual world *of pure consciousness*, or of *thinking*."[177] According to Hegel, there are two opposing moments to this pure consciousness: faith[178] and pure insight. On the one hand, both faith and pure insight represent the cultural subject returning to itself from the actual world in an effort to overcome its alienation: "Just as faith and pure

---

176. *PS*, 316; §521.

177. *PS*, 321; §527. Once again, it must be reminded that unlike stoic consciousness in the stage of self-consciousness and virtuous consciousness in the stage of reason, pure consciousness here is a shape of consciousness in the stage of spirit, that is, a universal subject in community with others. Thus, although pure consciousness as faith and pure insight has a negative relationship to the actual world as it immediately appears, it indeed carries the actual world within itself inasmuch as it seeks to find the pure essence of that world.

178. It should be noted that Hegel distinguishes faith from religion that will be dealt in the next chapter of the *Phenomenology* entitled "Religion." Faith here refers merely to a belief in something that consciousness recognizes to be not in and for itself but beyond the actual world. See *PS*, 322; §528.

insight belong in common to the element of pure consciousness, so also are they in common the return from the actual world of culture."[179] On the other hand, faith and pure insight are opposed to each other. Faith, though it is the transcendence of the actual world as pure consciousness, still has a *positive* or given content as an irreducible objectivity which must be taken to be an object of faith; by contrast, pure insight is immediately self-conscious and characterized by its movement to *negate* all alienating objectivity or otherness, and thus has no content of its own.[180] Pure insight, then, wages war against faith by considering the given content of faith that seems irrational and extrinsic as merely a vanishing *moment* of its own self-conscious movement of absolute negativity. For Hegel, pure insight turning against faith in this way comes to be called "the Enlightenment" (*Aufklärung*) whose fundamental call to all humans is as follows: "*be for yourselves* what you all are *in yourselves—rational*."[181]

By opposing itself to faith and negating the given positive content of faith that appears to be irrational and alien to itself, the subject as the pure insight of the Enlightenment now seeks to overcome alienation and achieve self-actualization. As such, the subject of the Enlightenment is in itself the "category" or "concept," whose essence is "absolute negativity," in which "knowing and the *object* of knowing are the same," and thus "what pure insight pronounces to be its other, what it asserts to be an error or a lie, can be nothing else but its own self."[182] At first, however, it is aware of the object not yet as its own in which it finds itself, but as "something that exists totally independently of it," namely, as the content "*given* in faith."[183] In this connection, the subject of the Enlightenment sees faith as "a tissue of superstitions, prejudices, and errors" perverting primarily the general mass of society, and thus severely criticizes it.[184]

---

179. *PS*, 324; §530.

180. See *PS*, 329: §541: "Since faith and insight are the same pure consciousness, but are opposed as regards form—the essence is for faith [mere] *thought*, not *concept*, and therefore the sheer opposite of *self*-consciousness, whereas for pure insight the essence is the *self*—their nature is such that each is for the other the sheer negative of it."

181. *PS*, 328; §537.

182. *PS*, 333; §548.

183. *PS*, 334; §5485. Emphasis mine.

184. *PS*, 330; §542. For Hegel's detailed exposition of the Enlightenment's criticisms against faith, which are based on the three characteristic moments of faith, namely, God as its object, the ground of its belief, and its service and practice, see *PS*, 336–40; §551–56. Simply put, according to Hegel, the Enlightenment provides largely three criticisms against those three moments of faith: faith as anthropomorphic

Yet, as Hegel points out, in criticizing faith the subject as the pure insight of the Enlightenment is bound to be caught in the mire of self-contradiction. It is in attacking faith that *itself* ends up doing what it attacks; for instance, criticizing faith for taking the content of its own subjective, anthropomorphic belief to be absolutely true amounts to a criticism of itself, in that what the pure insight of the Enlightenment itself does is also treating its own thoughts as something essentially absolute and not just subjective. For Hegel, as expected, this contradiction arising from the struggle of the Enlightenment with faith does not merely remain something purely negative, but rather leads to a positive dialectic whereby the subject of the Enlightenment could be *more* enlightened. That is, the subject in its unconscious activity of pure concept becomes aware of itself *as* its own contrary, experiencing that faith is, in essence, not something completely different from itself.[185]

Taking every determinate content of faith to be the product of its own thought, i.e., "as something *finite*, as a *human essence and representation*," the subject as the pure insight of the Enlightenment regards any transcendent notion of "*absolute essence*," to which faith directs itself, as a "*vacuum* to which no determinations, no predicates, can be attributed."[186] In this way, it negates everything that lies beyond *sense-certainty*[187] and so ends up absolutizing its *human* essence and reality that are indeed sensuous, immediate, and finite. That is to say, it claims that the human being in her sensuous existence is the highest, absolute being and the ultimate measure of the value of all things, and thus that all things exist *for* the human being. For the subject of the Enlightenment, everything that is *in itself* is *for an other*, in other words, all things are *useful* to the human being: "What is useful, is something with an enduring being *in itself*, or a thing. This being-in-itself is at the same time only a pure moment;

---

projectionism, faith as ill-founded belief based upon the represented content of quasi-historical narratives, and faith as foolish and wrong ascetic practice.

185. Along similar lines, Hegel calls faith an "*unsatisfied* Enlightenment" (PS, 349; §573).

186. PS, 340; §557.

187. See PS, 340–41; §558, where Hegel points out that the Enlightenment's appeal to sense-certainty here does not mean its sheer returning to the first form of consciousness as object-consciousness: "Here, however, it is not an *immediate*, natural consciousness; rather, it has *become* such a consciousness to itself. . . . Grounded on the insight into the nothingness of all other shapes of consciousness, and hence of everything beyond sense-certainty, this sense-certainty is no longer mere 'meaning,' but rather the absolute truth."

hence it is absolutely *for an other* . . ."[188] This anthropocentric, utilitarian principle of the Enlightenment, which says that things are valuable in themselves only insofar as and to the extent that they are useful to the human being, is also applied to the relationships among human beings themselves. Just as everything is useful to the human being, so too are human beings useful to each other, and in this way human relationships are constituted by the mutual usefulness of individuals to each other. Consequently, the world wherein the self-alienated cultural subject as the pure insight of the Enlightenment has found its essence is the world of *utility* in which it seeks to relate itself to nature, society, and even religion in such a way that they serve as a useful device or means for satisfying its own will and interest.

Nevertheless, utility is indeed a predicate of the object and not of the subject. In this respect, the fact that the object is useful to the subject does not mean that the subject always and already takes *actual* possession of that object. In other words, in the world of utility there remains a gap between the subject and the object that is *potentially* useful to the subject. Therefore, for the subject to find itself in what is for it, it has to do more than just regard everything useful. For this reason, Hegel observes, the subject of the Enlightenment must become the subject of "*absolute freedom*"[189] which "grasps the fact that its certainty of itself is the essence of all the spiritual masses, or spheres, of the real as well as of the supersensible world, or conversely, that essence and actuality are consciousness' knowledge of *itself*."[190] For the subject of absolute freedom, all objectivity, reality, or substance, which has been alien to itself, is now its own will and work that are simultaneously the universal will[191] of all individuals and their common work. Hence, for Hegel, as for Rousseau, absolute freedom requires that there be no distinction between universal will and all individual wills.[192]

188. PS, 354; §580.

189. Here "absolute freedom" refers, more precisely, to absolutely abstract or negative freedom as the absolute abstraction or flight from every determinate content. For Hegel's exposition of absolute freedom in this sense of negative freedom, see PR, 37–39; §5.

190. PS, 356; §584. According to Hegel, this absolute freedom was pursued historically in the French Revolution.

191. Hegel has Rousseau's "general will" (*volonté générale*) in mind at this point.

192. In the same vein, Rousseau stands against any kind of representative democracy: "Be that as it may, the moment that a people provides itself with representatives, it is no longer free; it no longer exists" (Rousseau, *Social Contract*, 129).

However, the following question is of necessity raised: "Who then *actually* determines this universal will?" For, in reality, there seems no existing will that is in and of itself truly universal. Each and every individual as the subject of absolute freedom claims that its own will is *immediately* equated with universal will, and that it directly participates in the work of one and all in which it finds itself without limiting its participation to a particular sphere. Yet, as this universal will makes itself into an *actual* political object or substance, i.e., "the laws and functions of the state" in the course of the subject's *actions*, its claim to be universal cannot help but remain merely abstract in the sense that this universal will and freedom would be "free from singular individuality, and would apportion the *plurality* of *individuals* to its various constituent parts."[193] Furthermore, for the state or, more exactly, the government presumed to be an embodiment of the universal will of all individuals turns out to be nothing but a faction, an embodiment of the particular, contingent will of someone or some group that happens to take power. Consequently, Hegel argues, the subject of absolute freedom, which claims to abstract universality in the sense of the *immediate* passing over of its own particular will to universal will and so imposing on the rest of the world its own unsublated particularity that is opposed to the freedom and will of other concrete individuals, leads ultimately to the reign of universal terror. It is because anyone who diverges from the *presumed* universal will of the regime, which is indeed the particular will of one individual or group in power, must be eliminated under the cloak of unanimity, if the ideology of absolute freedom is to be upheld.[194]

As experiencing a great opposition between its claim to be universal (absolute freedom) and the actual consequence (universal terror) in the sense that absolute freedom as abstract universality, devoid of appropriate content, can only bring about the terror of death to individuality, the self-alienated cultural subject has learned that it must transcend its claim to absolute freedom, which tries to actualize itself *immediately*, and so

---

193. *PS*, 358; §588. For this reason, Hegel observes, Rousseau's general will, in principle, can create no positive work because any positive social substance (e.g., laws or institutions) would stand opposed to the individuality of actual self-consciousness. The only work possible for the general will is thus the negative work of destroying the will of individuals; see *PR*, 276–78; §258 A.

194. According to Hegel, this experience was exhibited historically in the Reign of Terror in the French Revolution. See also *PR*, 39; §5 A.

move itself to a new form of communal-spiritual subjectivity in a new world. I would call this "the moral subject" in the world of morality:

> Just as the realm of the actual world passes over into the realm of faith and insight, so does absolute freedom pass over from its self-destroying actuality into another land of self-conscious spirit where, in this non-actuality, freedom counts as the truth. In the thought of this truth spirit refreshes itself, insofar as spirit *is* and remains *thought*, and knows this being which is enclosed within self-consciousness to be the perfected and completed essence. There has arisen the new shape of spirit, that of the *moral spirit*.[195]

The Moral Subject

Negating the immediate identification of its particular, contingent individuality (individual will) with abstract universality (general will), while, at the same time, preserving its immanent demand to pursue genuine freedom in the sense of the spiritual unity of itself and the world, the subject now transcends itself into moral subjectivity. For the moral subject, the universal and objective substance, which has turned out to be something alien to itself in the world of culture, even to the extent of the terror of death in the moment of the Enlightenment's absolute freedom, is *interiorized*, and the absolute essence lies within itself. Thus, rather than desiring neither political power or economic wealth in *this* world nor faith or pure insight in *that* world, the subject now only desires itself in its universal self-certainty as its object in the world of morality. This world of morality, as Hegel indicates, is different from the earlier ethical world (e.g., Greek *Sittlichkeit*) in that the world of morality is the *mediated* or *sublated* synthesis of the ethical world (the immediate unity of subject and object) and the world of culture (the split of subject and object).[196]

The moral subject, at first, takes the form of Kantian "pure duty," which is not alien to itself, nor imposed from without, but intrinsic to itself as its *own* object, substance, or essence in its *formal* universality that is empty of specific content.[197] The moral subject as the subject of pure

---

195. PS, 363; §595. For Hegel, this movement was reflected historically in a transition of the world of the French Revolution based on Rousseau's general will to the moral world of German idealism based on Kant's and Fichte's moral will.

196. PS, 364; §597.

197. Kant formulates the formal principle of the moral law as pure duty in the

duty claims that it "knows duty as the absolute essence" and performs it *freely*,[198] making itself indifferent to, or independent of, "nature" (i.e., the necessitation of sensuous impulses and inclinations), which is considered as morally irrelevant, inessential "otherness," though *perpetually present within itself*.[199] However, as hinted at the last four italicized words of the preceding sentence, the complete mutual independence or indifference of duty/morality and nature/reality is not something feasible, for it is the very same subject that itself counts duty *as* essential and nature *as* inessential, both existing *within* itself. In other words, these two points of view—that "nature and duty are mutually indifferent to each other" and that "nature as inessential is subordinate to duty as essential"—are contradictory.[200] Aware of this contradiction fundamentally rooted in the conflict between morality (pure duty, pure will, freedom) and reality (nature, sensibility) *within* itself as "*one consciousness*," the moral subject of Kantian pure duty must resolve it not simply by exterminating natural sensuousness—"since sensibility is itself a moment of the process producing the unity, viz., the moment of *actuality*"[201]—but by "necessarily" *postulating* "the harmony of morality and nature," i.e., the conformity of sensuous nature to the demands of morality, yet not in the world of here and now but in the world *beyond*.[202] More specifically, according to Kant,

---

following way: "*So act that the maxim of your will could always hold at the same time as a principle in a giving of universal law*" (Kant, "Critique of Practical Reason," 164).

198. Freedom here means "complete spontaneity," the power to fulfill pure duty, independently of natural inclinations and external causes or motivations.

199. PS, 365; §599–600.

200. See PS, 365–67; §600: "This relation [between duty/morality and nature] is based, on the one hand, on the complete *indifference* and independence of *nature* and of *moral* purposes and activity with respect to each other, and, on the other hand, on the consciousness of the sole essentiality of duty and of the complete dependence and inessentiality of nature. The moral worldview contains the development of the moments which are presented in this relation of such entirely conflicting presuppositions."

201. PS, 367–68; §603. Hegel continues, "Consciousness has, therefore, itself to bring about this harmony and to be making continuous progress in morality. But the *consummation* of this progress *has to be postponed to infinity*; for if it actually came about, this would do away with the moral consciousness. For *morality* is only moral *consciousness* as negative essence for which sensibility is only of *negative* significance, is only *not in conformity with* pure duty. But in that harmony, *morality* qua *consciousness*, or its *actuality*, vanishes, just as in the moral *consciousness*, or in the actuality, its *harmony* vanishes." What Hegel implies here is that in the concept of "duty" *per se* there is the intrinsic thought of hindrances and obstacles to be overcome, which are natural, sensuous impulses and inclinations for Kant.

202. PS, 366–67; §602.

the eventual harmony of morality and nature entails the two specific postulates: the immortality of the soul and the existence of God. As for the first postulate (the immortality of the soul), Kant argues that "no rational being of the sensible world is capable at any moment of his existence" of attaining the complete conformity with the demands or laws of morality, but "it can only be found in an *endless progress*" toward that ideal, and this endless progress is "possible only on the presupposition of the *existence* and personality of the same rational being continuing *endlessly*."[203] Hence, the immortality of the soul must necessarily be postulated for the harmony of morality and nature. As for the second postulate (the existence of God), it seems clear that such harmony, however, is beyond the power of any finite moral subject to achieve. What is postulated for the integral fulfillment of morality in the sense of the complete conformity of nature to moral laws is an agency that can *guarantee* this harmony between the intelligible world of morality (freedom) and the sensible world of nature (happiness), and such an agency, for Kant, is "God" as the supreme being who is the cause of nature and at the same time governs it according to moral laws.[204]

Accordingly, in order to fulfill Kantian pure duty in the community of morality, the subject ought to postulate the unity of duty and nature, of morality and happiness, which is to be placed *outside* or *beyond* itself. However, as the moral subject claimed at the outset, the realm of duty and morality is at the same time something that it "itself *consciously produces*" as its own object and essence, and thus it is also "equally posited" as "existing in the interest of, and by means of," the subject itself.[205] After all, the moral subject of Kantian pure duty reveals its fundamental contradiction which Hegel describes with the notion of "dissembling replacement" (*Verstellung*):

> The way in which consciousness proceeds in this development, is to establish one moment and to pass immediately from it to another, sublating the first; but now, as soon as it has *set up* this second moment, it also *displaces* it again, and instead makes the

203. Kant, "Religion," 58.

204. See Kant, "Religion," 58–60. In this sense, for Kant, the existence of God is not a matter of rational demonstration or intellectual intuition, but a postulate which is morally necessary in fulfilling our duty; that is to say, the postulate of the existence of God is a matter of "moral religion" or "rational belief," rather than a matter of speculative knowledge.

205. *PS*, 374; §616.

> opposite into the essence. At the same time, it is *also* conscious of its contradiction and *dissembling*, for it passes from one moment, *immediately* in *relation to this very moment*, over to the opposite.²⁰⁶

According to Hegel, this antinomy or contradiction—arising from dissembling displacements between morality and happiness, pure will and sensuous impulse, the one pure duty and many duties, etc.—that the moral subject of Kantian pure duty is bound to face explicitly comes to the fore in the process of its "moral action" to fulfill duty. When the moral subject of duty *acts*—and it indeed *cannot not* act because the necessity of action is *inherent* in the very idea of duty—it in fact actualizes and even enjoys, though not completely, the harmony between duty/morality and nature/happiness, which it has nonetheless postulated as something beyond itself, "for acting is nothing other than the actualization of the inner moral purpose . . . or of the harmony of the moral purpose and actuality itself."²⁰⁷

Consequently, the moral subject of Kantian pure duty finds itself hypocritical as it has become aware, in the process of its own moral action, that "the accomplishment of morality is posited in the fact that what has just been determined as morally null is present within it and intrinsic to it."²⁰⁸ Before acting, the subject claims that the harmony between duty and nature, reason and sensibility, morality and happiness, is something to be posited in the world beyond; however, when it actually acts, which is inevitable in the course of real life, it indeed actualizes the presence of this harmony that has been postulated to take place outside itself. The moral subject, aware of such hypocrisy and contradiction, is compelled to give up its initial moral worldview, i.e., its immediate preoccupation with Kantian pure duty, and to flee back into itself, which gives rise to another moment of morality. According to Hegel, this new moment of the moral subject is "conscience" (*Gewissen*), which, as we are going to see shortly, will bring the moral subject to its ultimate contradiction and

---

206. *PS*, 374; §617.

207. *PS*, 375; §618. "Action," as has been consistently pointed out, involves the unification of all the traditional dualisms—particularly, in this context, of reason and sensibility, of duty and nature, of morality and happiness.

208. *PS*, 382; §630. For Hegel, any kind of purist position, which seeks to separate reason from sensibility, duty from nature, morality from happiness, etc., leads to hypocrisy, for it rules out the very possibility of action; however, we humans cannot avoid acting in real life.

crisis and, in turn, give way to the final stage of subjectivity, that is, absolute subjectivity.

The moral subject, as it has been forced to abandon all the postulates of harmony which failed to resolve the internal contradiction of pure duty (moral reason) and sensuous nature, now returns to itself and becomes "conscience," in which, Hegel observes, it attempts to overcome that inner contradiction in such a way that those opposing elements in their brute otherness to each other are made into sublated moments of itself. The moral subject of conscience claims that it is an acting, concrete moral spirit, immediately certain of itself, that knows and wills itself in its particular existence (*Dasein*) *as* actuality and *as* universality, without separating what appears moral to itself (the for-itself) from what is moral in actuality (the in-itself): "It itself is what is, in its contingency, completely valid in its own eyes, and knows its immediate individuality as pure knowing and action, as true actuality and harmony."[209] Therefore, conscience is, in its immediate unity, "moral *action* qua action" that "fulfills not this or that duty, but knows and does what is concretely right," with its own conviction that it *is* moral.[210] In this respect, Hegel emphasizes, it is quite different from the preceding moment of moral subjectivity, i.e., Kantian pure duty in its bare form of universality which is indifferent to concrete, particular content, keeping itself separate from sensuous nature and reality, and should not *ipso facto* act:

> According to this latter view [the Kantian view of morality as pure duty], I act morally when I am *conscious* of accomplishing only pure duty and *nothing else* but that, and this means, in fact, when *I do not* act. But when I actually act, I am conscious of an *other*, of an actuality, which is already in existence, and of an actuality I want to produce, so I have a *determinate* purpose and fulfil a *determinate* duty; and in this there is something *other* than the pure duty which alone should be intended.[211]

On the contrary, for the moral subject of conscience, the realization of morality no longer consists in a beyond, but in its very concrete moral action that is grounded upon nothing other than the immediate conviction of its own morality.

---

209. *PS*, 384; §632.

210. *PS*, 386; §635. In this sense, for Hegel, conscience is morality in its culmination, which never leaves itself to something other than itself.

211. *PS*, 386; §637.

It is important to note that the moral subject of conscience, which takes itself to be the essence of morality and so acts with its own conviction that its action is always moral, is without doubt the individual,[212] but this individual has already been *spirit* in this stage of communal-spiritual subjectivity, that is, spirit as the I that is We and the We that is I. In other words, it considers itself as the universal and, more specifically, its own individual, subjective moral conviction and action as objectively binding, as something to be recognized as valid by the whole community of conscientious individuals. In this sense, the universality of pure duty is not simply negated, but, at the same time, preserved in conscience; however, in lieu of being an abstract, formal universality in its sheer externality and transcendence (being-in-itself) as in Kantian morality, the universality of conscience is something concretely actualized in the subject itself, existing as a *moment* of its moral action (being-for-others).[213] At this point, it seems as though the subject returns to ethical subjectivity in its immediate identity with substantial universality, namely, with the laws and customs of the community to which it naturally belongs. Yet, as Hegel points out, there is a big difference between the immediate ethical subject and the moral subject of conscience, in that the latter, unlike the former, has gone through the mediation of the world of culture (the cultural subject) whereby it could develop into subjectivity that is certain of itself. Accordingly, the moral subject of conscience preserves within itself the moment of "substantiality" from the ethical world and the moment of "external existence" from the world of culture, as well as the moment of "self-knowing essentiality of thinking" from the moral world of Kantian pure duty, and in this way it becomes absolute negativity "because it knows the moments of consciousness as *moments*, and dominates them as their negative essence."[214]

However, as anticipated, the moral subject of conscience, as it acts upon its own moral conviction, soon finds itself facing a predicament. When the moral subject of conscience *acts*—and, as indicated earlier, it cannot avoid acting—out of its own moral conviction, it cannot help but disclose the arbitrary and particular character of its own action. The moral subject *knows* that insofar as "the moment of *universality*" exists in conscience, "conscientious action requires that the actuality before it

212. Remember that "individuality is the principle of actuality" for Hegel.

213. See PS, 387; §638, where Hegel quotes Jacobi along these lines: "It is now the law that exists for the sake of the self, not the self that exists for the sake of the law."

214. PS, 389; §641.

should be grasped in an unrestricted manner, and therefore that all the circumstances of the case should be accurately known and taken into consideration."[215] However, it is also aware that *in reality* "it does not grasp all the circumstances" in which its action is to take place, and thus that its presumed universality is an empty claim in the sense that "its pretense of conscientiously weighing all the circumstances is vain."[216] Nevertheless, since it must act no matter what, the moral subject has to make a decision *on its own*, for it as *conscience* does not rest on any authority, criterion, or content external to itself, and, in turn, its self-determination and action thereupon is necessarily bound by its own immediate, particular, contingent, and arbitrary content, rather than mediated by universal content.

Furthermore, since the essence of morality, for the subject of conscience, lies in its moral action based upon the immediate self-certainty and individual conviction that what it is doing is always good and universally valid, any content, insofar as it is considered as its own, can be essentially moral and must be recognized by all other individuals as moral. In this way, morality turns into a pure form with which every content can be associated, freed of any determinate duty; "for whatever the content may be, it contains the *blemish of determinateness*," and therefore every content "stands on the same level as any other."[217] Hence, one's moral, conscientious action must always be "a *determinate* action," being-for-others, externalizing its own determinate, particular content to others. Yet, Hegel contends, the problem is that there is no guarantee that all other conscientious people could also identify themselves with *this* particular content of *this* determinate action and thereby necessarily recognize it; rather, in reality, they, who also regard themselves equally as certain of its own consciences, doubt, displace or dissemble, criticize, and even "nullify it by judging and explaining it in order to preserve their own self."[218] After all, the moral subject of conscience falls into contradiction, experiencing within itself the discrepancy between the intended universality of moral conviction with self-certainty (the *immediate* unity of being-in-itself and being-for-itself) and the actual particularity of moral action as its externalization (being-for-others)—in more practical terms, a dilemma of *whether* it remains true to its own conscience but gives up recognition

---

215. *PS*, 389; §642.
216. *PS*, 389–90; §642.
217. *PS*, 392; §645.
218. *PS*, 394–95; §648–49.

of others *or* it recognizes the conscientiousness of others but violates its own conscience.

The moral subject, having experienced this contradiction of conscience, now withdraws from conscientious action into "the intuiting of its own divinity,"[219] i.e., the contemplation of its inner conviction and pure intention as a divine voice, in order to hold true to its inner demand of knowing itself as universality. This movement constitutes a new moment that Hegel calls the *"beautiful soul"* (*schöne Seele*).[220] Hegel portrays what the beautiful soul looks like as follows:

> It lacks the power to externalize itself, the power to make itself into a thing, and to endure being. It lives in dread of besmirching the splendor of its inner being by action and existence; and, in order to preserve the purity of its heart, it flees from contact with actuality, and persists in its obstinate impotence to renounce its own self which is reduced to the extreme of ultimate abstraction, and to give itself substantiality, or to transform its thinking into being and put its trust in the absolute difference [between thinking and being].[221]

The beautiful soul, afraid of contaminating itself and so refusing to act, is nothing else than a judging consciousness that, without allowing itself any externalization through acting, only criticizes acting conscience for its seemingly oxymoronic stance, an oxymoron because acting means *particularizing* itself, while conscience refers to that which is immediately certain of itself as *universality*. What the moral subject of the beautiful soul claims is that its only undertaking is to judge the presumed conscientious actions of others by uncovering their hypocrisy and evilness, namely, that they are not acting conscientiously—acting not out of genuine convictions in their universality but out of individual motives in their particularity.[222]

---

219. *PS*, 397; §655.

220. *PS*, 400; §658. The term "beautiful soul" also appeared in the works of Hegel's contemporaries such as Schiller, Goethe, Novalis, Rousseau, etc.

221. *PS*, 399–400; §658. See also *PR*, 47; §13 Z.

222. Hegel wants us to pay attention to the fact that this judgment or critique is indeed carried out in "language" which is regarded as the true mode of expression that preserves not only subjectivity/particularity but also objectivity/universality; that is, in language the subject is this or that particular individuality *as* universal subjectivity. For Hegel's own argument on this, see *PS*, 395–96; §652–53.

However, as has been repeatedly indicated, the beautiful soul as the moral subject must act at any rate, which is manifested precisely in its own *activity* of judging, and thereby give empty universality a determinate content drawn from itself as particular individuality; in other words, judgment is itself a mode of action in the sense that when one judges something or someone, it necessarily bases its judgment on its own determinate, particular standards or criteria. In this way, the beautiful soul cannot help but find itself in an inverted situation where it is rather judged to be hypocritical and evil by those who it has judged to be so, for it does exactly what it accuses acting conscience of doing. That is to say, insofar as the subject is judging, it must engage itself in the otherness of the world and so, of necessity, become particular, which has been counted by itself as evil.[223] Consequently, the moral subject gets caught up in a dilemma, specifically the conflict between an acting self (conscience) and a judging self (beautiful soul), i.e., the contradiction between "what is for itself and what is for others" within itself as the individual, and more essentially "the opposition of individuality to other individuals, and to the universal" in a community or society.[224]

Experiencing in its final moment (beautiful soul) another repeated failure to achieve the unity of its own particular individuality with universality, which, according to Hegel, is indeed the highest crisis possible at the stage of communal-spiritual subjectivity,[225] the moral subject now becomes aware that the predicament of morality, i.e., the conflict of particularity and universality, cannot be resolved simply by choosing *either* acting conscience *or* judging beautiful soul in their immediate opposition, but instead only if these two oppositions reconcile themselves to each other. More specifically, Hegel observes, this reconciliation takes place in the form of "forgiveness" (*Verzeihung*), in which each side negates or renounces itself in a way that confesses the inadequacy of its

---

223. This Hegelian dialectic of judging beautiful soul and acting conscience is in a similar vein to the earlier dialectic of master and slave and of noble consciousness and base consciousness in terms of the dialectic of universality and particularity.

224. *PS*, 400–401; §659.

225. See *PS*, 406–7; §668, where Hegel vividly describes the crisis in which the moral subject of the beautiful soul is stuck: "The beautiful soul, lacking actuality, caught in the contradiction between its pure self and the necessity of that self to externalize itself into being and to change itself into actuality, in the *immediacy* of this entrenched opposition . . . this beautiful soul, then, as the consciousness of this contradiction in its unreconciled immediacy, is disordered to the point of madness, wastes itself in yearning, and pines away in consumption."

own absolute claim in its immediacy, namely, the merely *particular* individuality of acting conscience and the purely *abstract* universality of judging beautiful soul, and thus they recognize each other equally as a *moment* of total truth as *concrete universality*, of what Hegel characterizes as Absolute Spirit.[226] In this way, Hegel argues, the mutual forgiveness and reconciliation lead the subject to develop into a new and, indeed, final stage of subjectivity which finds its true essence in the realm of Absolute Spirit. I would call this "absolute subjectivity," truly spiritual and universal subjectivity in its fullest sense, which is neither the abstractly universal, infinite I nor the merely particular, finite I, but the very sublated unity of these two I's in their difference:

> It is the *actual* I, the universal knowing *of itself* in its *absolute opposite*, in the knowledge which remains *internal*, and which, on account of the purity of its separated being-within-itself, is itself the completely universal. The reconciling *Yes*, in which the two I's let go of their opposed *existence*, is the *existence* of the *I* expanded into duality, which therein remains identical with itself and, in its complete externalization and opposite, has the certainty of itself—it is God that appears in the midst of those who know themselves as pure knowledge.[227]

Absolute Subjectivity: "Religion" and "Absolute Knowing"

From the very beginning of the journey, as Hegel emphatically insists, there has been a sort of irresistible drive built into the immanent structure of the human subject, namely, searching for the essence or truth in

---

226. *PS*, 407–8; §670: "The forgiveness which it [judging beautiful soul] extends to the first consciousness [acting conscience] is the renunciation of itself, of its *unactual* essence, the essence which it equates with that other consciousness which was *actual* action, and it recognizes as good that which thought characterized as bad, viz., action; or rather, it abandons this distinction of the determinate thought and its determining judgment existing-for-itself, just as the other abandons its own, existing-for-itself, determining of action. The word of reconciliation is the *existing* spirit, which intuits the pure knowledge of itself qua *universal* essence in its opposite, in the pure knowledge of itself qua *individuality* that is absolutely within itself—a reciprocal recognition which is *absolute* spirit." Interestingly, Pinkard adopts the Kantian "mutual acknowledgement of radical evil" as the condition for forgiveness; see Pinkard, *Hegel's Naturalism*, 142.

227. *PS*, 409; §671.

which it is fully present to itself (*Beisichselbstsein*)[228]—not just at the individual level, but more fundamentally at the communal level. As it moves from communal-spiritual subjectivity, consisting of the ethical subject, the self-alienated cultural subject, and the moral subject in their logically necessary sequence, to a new shape of subjectivity where it continues to be conscious of itself as spirit, but now in a different dimension, the subject becomes clear that the essence it must now look for is not just any kind of universal substance, but something that can embrace universal subjectivity and universal objectivity in their totality, i.e., the absolute essence in which all individual subjects find themselves and find one another.[229] It is in this sense that Hegel calls this essence the Absolute, and more exactly "Absolute Spirit." Unlike the initial spiritual community of the ethical order (Greek *Sittlichkeit*), this is truly *absolute* in that its content is not limited by, or relative to, anything other than itself, i.e., any natural, given differences or any other extraneous factors—such as one's gender, kinship, and nationality in their immediate particularity. In the same vein, no human customs, laws, and institutions objectified in human history, which are still burdened with unsublated externality, otherness, and alienations of various kinds, can fulfill the role of this absolutely universal and spiritual essence. Indeed, Hegel argues, only the divine ("God") can do, which means he is also saying that God must be understood *as* "Absolute Spirit" and no longer as an immutable substance. With the emergence of the concept of God as Absolute Spirit in its concrete universality par excellence, in which all human beings are identified as *its* others or its *self-expression*, the subject develops itself into "absolute subjectivity" that is conscious of itself as being concretely universal too in and through participating in Absolute Spirit.[230] In fact, as pointed out from the very beginning, absolute subjectivity in the realm of Absolute Spirit has always been present as the immanent telos in all developmental stages and forms of the human subject.

228. This is precisely what Hegel means by "freedom."
229. As discussed above, it was the "mutual forgiveness and reconciliation" that made possible this passage to the new and final form of subjectivity, precisely because by forgiving and reconciling each other, each subject encounters in its hitherto opposite others knowledge of itself as universal and essential; in other words, all individuals are aware of the I that is We, and the We that is I.
230. In the next chapter (chapter 5), I will further articulate the importance and necessity of the concept of God as Absolute Spirit in Hegel's vision of spiritual subjectivity.

According to Hegel, the sphere of Absolute Spirit contains within itself two distinguishing moments in their progression, viz., Religion and Absolute Knowing (Philosophy),[231] and hence, in accordance with this, I divide absolute subjectivity into its two moments which I would call "the religious subject" and "the philosophical subject" respectively. Before dealing with each moment of absolute subjectivity, it must be noted that both "the religious subject" and "the philosophical subject" here go beyond their conventional meaning, character, and scope. Since religion and philosophy, for Hegel, are not one sphere among other spheres but their ultimate ground, truth, and fulfillment, the religious and philosophical subjects contain within themselves all the stages and forms of human subjectivity in its spiritual, teleological, dialectical movement as *sublated moments*. It is in this very sense that I call them "absolute subjectivity."[232]

The Religious Subject

As discussed above, the concept of God as Absolute Spirit, "spirit that knows itself as spirit,"[233] begins to emerge as the truly universal essence in the midst of the moral subjects' reciprocal recognition arising from mutual forgiveness and reconciliation.[234] However, although the subject now finds itself in every other subject, each knowing itself as universal

---

231. In the *Phenomenology* Hegel places "art" as a moment of religion; it is much later that he separates it from religion and so grasps the Absolute Spirit in three stages, namely, art, religion, and philosophy.

232. In a similar vein, for example, Hegel calls religion "the absolute object . . . the region of eternal truth and eternal virtue, the region where all riddles of thought, all contradictions, and all the sorrows of the heart should show themselves to be resolved, and the region of the eternal peace through which the human being is truly human" (*LPR I*, 149).

233. *PS*, 410; §673. Although God has appeared in the preceding stages and forms of consciousness, for example, in the unhappy consciousness at the stage of self-consciousness and in the faith of self-alienated spirt, Hegel observes that its full conception emerges at this stage for the first time, that is, God as Absolute Spirit, "Spirit in-and-for-itself." For Hegel's detailed descriptions about this, see *PS*, 410-12; §672-77.

234. For Hegel's remarks on the moral roots of religious consciousness elsewhere, see *EM*, 250; §552 A: "Genuine religion and genuine religiosity emerge only from ethical life and they are the ethical life at *thought*, i.e., becoming conscious of the free universality of its concrete essence. Only from ethical life and by ethical life is the Idea of God known as free spirit; it is therefore futile to look for genuine religion and religiosity outside the ethical spirit."

and essential, and in this way has Absolute Spirit as its object, it confronts this object as something beyond itself, though not completely other than and external to itself. This distinction between subject and object gives Absolute Spirit a *transcendent* divine character, and thus allows the human subject to take the form of *religious* consciousness. Therefore, the religious subject is fundamentally characterized as knowing itself to be universal and essential in and through its relationship to the transcendent divine object.[235] For Hegel, this transcendent character of the divine object in relation to the human subject (religious consciousness) is what makes religion bring in the form of "representation" (*Vorstellung*).[236] The religious subject *represents* the divine object to itself precisely because the divine object appears as something beyond itself, even though it relates to the divine object as that in which it finds its true essence.

The telos of religion, namely, the consciousness of the unification of the infinite, divine spirit (God) and the finite, human spirit[237] is neither immediately given nor readily comprehensible, but rather the religious subject must gradually grow into it through the multiplicity of its phenomenal forms. For Hegel, the growth of the religious subject intrinsically corresponds to the progress of its consciousness of the divine object, that is, to the gradual spiritualization and universalization of its conception of God as Absolute Spirit.[238] In this progressive development, the religious subject at each level of growth experiences inherent predicaments in light of the telos or concept of religion and gets over them in a way that moves to a higher form with a new conception of both the divine and the human. Before discussing how the religious subject dialectically develops into its particular forms in proportion to its progressive consciousness of

235. Along the same lines, Hegel defines "religion" as "the relation of human consciousness to God" (*LPR I*, 150).

236. *PS*, 412; §678.

237. According to Hegel's philosophy of religion, this is what constitutes the "concept of religion," namely, religion as the relation of the divine spirit and the human spirit, which involves the intrinsic unity of the movement of the divine spirit seeking to express itself in the reality of the finite, human spirit and the movement of the human spirit seeking to realize itself in the infinite, divine spirit as its essence; see *LPR I*, 178–80.

238. See *LPR II*, 515: "The principle by which God is defined for human beings is also the principle for how humanity defines itself inwardly, or for humanity in its own spirit. An inferior god or a nature god has inferior, natural and unfree human beings as its correlates; the pure concept of God or the spiritual God has as its correlates spirit that is free and spiritual, that actually knows God." Min calls this principle the "principle of coherence" (Min, "Hegel's Dialectic," 9).

the divine in its content, it must be noted again that each form of religious subjectivity is a moment of *spirit* which as such involves "community," and in this stage "religious" community.

As always, the religious subject in its initial form or moment, where the concept of religion is merely and abstractly posited, is characterized by its *immediacy* (the in-itself). It claims to find its true essence in a divine object that is immediately present, and, according to Hegel, this claim is exemplified historically in "natural religion" (*natürliche Religion*). At this level, the divine object (God), which the religious subject worships as the member of a religious community, is *represented* as something sensuous and given in nature, a being as yet without self-consciousness and interiority—though not simply taken in its purely physical, natural character without any sort of meta-physical, spiritual significance in its universality. The religious subject belonging to the community of natural religion sees divinity in nature, first in "light" (e.g., the religions of Persia), then in "plants and animals" (e.g., the first religions of India), and lastly in the "works of the artisan" (e.g., the religions of Egypt).[239]

Particularly, in the religion of the artisan (*Werkmeister*) which Hegel considers the last moment of natural religion, the religious subject becomes aware that divinity cannot exist in an immediately given, natural form, and so instead venerates or worships objects that the artisan produces. Since the artisan's works, which are now seen as the divine object, are no longer something immediate and given in nature but rather something mediated and produced, it seems reasonable to say that the religious subject at this level has already left natural religion behind and moved to the next form of religion, namely, the religion of art. However, Hegel observes that although the content of the divine object as the absolute essence begins to lose the character of natural immediacy in the religion of the artisan, it still remains the moment of natural religion and not as yet that of art-religion; for the works of the artisan as representing the divine—be it obelisk, pyramid, sphinx, etc.—cannot communicate to the religious subject in human terms. In other words, those representations of the divine that the artisan produces are still an "instinctive operation, like that of bees building their cells," "without having yet grasped the thought of itself," which relies upon natural forms of one sort or another.[240] Therefore, in whatever the artifact might be as the

---

239. For Hegel's detailed discussions of each phase, see *PS*, 418–20 (§685–88), 420–21 (§689–90), and 421–24 (§691–98), respectively.

240. *PS*, 421; §691.

representation of the divine, the religious subject finds itself confronting a divine essence that is alien to its genuine spiritual and universal truth, and consequently it must move from natural religion, both in its moment of given, natural immediacy and in its moment of artificial mediation, to a new form of religion, that is, "religion of art" (*Kunst-Religion*) where the artisan becomes an artist inasmuch as its works that represent the divine come to have an expressive function in human language.

The religious subject that has moved from the community of natural religion to that of art-religion now seeks to find as its essence the divine object (God) in the form of art. For Hegel, this new and higher moment of religion was exemplified historically in Greek religions, wherein the divine is represented as something more spiritual, raised above the natural, with ethical (*sittlich*) characteristics. More precisely, the religious subject in the community of art-religion regards the nation or people (*Volk*), rather than nature, as the place where it relates to the divine object: "These ancient gods . . . are supplanted by shapes which in themselves only have a dimly reminiscent echo of those Titans, and which are no longer natural beings, but lucid, ethical spirits of self-conscious peoples."[241] In the religion of art, moving beyond the religion of the artisan, divinity takes on the human form with spiritual, self-conscious activity, and is *ipso facto* closely connected with the human community. However, at first, it is difficult for the religious subject to find itself as spiritual, universal self-consciousness, as the I that is We and the We that is I, in this anthropomorphic form of divinity created by the artist, because what the religion of art produces at this level as representing the divine are anthropomorphic sculptures or statues which lack actual self-consciousness. As it becomes aware that the sheer static, inorganic reality of representation needs to be surmounted by the actuality of self-consciousness, the religious subject now seeks for something different from sculptures standing mute as a means for representing the divine, that is, something as the spiritual, universal essence in which it also finds itself as spiritual, universal subjectivity. According to Hegel, this new form of art engages directly with *language* and more specifically the "hymn," in and through which members of the religious community communicate with the divine that *speaks*:

> The work of art therefore demands another element of its existence, the god requires another mode of coming forth than

---

241. *PS*, 428; §707.

this ... This higher element is *language* ... language is the soul existing as soul. The god who therefore has language as the element of his shape is the work of art that has in itself a soul, that possesses immediately in its existence the pure activity which, when it existed as a thing, was in contrast to the god.[242]

However, the religious subject that worships the divine through the hymn soon comes to reveal that it relates itself to the divine in the hymn only in an impermanent way, in contrast with the permanence of the sculpture.[243] Thus, it needs to move to the next development of art-religion that Hegel calls the "*cult*" (*Kultus*), in which the opposition between the two moments of "the *abstract* work of art"[244] is sublated into a *dialectical* unity, the unity of "the divine shape *in motion* in the pure sentient element of self-consciousness" (hymn) and "the divine shape *at rest* in the element of thinghood" (sculpture).[245] Members of a cultic community worship together the divine through religious rites or services, where they, for example, sing hymns together before the statues in the temple in order to receive and serve the divine. In the process of various cultic activities, Hegel observes, the religious subject as the member of the art-religion community renounces their particularity and draws nearer to the divine, and, in turn, the divine takes off its abstract universality or mere remoteness and obtains consciousness of itself.[246] In this way, it is in

---

242. *PS*, 429–30; §710. Hegel proceeds to argue that the language of the hymn is more advanced than that of the oracle in that the latter utters contingent matters and arbitrary decisions that concern a particular individual who claims to speak in the voice of the divine, whereas the former speaks something that is universally shared by all who partake in it; see *PS*, 430–32; §711–12.

243. See *PS*, 432; §713: "Whereas the statue is an existence at rest, speech is a vanishing existence; and whereas in the statue objectivity is set free and lacks an immediate self of its own, in speech, by contrast, objectivity remains too much enclosed in the self, falls too far short of a lasting shape and is, like time, no longer immediately present in the very moment of its being present."

244. For Hegel, both the sculpture and the hymn are *abstract* in that each represents the divine object as something isolated from its internal, constitutive relations; that is to say, the former only takes on pure objectivity, while the latter only pure subjectivity.

245. *PS*, 432; §714.

246. See *PS*, 433–38; §718–24, where Hegel describes various religious, cultic rites and practices as a dialectical movement that develops from abstract to more and more concrete in terms of the unity between the human and the divine—from the sacrifice of the worshippers' own material possessions through their communal labor to construct holy temples to their mysteries.

the cult that the religious subject enjoys immediate unity with the divine essence.

Yet, as the religious subject has engaged in the cult *specific* to its own religious community, it becomes aware of its intrinsic limit which consists in its insufficiency as the medium of the actualization or revelation of the divine as the *absolute* spiritual essence: "Its self-conscious life is only the mystery of bread and wine, of Ceres and Bacchus, not of the other, the strictly higher, gods whose individuality includes as an essential moment self-consciousness as such."[247] Furthermore, the cult in which the religious subject participates is not only specific to its own religious community as art-religion, but also *distinguished* from its ordinary affairs; in other words, its cultic practices do not encompass the totality of human actuality *as* divine actuality. It is for this reason that Hegel places the cult in the realm of the abstract work of art, along with the sculpture and the hymn; though, as stated earlier, it is at the same time construed as the sublated unity of them.

To overcome this inadequacy that the religious subject experiences as it engages in the cult, it now moves to the next moment of the art of religion, namely, "the *living* work of art." As indicated, the living work of art is a necessary outcome, both positive and negative, from the experience of the cult. Thus, the living work of art is directed at providing the religious subject with a product that involves the whole essential activity of the divine *in* the human and of the human *in* the divine, while at the same time preserving the moment of joyous communion between the two experienced in the cult. Knowing that the human being is at one with the divine essence, the religious subject seeks a *living* embodiment of the divine represented in human form, i.e., an acting divinized individual, and this it finds in the athlete champion or the handsome warrior, who is "an ensouled, living work of art that matches strength with its beauty."[248] However, the religious subject soon comes to realize that the athlete or warrior's powerful physicality cannot properly represent the divine essence because in it only the corporeality or exteriority of the divine is realized without interiority. The religious subject, therefore, turns to a more adequate form that Hegel calls "the *spiritual* work of art," which is

---

247. *PS*, 438; §724.
248. *PS*, 438; §725.

once again the form of language where "inwardness is just as external as externality is inward."[249]

To put it concretely, in the spiritual work of art the divine object is represented in the language of literature, which is in principle open to all and not just exclusive to a specific politico-religious community. The religious subject, which seeks to witness its unity with the divine in literary forms where it sees the divine and the human equally as spiritual, universal self-consciousness, takes "epic" as the first form, followed by "tragedy" and "comedy."[250] In the epic, as exemplified in Homer's epics (*Iliad* and *Odyssey*), the divine (the Olympian gods) is essentially represented as "the universal" and "the positive" vis-à-vis the human heroes (Agamemnon, Achilles, Ulysses, etc.), that is, "as the *irrational void of necessity*" that controls or manages the actions and destiny of "the *individual self* of mortals."[251] By contrast, in the tragedy, as exemplified in Aeschylus and Sophocles's tragedies, human beings appear more in control of their actions, in the sense that they are themselves "*self-conscious* human beings who *know* their own rights and purposes, the power and the will of their determinateness, and who know how to *say* them."[252] Nevertheless, as with the epic, a sense of impotence in relation to the divine is still present in the tragedy too;[253] it "clings to the consciousness of an *alien fate*."[254] Thus, in the tragedy the religious subject no longer regards the divine as the agent controlling the lives of human individuals, but nonetheless remains at the level of representing the divine as a fate that lacks

---

249. PS, 439; §726. As Hegel points out in the next sentence, the form of language at this point is "neither the language of the oracle, wholly contingent and singular in its content, nor the emotional hymn sung only in praise of a singular god; nor is it the contentless stammer of Bacchic frenzy."

250. To be sure, Hegel has in mind here the different genres of ancient Greek literature, namely, Greek epic, tragedy, and comedy. Yet, as Hegel does, it is necessary for us to look into the logical structure and movement operating behind each of these literary forms, i.e., the movement from substance to subject, which is not just confined by any exclusive connection to particular historical reality. In a similar vein, Winfield distinguishes these three literary forms by type of narration: Epic "employs third-person narration"; tragedy "supplants third-person narrative with the actual speech of interacting characters"; and comedy "employs the first-person narration" (Winfield, *Hegel's Phenomenology of Spirit*, 338).

251. PS, 443, §731.

252. PS, 444, §733.

253. For Hegel, such powerlessness in Greek tragedy is manifested particularly "in the *chorus of the elders*" (PS, 444; §734).

254. PS, 445; §734.

its own self-consciousness. Lastly, in the comedy, as exemplified in Aristophanes's comedies, it is disclosed that there is none other than the self of human actors behind all the representations of the divine in its seemingly fateful workings, which is manifested as they take off their masks. In this way, the divine and the human, which were separated in the epic and the tragedy, are now united, but in such a way that human beings laugh at the divine in its claim to be universal ethical power and that the former ironically turns out to be the destiny of the latter. Therefore, as it finds itself in unity with the workings of fate which have been taken to be the absolute spiritual essence, the religious subject no longer sets the divine essence apart from itself: "What this self-consciousness intuitively beholds is that whatever assumes the form of essentiality over against it, is instead dissolved in it—in its thinking, its existence, and its action—and is at its mercy."[255] In short, through the dialectical movement of the religion of art, which culminates in the spiritual work of art in its form of comedy,[256] the religious subject has now elevated itself to the divine, the absolute spiritual essence into which all substance is resolved, and to the extent that it advances the non-religious proposition that *"The self is the absolute essence"*[257] and that *"God is dead."*[258]

In effect, however, what the religious subject, being certain of itself as the absolute essence for a moment, finds itself confronting is the very opposite of such self-certainty, namely, a finite, contingent, mortal individual. When it claims to be present to itself, it at the same time finds itself alienated from itself; when it believes that it has reached itself, it soon discovers that it has become lost. In this way, the religious subject comes to see itself not just as "happy consciousness" which is characteristic of the

---

255. *PS*, 452; §747.

256. Throughout the succession of forms from natural religion to art-religion, as has been examined, the conception of the divine as the absolute essence has passed from the form of substance into the form of subject. Hegel characterizes this movement as the "incarnation of the divine essence," which begins in earnest with an anthropomorphic statue and culminates with an actual self-conscious individual in the comedy (*PS*, 453; §748). In addition, this development from substance to subject precisely squares with Hegel's main thesis of the *Phenomenology*, which is expressed in its Preface, that the truth as the Absolute must be grasped "not only as *substance*, but equally as *subject*" (*PS*, 10; §17).

257. *PS*, 453; §748.

258. *PS*, 455; §752. As will be seen, this negative expression of the death of God is preserved in the next form of religion (revealed religion) in a positive way: that the God as substance dies, which indeed paves the way for the God as spirit.

comedy, but more essentially as "unhappy consciousness," the consciousness of the existentially intrinsic cleavage between divine and human, infinite and finite, universality and particularity.[259] This self-consciousness as unhappy consciousness leads to the knowledge of a "*total* loss,"[260] "the loss of substance as well as of the self,"[261] which in turn amounts to the awareness that human existence as such is evil.[262] Since the religion of art cannot resolve this highest, greatest alienating contradiction, the religious subject now must transcend into the higher form of religion in which it can truly find the absolute unity with itself in God as spiritual, universal subjectivity without any alienation from itself.[263] This new form of religion is what Hegel characterizes as the absolute, consummate, final, highest, perfect, or ultimate form of religion, namely, "revealed religion" (*offenbare Religion*).[264]

As alluded to above, the revealed religion must present the concept of God, the absolute essence, not merely as substance but as *spirit*, for only spirit can be truly *absolute* in that it can relate itself to others (being-for-others; immanence) while at the same time remaining present to itself (being-for-itself; transcendence). Only in such God that *is* spirit, the human subject can also become truly spiritual in the sense of finding itself in others (individuality) and others in itself (universality) without

---

259. This dialectic of happy consciousness and unhappy consciousness is analogous to the earlier movement of the thinking subject (stoicism and skepticism) to the split subject (unhappy consciousness). Yet it must be noted again that this time the similar dialectical movement takes place not at the individual level but at the communal level.

260. *PS*, 455; §753.

261. *PS*, 455; §752.

262. For Hegel's detailed exposition of what he means by that "*humanity is by nature evil*," see *LPR III*, 295–300; "the cleavage is all within the subject, that the subject is evil, that it *is* the split and the contradiction—yet not a contradiction that simply falls apart, but rather one that simultaneously holds itself together" (*LPR III*, 295–96).

263. As Hegel says that "spirit is all the greater, the greater the opposition from which it returns into itself" (*PS*, 206; §340), the greatest contradiction leads to the highest form of spirit, both the divine spirit and the human spirit.

264. As Harris points out, "revealed" is not quite an accurate translation for the German word used by Hegel, *offenbar* ("revelatory"); "revealed" is rather a translation of *geoffenbart*; see Harris, *Hegel's Ladder*, 649. Unfortunately, in English translations these terms are not consistently distinguished, which nonetheless could be justified to some degree, because what is revealed (*geoffenbart*) in Christianity is first and foremost the fact that God is intrinsically revelatory (*offenbar*); see Hodgson, *Hegel and Christian Theology*, 92–93.

unsublated alienations. For Hegel, this revealed religion as the absolute, consummate, highest form of religion is historically manifested in Christianity, and thus it is only in and through Christianity that the human subject is to attain its ultimate truth or telos, i.e., absolutely spiritual and universal subjectivity—at least in terms of *content*.[265] In this regard, I believe, it would be necessary to take a closer look into the reason why Hegel identifies Christianity as the revealed or absolute religion, in which the concept of religion—the unification of the divine and the human in their universal spirituality—finds its adequate actualization beyond all alienating limitations that have still remained in other forms of religion prior to it (natural religion and art-religion).[266]

Simply put, Hegel argues, Christianity is the revealed religion in that it proclaims the content of reconciliation or unification between infinite and finite, divine and human, God and the world by *revealing* the concept of God *as* "Absolute Spirit" in its dialectical movement. Despite its gradual spiritualization in the movement of religion, the divine (God) has remained merely one being alongside other finite beings and thus not as yet truly infinite and absolute. Distinctive from this conception of the divine in other religions, however, the God of Christianity is not just substance but equally subject or, more precisely, Absolute Spirit and as such essentially "trinitarian." In its trinitarian movement God not only posits itself as eternal substance (affirmation) but also differentiates itself from itself by positing something *other* than itself as *its own* other (negation); yet, at the same time, it returns to itself by finding itself in this very otherness (negation of negation). Identity with itself (God as *being-in-itself*, which is represented as God the Father), differentiation from itself (God as *being-for-itself* in and through being-for-others, which is represented as God the Son), and the reconciliation or unification of identity and difference/otherness (God as *being-in-and-for-itself*, which is represented as God the Holy Spirit): these three *moments* constitute God as Absolute Spirit.[267]

---

265. The reason that Hegel confines the absoluteness of Christianity only to its content, as opposed to its form, will be discussed later.

266. See PS, 461; §761: "The hopes and expectations of the preceding world pressed forward solely to this revelation, to intuit what absolute essence is, and in it to find itself."

267. For Hegel's speculative exposition on the Christian doctrine of the Trinity as the representation of the dialectical process of Absolute Spirit, see PS, 464–67; §769–73. I will also deal with this more in the following chapter.

These three moments suggest that the God of Christianity is not simply a transcendent being out there that only enjoys its eternal identity with itself outside the world, but, first of all, the creator that posits, which means "creates" in Christian representational language, the other of itself, the world (nature and the human being), from within itself as its own self-externalization or self-expression, yet without abandoning its identity with itself. In this way, "creation" represents the process whereby the absolute, infinite being becomes other to itself, through which God, who is infinite, finitizes himself and, in turn, makes the finite world (creature) to be a necessary moment of his own infinite life.[268] According to Hegel, in the finite world the human being alone is an adequate other of God as his self-expression precisely because the human being, unlike nature, is only a self-conscious, free spirit, though finite spirit, in which God, who is infinitely self-conscious, free spirit, can be fully present to himself.[269] Yet this does not mean that the human being is *explicitly* free, self-conscious spirit from the outset of creation; it must rather grow into such being, making its implicit spirituality (*imago Dei*) explicit in actuality. In this connection, Hegel interprets the biblical story of the Fall as the representation of humanity's alienation, its separation from God, which is a necessary movement from natural humanity (the state of innocence; immediate existence) to spiritual humanity (self-consciousness; being-within-itself), that is, as the essential moment toward making *explicit* humanity's *implicit* unification or reconciliation with God.[270]

More importantly, Hegel emphasizes that all of this leads to the Christian doctrine of the Incarnation.[271] The incarnation of God is, first and foremost, what makes Christianity the absolute religion in the sense that it epitomizes the fulfillment of the concept of religion, the unification of the divine and the human. God in its trinitarian movement becomes human in such a way that the eternal Son of God the Father becomes incarnate as a temporal-historical Son in Jesus of Nazareth. Therefore,

---

268. For Hegel's speculative interpretation of the biblical story of creation, see *PS*, 467; §774, and *LPR III*, 290–94.

269. Hegel's dictum that "*Self-consciousness achieves its satisfaction only in another self-consciousness*" (*PS*, 110; §175) is applied in this phase, at the highest possible level.

270. For Hegel's speculative interpretation of the biblical story of the Fall, see *PS*, 467–70; §775–77; *LPR III*, 300–304.

271. In a similar vein, Lauer states that "for Christian theology creation, fall, incarnation, and redemption are part and parcel of one and the same movement" (Lauer, *Reading of Hegel's Phenomenology*, 281).

Jesus Christ, in whom the union of the divine and the human has fully and completely come to pass as a concrete spatio-temporal event, is both the finite other of God and God himself.[272] It is through this incarnation of God in the finite otherness of an actual human individual that people first become explicitly aware of God as Absolute Spirit, the absolute totality of the divine and the human, the infinite and the finite, universality and particularity, in which they can find themselves. In other words, in and through the incarnation of God people intuitively perceive the unity of the divine essence with their own because it is given before them in the form of immediate existence, as a present, immediate individual. In this regard, Hegel argues, the implicit unity of God and humanity is made explicit in its full-fledged form in Christianity because the foundation of Christianity is laid upon the historical fact of the Incarnation:

> This, that absolute spirit has given itself the shape of self-consciousness *in itself* and therefore also for its *consciousness*, now appears in the following way. The *faith of the world* is that spirit *is immediately present* as a self-consciousness, i.e., as an *actual man*, that spirit is for immediate certainty, that the faithful consciousness *sees*, *feels*, and *hears* this divinity. Thus, this self-consciousness is not imagination, but is *actual in the believer*. Consciousness, then, does not start from *its* inner, from thought, and unite *within itself* the thought of God with existence; on the contrary, it starts from an existence that is immediately present and recognizes God therein.[273]

In short, for Hegel, it is the incarnation of God in Jesus Christ that is "the simple content of the absolute religion" of Christianity in which the divine is *revealed* essentially as Absolute Spirit, i.e., as "*self-consciousness*" that knows itself in the externalization or otherness of itself—"the essence that is the movement of retaining its self-identity in its otherness."[274] This

---

272. "Of this spirit, which has abandoned the form of substance and enters into existence in the shape of self-consciousness, it may therefore be said—if we wish to employ relationships derived from natural generation—that it has an *actual* mother but a *father* who exists *in itself*. For *actuality* or self-consciousness, and the *in-itself* as substance, are its two moments through whose reciprocal externalization, each becoming the other, spirit enters into existence as their unity" (PS, 457; §755).

273. PS, 458; §758. See also LPR III, 115: "The consummation of reality in immediate singular individuality [is] the most beautiful point of the Christian religion. For the first time the absolute transfiguration [of finitude is] intuitively exhibited [so that everyone can] give an account of it and have an awareness of it."

274. PS, 459; §759.

dialectical or conceptual necessity constitutes the speculative significance of the Incarnation for Hegel.[275]

According to Hegel, however, this self-revelation of God in Jesus Christ (the Incarnation) is still *immediate* and therefore not yet fully spiritual and universal, for God is at this level "*this individual* self-consciousness in opposition to the *universal* self-consciousness," where spirit does not yet exist as universal subjectivity in the same way that it does as the individual subject (Jesus Christ).[276] In other words, the concept of religion, i.e., the unification of the divine and the human by way of the consciousness of God as Absolute Spirit, has been achieved only in one particular individual and not equally in all human subjects.

To fully reveal the essence or truth of God as Absolute Spirit, therefore, God's immediate, sensible presence in a here-and-now should be sublated into his *spiritual* presence in the universal community of all human spirits. To this end, God must give up his immediate incarnation present in this world, that is, the Son of God must himself die as the particular individual with all natural finitude, negativity, and sins of the world, and then resurrect himself as the absolute universality of spirit (the Holy Spirit) with new infinite life and love: "This death [of the Son] is, therefore, its resurrection as [the Holy] Spirit."[277] In this way, people can know that God's existence is more than "this objective singular individual," that is, "the *universal self-consciousness* of the community."[278] According to Hegel, it is in the religious community of believers called the Church, the Kingdom of God or the Kingdom of the Spirit, that God, while remaining identical with himself, continues to be *universally* present to all his human others, assisting them in *subjectively* (by faith and in

---

275. Along these lines, Hegel problematizes the so-called "quest for the historical Jesus," which is preoccupied with purely historical questions about the life of Jesus of Nazareth: "What results from this impoverishment of the life of spirit, from getting rid of the representation of the community and its action with regard to its representation, is not the concept, but rather bare externality and singularity, the historical manner of immediate appearance, and the spiritless recollection of a fancied singular shape and its past" (*PS*, 463; §766).

276. *PS*, 461–62; §762.

277. *PS*, 471; §779. For Hegel's detailed exploration on the speculative meaning of the biblical story of the death of Jesus Christ followed by his resurrection and ascension, see *PS*, 475–76; §784–85; *LPR III*, 322–28.

278. *PS*, 462; §763.

cult) appropriating the reconciliation of the divine and the human that has accomplished *objectively* in Jesus Christ.[279]

It is precisely because of these Christian discourses on the full dialectical nature of God as Absolute Spirit in its trinitarian movement that Hegel identifies Christianity as the revealed and absolute religion. The divine being that is not grasped as Absolute Spirit is "merely the abstract void, just as spirit that is not grasped as this [trinitarian] movement is only an empty word."[280] In the end, the concept of Absolute Spirit, which first emerged for the subject as it entered into the sphere of religion, is fully manifest *in content* to the religious subject in and through Christianity, that is, the Absolute Spirit (God) in its dialectical, trinitarian movement in or under which all human subjects can find themselves and find one another without alienation.

However, as Hegel insists, the revealed or absolute religion of Christianity still remains burdened with shortcomings, some kind of alienating dualism, because of which the human subject cannot be completely present to itself therein. For all its doctrines and practices identifying God as Absolute Spirit in its trinitarian movement, which is indeed what makes Christianity the absolute religion, this content is presented "in the form of *representational thinking*," portrayed in the story by employing terms, for example, like the Father, the Son, creation, fall, incarnation, crucifixion, resurrection, etc., as represented in narrative histories.[281] In

---

279. For Hegel, as will be discussed, this subjective appropriation of objective reconciliation is to be fully achieved by philosophy, which is the witness of spirit in its highest form. It is in this sense that Hegel says, "philosophy is itself the service of God" (*LPR I*, 153).

280. *PS*, 465; §771.

281. *PS*, 477; §787. "But the religious community's representational thinking is not this *conceptual* thinking; it has the content without its necessity, and instead of the form of the concept it brings into the realm of pure consciousness the natural relationships of father and son. Since this consciousness . . . remains at the level of *representational* thinking, the essence is indeed revealed to it, but the moments of the essence, on account of this synthetic representation, partly themselves fall asunder so that they are not related to one another through their own concept, and partly this consciousness retreats from this, its pure object, relating itself to it only in an external manner" (*PS*, 465–66; §771). As shown in the words of "representational thinking," Hegel regards "representation" or "representing" as *thinking* or, more exactly, the initial form of thinking in its movement, which, however, remains one-sided, still linked to images in their immediate givenness, and therefore is to be sublated into conceptual or speculative thinking, a thinking in its fullest sense. In this respect, representation stands somewhere between immediate intuition or mere acceptance of what is given and conceptual comprehension. For Hegel's view on the function of "representation"

other words, the content of unification between divine and human on the basis of the concept of God as Absolute Spirit has become revealed and made manifest in Christianity only *in itself*, as something *given*, as a narrated *re*-presentation, and thereby still external and other to the religious subject itself, and not yet "in and for itself" as something with which it fully identifies itself. In the revealed religion, the religious subject is conscious of God as Absolute Spirit, but not as yet actually finds itself in that Absolute or conscious of Absolute Spirit as its own essence. This is so because the Absolute is still represented to itself as something given, thus extraneous and transcendent, that is, as the object of faith—as witnessed in the Christian doctrine of the hiddenness or mystery of God and so forth. After all, the otherness between its consciousness of God and its consciousness of itself remains unsublated:

> While this unity of essence and the self has come about *in itself*, consciousness too still has this *representational thought* of its reconciliation, but as a representation. It obtains satisfaction by *externally* adding to its pure negativity the positive meaning of the unity of itself with the essence; its satisfaction thus itself remains burdened with the opposition of a beyond. Its own reconciliation therefore enters its consciousness as something *distant*, as something in the distant *future*, just as the reconciliation which the other *self* achieved appears as something in the distant *past*.[282]

The religious subject, which has end up facing the gap between what it intends (absolute unification with God) and what it actually experiences (the discrepancy between its consciousness of the Absolute and its self-consciousness), comes to recognize that in order to resolve this last predicament on the path toward its goal or truth, i.e., absolute subjectivity in its full sense, it now has to sublate itself to a higher—indeed, the highest—level of subjectivity that I would call "the philosophical subject."

The Philosophical Subject

The philosophical subject, which is identical with the religious subject *in content* but different *in form*,[283] has the absolute "form" adequate to

---

in terms of thinking, see Lauer, *Hegel's Concept of God*, 9–10.

282. *PS*, 478; §787.

283. "It must be said that the content of philosophy, its need and interest, is wholly

the absolute "content" that has been manifest to the religious subject of Christianity in the form of representational thinking: "Truth is the *content*, which in religion is still not identical with its certainty. But this identity consists in the content receiving the shape of the self."[284] This absolute form is what Hegel identifies as the "conceptual thinking" (*begreifendes Denken*),[285] or speculative reason, whereby the content is elevated from something merely given to something equal to the subject's own activity; for the concept is "the knowledge of the self's act within itself as all essentiality and all existence, the knowledge of *this subject* as *substance* and of the substance as this knowledge of its act."[286] Thus, it is the philosophical subject's task to unfold *in concept* the *speculative meaning* of what the religious subject experiences in representational, metaphorical forms, and only in so doing its unification or reconciliation with the Absolute (God) is realized in the most absolute, complete, ultimate, universal dimension.[287]

In fact, according to Hegel, this new form is something that has already, though implicitly, been reached by the subject in the previous stage, that is, by the moral subject as typical modern consciousness, and thus it only needs to be *re*-cognized explicitly in conjunction with what it has experienced in the revealed religion.[288] Along these lines, Hegel

in common with that of religion. The object of religion, like that of philosophy, is the eternal truth, God and nothing but God and the explication of God.... Thus religion and philosophy coincide in one. In fact, philosophy is itself the service of God, as is religion. But each of them, religion as well as philosophy, is the service of God in a way peculiar to it... They differ in the peculiar character of their concern with God" (*LPR I*, 152–53).

284. *PS*, 485; §798.

285. For Hegel, as mentioned earlier, the conceptual thinking is interchangeable with the rational, dialectical, or speculative thinking.

286. *PS*, 485; §797.

287. It should be very clear by now that this undertaking takes place not at the individual level but at the communal level, according to Hegel's conception of the "spirit acting in the community." In other words, although each subject needs to make the content its own by clarifying, articulating, and internalizing its conceptual significance, this is done not based on purely an individual interpretation or judgment in its particularity and arbitrariness, but in communion with other subjects—and, in principle, all human subjects—by the witness of the Spirit of God.

288. See *PS*, 484; §796: "This concept gained its fulfillment, on the one hand, in the *acting* spirit certain of itself [morality], and on the other, in *religion*: in religion it acquired the absolute *content as content* or in the form of *representational thinking*, the form of otherness for consciousness; in the former shape, on the contrary, the form is the self itself, for it contains the self-certain spirit that *acts*; the self accomplishes the

also remarks that the revealed religion of Christianity has the true "content" but without an adequate form corresponding to it, while modern consciousness has the true "form" but without an adequate content corresponding to it. What is required, therefore, is to sublate this opposition between the purely formal subjectivism of modern consciousness (the for-itself) and the dualistic objectivism of the revealed religion (the in-itself) into a "philosophy," to wit, Hegel's own dialectical, rational, or speculative philosophy that can truly reconcile the true subjective form of modern consciousness with the true objective content of the revealed religion (the in-and-for-itself):[289]

> The *content* is the true content, but all its moments, when posited in the medium of representation, have the character of being uncomprehended [in terms of the concept], of appearing as completely independent sides which are *externally* related to each other. For the true content also to receive its true form for consciousness, the higher formative development of consciousness is necessary; it must elevate its intuition of absolute substance into the concept, and equate its consciousness with its self-consciousness *for itself*, just as this has happened for us, or *in itself*.[290]

Hegel calls this last form of spiritual subjectivity (the philosophical subject) "absolute knowing" (*absolute Wissen*)[291]—"the spirit which at the same time gives its complete and true content the form of the self and thereby realizes its concept while remaining in its concept in this

---

life of absolute spirit."

289. Thus, it seems reasonable to say that Hegel's philosophy is "theological" in the sense that its content is the same as that of religion, i.e., the Absolute Spirit that is indeed identical with the God of Christian faith. In this respect, Hegel's own philosophy could be equated with his "theology" or, more exactly, "speculative theology," as opposed to positive theology, in which revealed religious content (*theos*) and conceptual form (*logos*) are inextricably interwoven. Along the same lines, Lauer observes, what Hegel sets forth is not "*philosophized* theology that he has dispensed with faith," as some left-wing Hegelians seem to argue for, but "*theologized* philosophy to such an extent that . . . it cannot dispense with faith, that is, with faith's content" (Lauer, *Hegel's Concept of God*, 11).

290. PS, 463; §765.

291. As Winfield points out, "absolute knowing" would be a better translation for *absolute Wissen* than "absolute knowledge," in that "absolute knowing ends up being not a determinate body of knowledge but a knowing that eliminates the structure of consciousness as the framework to which knowing is confined" (Winfield, *Hegel's Phenomenology of Spirit*, 365–66).

realization."²⁹² By "absolute knowing" (i.e., philosophy) Hegel does mean neither all-knowing (omniscience) in the crude, empirical sense of the term nor knowledge of some transcendent, other-worldly being, but rather the *conceptual*, speculative, or rational grasp of the essential *structure* of all things that are, i.e., of the *dialectical* movement of all reality that has appeared in history, in contrast to the representational understanding that looks at them as happening side by side (*nebeneinander*) and one after another (*nacheinander*) without any internal relatedness. Hence, the philosophical subject as absolute knowing discloses the inner logic of all phenomena, namely, their internal, constitutive relationship, immanent necessity, and universal significance, in a way that *conceives* them, so to speak, under the logic of Absolute Spirit (*sub ratione Dei*) in its dialectical movement, that is, as self-expressive moments of God as Absolute Spirit. In other words, the human subject is to reach the philosophical subject as absolute knowing when it absolutely finds itself as well as all others contained in the unity of God and at one with that unity.

The philosophical subject does not render the religious subject otiose, but rather illuminates the inner logic and coherence of its representations. In more Hegelian terms, the philosophical subject as absolute knowing is the *sublation* of the religious subject—*negating* the inadequate form of religious representation and *transcending* into the absolute form of philosophical conceptualization while *preserving* the absolute content of the revealed religion, that is, God as Absolute Spirit in its trinitarian movement.²⁹³ Thus, contrary to general suspicion, the transition of the religious subject (Religion) to the philosophical subject (Absolute Knowing) does not destroy the positive content of religion as such, revealed religious truths; rather, it elevates and trans*forms* the content—which, for the religious subject, is simply given and thus only represented in finite,

292. *PS*, 485; §798.
293. For Hegel's own statement that religion and philosophy are identical in content but different in form, among many textual sources, see *LPR I*, 152–53: "the content of philosophy . . . is wholly in common with that of religion. The object of religion, like that of philosophy, is the eternal truth, God and nothing but God and the explication of God. Philosophy is only explicating *itself* when it explicates religion, and when it explicates itself it is explicating religion. . . . But each of them, religion as well as philosophy, is the service of God in a way peculiar to it . . . They differ in the peculiar character of their concern with God." *EL*, 28; §1: "It is true that philosophy initially shares its objects with religion. Both have the *truth* for their object, and more precisely the truth in the highest sense, in the sense that *God* and God *alone* is the truth. Moreover, both treat the sphere of finite things, the sphere of *nature* and the *human spirit*, their relation to each other and to God as their truth."

particular experience tinged with accidentality and contingency—to the level of conceptual, rational necessity and universality whereby the subject can know the true essence of itself and of all others universally *as* spirit, as "a vehicle of the self-knowledge of *Geist*,"[294] that is, as a *moment* of God.[295] In this sense, the philosophical subject must be considered to be "absolute subjectivity" par excellence, i.e., as the absolutely spiritual and universal subject of the *I that is We* and of the *We that is I*: "it is the *I*, which is *this I* and no other, and it is just as much the immediately *mediated*, or the sublated *universal* I."[296]

According to Hegel, the highest point reached by the dialectic is the place where the richest and most concrete universal comes into being, and, in this respect, the philosophical subject (absolute knowing) as the highest form of subjectivity is as such *concreate universality*, which includes within itself, as sublated moments, all other stages and forms of spiritual subjectivity in its dialectical and teleological movement:

> The *goal*, absolute knowing, ... has for its path the recollection of the spirits as they are in themselves and as they accomplish the organization of their realm. Their preservation, regarded from the side of their free-standing existence appearing in the form of contingency, is history; but regarded from the side of their conceptually comprehended organization, it is the *science* (*Wissenschaft*) of *appearing knowing*. The two together, comprehended history, form the recollection and the Calvary of absolute spirit, the actuality, truth, and certainty of its throne, without which it

---

294. Taylor, *Hegel*, 137.

295. This also has to do with Hegel's view on the relationship between faith and reason. Hegel certainly rejects the long-held position of the reason-faith dichotomy. For Hegel, reason, to wit, speculative reason, unlike the understanding, does not simply cancel out religious faith, but instead *sublates* it in the sense that faith in religious content (revelation) is *preserved* as a moment of philosophical knowledge, which is not only rationally permissible but necessary. In this respect, Hegel's commitment to rationality is not a rationalism which claims that human reason (here, in the sense of the understanding) is the only source of knowledge and the only criterion of all truths and values. Hegel's speculative reason is not one that simply opposes and prescinds from faith in divine revelation, along with its constitutive features of intuition, feeling, passion, commitment, representation, etc., but rather one that relates to, includes, and, more properly, *sublates* them—in its triple meaning of negating, transcending, and preserving. This point seems to be what Kierkegaard and other critics miss in their criticisms of Hegel.

296. *PS*, 486; §799.

would be lifeless and alone; only—from the chalice of this realm of spirits foams forth for Him his own infinity.[297]

Moreover, it seems worth mentioning that absolute knowing (the philosophical subject) could be considered as "more a goal than an achievement" for Hegel, as stated in the quote above, that is, "on the way" toward the goal whose achievement "in religious terms could only be the beatific vision."[298]

In conclusion, as we have discussed throughout two chapters, a long journey—indeed, a spiritual journey driven by a teleological-dialectical movement—is necessary for the human being to develop into the stage of Hegelian absolute-universal subjectivity. Importantly, it is in virtue of religion and philosophy that the human subject can and should arrive at this destination (telos), where it, most importantly, participates in the life of God as Absolute Spirit—first in the manner of religious representation, then of philosophical concept. In other words, Hegel's absolute subjectivity exists only where the human subject is recognized as having its essence or truth in God. In this way, the human being at this stage of absolute subjectivity is meant to be truly spiritualized, divinized, and liberated in the sense that she no longer experiences any *alienating* discrepancy between subjective knowing and objective reality, between individual certainty and universal truth, between I and We, between human and divine, and so forth—the discrepancy upon which all preceding stages and forms of subjectivity have rested in its developmental movement.

---

297. PS, 493; §808. In the same vein, Hegel gives a definition of "philosophy" in the Introduction to the *Phenomenology* as "the actual cognition of what truly is" (PS, 46; §73). In contrast to the *Phenomenology*, the more full-blown, positive account of philosophy as the science of knowing is presented in his *Logic*, as Hegel alludes to PS, 491; §805: "Spirit, therefore, having won the concept, unfolds its existence and movement in this ether of its life, and it is *science*. In science, the moments of its movement no longer exhibit themselves as determinate *shapes* of *consciousness* [as in the *Phenomenology*], but—since the difference of consciousness has returned into the self—as *determinate concepts* [as in the *Logic*] and as the organic self-grounded movement of these concepts." For a further argument on the preparatory role of the *Phenomenology* for the *Logic* within the whole enterprise of Hegel's philosophy, see Stern, *Hegel's Phenomenology of Spirit*, 223–25.

298. Hodgson, *Hegel and Christian Theology*, 115.

CHAPTER 5

Constructive Reflections on Hegelian Subjectivity

THIS CHAPTER PROVIDES MY constructive reflections on Hegelian subjectivity from a religious or theological point of view, which also includes my appraisal of a contemporary left-Hegelian reading of his philosophy of subjectivity. There are two sections to this chapter: one is a reflection on Hegel's view of God in connection with his conception of spiritual, universal subjectivity, where I emphasize the absolute necessity of the concept of God in his philosophy of subjectivity; and the other is a critical exploration on Žižek's reading of Hegelian subjectivity as radical negativity, where I argue that although I concur with Žižek in his emphasis on "negativity" as a kernel of Hegelian subjectivity, he nevertheless seems to miss the other aspect, equally constitutive and essential, that is, its *teleological* structure, due in large part to his failure to appreciate the significance and gravity of the concept of God proper in Hegel's philosophy of subjectivity as a whole.

Why *God* Is Essential to Hegelian Spiritual, Universal Subjectivity

In the last section of the preceding chapter (chapter 4), viz., "absolute subjectivity" comprising as its moments the religious subject and the philosophical subject, we have already discussed the significance of the concept of God, particularly of the God of Christianity, in Hegel's philosophy of spiritual subjectivity. Here I would like to further elaborate on that discussion, which would not only help us gain a better understanding of Hegelian subjectivity as such, but also render it more relevant to the contemporary context of globalization. In this regard, it seems necessary to first explore Hegel's conception of God in more depth.

Hegel's Concept of God

As conclusively disclosed in the preceding chapter, Absolute Spirit, another name for God, is *always* and *already* present throughout the entire movement of the human spirit in its self-determination and self-transcendence as both its alpha and omega, its primordial beginning and eschatological end.[1] For Hegel, God is indeed the a priori condition of the possibility for all stages and forms of human subjectivity in its developmental, i.e., dialectical and teleological, movement—from its being in the womb (subjectivity-in-itself) through its birth (subjectivity-for-itself) to its growth (subjectivity-in-and-for-itself). In this respect, Lauer seems surely correct in saying that "Hegel is clearly the most 'God-inebriated' of philosophers," in the sense that "Hegelian enterprise is an extraordinarily unified and grandiose attempt to elaborate one concept, which Hegel sees as the root of all intelligibility—the concept of God."[2] Thus, if we did not make sense of what Hegel means by God, it would be tantamount to being ignorant of the meaning and import of his philosophy as a whole.[3] In short, God is "the presupposition and the goal of all Hegel's thinking."[4]

As we plumb the depth of Hegel's concept of God, which is intimately bound up with his philosophy in general, and his philosophy of subjectivity in particular, the first thing we have to acknowledge is that Hegel has his own distinctive and unique, though not completely novel, view of God, just as all other philosophers and theologians have more or less different conceptions even when they speak of the same word *God*. How then does Hegel conceive of God? What kind of God does

---

1. "God is the beginning and end of all things. God is the sacred center, which animates and inspires all things" (*LPR I*, 150).

2. Lauer, *Hegel's Concept of God*, 20, 1.

3. "Only in the light of 'absolute Spirit' is anything Hegel says intelligible. . . in Hegel's view, 'absolute Spirit' is in fact to be identified with God and that, therefore, only if Hegel's 'Concept of God' is intelligible, will anything Hegel says be intelligible" (Lauer, *Hegel's Concept of God*, 19). In a similar vein, Hegel himself defines the content of his *Science of Logic* as "the exposition of God as he is in his eternal essence before the creation of nature and a finite spirit" (*SL*, 50).

4. Leighton, "Hegel's Conception of God," 601. See also *LPR I*, 367–68.

he attempt to set forth? In fact, shortly after Hegel's death in 1831, the controversy over his position on religion and particularly his view of God arose among his students and followers.[5] There were, broadly speaking, two camps: the so-called "right-wing Hegelians" who defended a reading of Hegel's God as compatible with traditional theism and the "left-wing Hegelians" who claimed that his God-talk was merely a literary technique to advance a fundamental humanism or, at best, a pantheism.[6] I am not going to discuss what each side precisely argues for and against, which is beyond the scope of my current concern, but, here, suffice it to say that in my judgment both right-wing and left-wing views are not *dialectical* enough to show Hegel's concept of God in its depth and breadth. Indeed, Hegel proposes a much more comprehensive understanding of God that does not simply absolutize either theism or humanism, either God's transcendence or immanence, and so forth, but instead integrates or, more precisely, *sublates* them in a very dialectical way. Along the same lines, the following two positions based on an *either-or* formula[7] are to be excluded as un-Hegelian. One is the *dualism* of traditional theism or deism in the sense that God is wholly transcendent to and separated from the world. The other is the *monism* of pantheism in the sense that God is exhaustively immanent in and identical with the world, which also tends to conversely lapse into a Feuerbachean humanistic atheism or atheistic subjectivism (God is simply a human projection) since all transcendence of God is dismissed there.[8]

---

5. For detailed surveys of this controversy, see Jaeschke, *Reason in Religion*, 349–421.

6. According to Beiser, this division continues today: among contemporary Hegel scholars the representatives of right-wing Hegelians are James Stirling, John McTaggart, Richard Kroner, Emil Fackenheim, John Findlay, Stephen Houlgate, and Alan Olson; and those of left-wing Hegelians are Walter Kaufmann, Georg Lukács, Roger Garaudy, Herbert Marcuse, Alexandre Kojève, and Robert Solomon. Beiser, *Hegel*, 124–25, 322n4, 323n5.

7. According to Hegel, this "either-or" conception seeing opposites as mutually external and exclusive is an attempt at the level of the "understanding" (*Verstand*), which is precisely what Hegel's dialectical, rational, speculative philosophy aims to overcome.

8. It is noteworthy that pantheism has two diametrically opposite faces: *acosmism* and *humanistic atheism*. Working from the ambiguous definition of pantheism that "God is all and all is God," Spinozistic acosmism seems to simply highlight the first proposition, "God is all," while humanistic atheism seems to only take up the second proposition, "All is God." As a result, the former eliminates the world, while the latter eliminates God.

Hegel's Sublation of Traditional Theism and Pantheism

It seems to be much easier to show that Hegel's God opposes the God of traditional theism. By traditional theism here Hegel means precisely that which posits God simply and exclusively as an utterly transcendent, immutable, infinite, and unknowable being or substance that is ontologically and epistemologically separated from us and the world in general, and thereby God and the world (including human beings) are merely *externally* related.[9] One of the fundamental reasons that Hegel is very critical of traditional theism of this kind is that although it firmly believes that God's utter transcendence and otherness vis-à-vis the finite world is the very hallmark of God's *infinity*, such a belief rather reduces God to something finite. As Hegel frequently points out through his well-known argumentation of the fallacy of the infinite-finite dichotomy, a divine being posited as wholly transcendent in relation to the world is not the true infinite at all.[10] An infinite that is only transcendent and thus merely externally opposed to the finite ironically makes the finite itself infinite by enabling the finite to exist on its own, and at the same time makes the infinite itself finite because the infinite stands over against the finite, which means that the infinite is bound to be limited by externality and otherness. This kind of the infinite, reified in itself and separated from the finite, is what Hegel calls "bad or spurious infinity" (*Schlecht-Unendliche*).[11]

In this regard, Hegel insists that to advocate the wholly transcendent God of traditional theism who is *utterly other* to the world without internal, meaningful relatedness of any kind is tantamount to finitizing the infinite God and infinitizing the finite world. This irony, i.e., the infinitization of the finite and the finitization of the infinite, emerges precisely because traditional theism remains at the level of the "understanding" (*Verstand*) which makes distinctions—such as finite and infinite, subject and object, human and divine, secular and sacred, and the like—and

---

9. It must be carefully noted that traditional theism discussed here is not exactly identical with classical *Christian* theism, but rather one that is heavily indebted to the Aristotelian philosophical idea of "unmoved mover" ("thought thinking itself"). In fact, classical Christian theism—for instance, presented by Augustine, Aquinas, and others—always tried to maintain the tension or dialectic between the transcendence and immanence of God in relation to the world.

10. For Hegel's in-depth discussions on the problem of the infinite-finite dichotomy, see *SL*, 137–50; *EL*, 149–52; §94–95; *LPR I*, 421–25; *LPR III*, 263–64.

11. There is another sense in which Hegel employs the word "bad infinity," which refers to an endless series of causes and effects.

then absolutizes or reifies these distinctions into stark separations and oppositions.[12] Additionally, not only is the conception of God as a sheer supernatural, transcendent Being logically or metaphysically incongruent and incoherent, which the foregoing Hegelian analysis of the fallacy of the infinite-finite dichotomy has sought to make clear, but it also runs counter to the scriptures that occasionally speak about God's love, suffering, and redemption for his creatures. Hegel seems to claim that traditional theism is based on an ancient, outmoded characterization of the divine as an absolute monarch by giving "unto God the attributes which belonged exclusively to Caesar" rather than Christ—to borrow a phrase from Whitehead.[13]

In short, Hegel rejects or, more exactly, *sublates*[14] traditional theism that views God as a wholly transcendent being who is set over against the world, separated from the realm of ordinary human experience. How are we, then, to make of God if not as the God of traditional theism (i.e., a sheer transcendent, unknowable being)? Before getting at Hegel's own position on that question, we need to look into how Hegel differentiates his view of God from the above-mentioned second extreme position of either-or conception, namely, "pantheism"[15] in the conventional, colloquial sense of the term. This is all the more necessary because the charge of pantheism, which was in Hegel's time commonly associated with atheism, was in fact frequently raised against Hegel by his contemporaries,[16] and, moreover, after his death these interpretations of Hegel's view of

---

12. For the same reason, Hegel criticizes the rationalist theology of the Enlightenment that takes the deistic view of God as an unknowable supreme being beyond the world, which divests God of all content. For Hegel's description of and critical attitude toward this Enlightenment deism, see *PS*, 340; §557; *EL*, 174–76; §112 Z.

13. Whitehead, *Process and Reality*, 342.

14. Hegel does not just simply negate traditional theism in its entirety, but also preserves it, precisely its sensibility of God's infinite, transcendent character in relation to the world, to which pantheism does little justice.

15. It is true, as Hartshone points out, that pantheism is the term that is difficult to define, for it is shrouded in ambiguity; see Hartshone, *Man's Vision of God*, 10. Hegel seems also aware of this ambiguity, given that he attempts to charge those who accuse him as a pantheist with having a bad, distorted conception of pantheism; see *LPR II*, 572–75. At any rate, as will be discussed, Hegel finds serious inadequacy and weakness in pantheism in general in terms of its view of God and of his relationship to the world.

16. Among Hegel's contemporaries it is F. A. G. Tholuck, a German Protestant theologian, who was a representative critic of Hegel as a pantheist. On his pietistic attacks on Hegel's pantheism, see Tholuck, *Lehre von der Sünde*, 231.

God as pantheistic were bolstered by left-wing Hegelians, such as D. F. Strauss.[17]

Historically, in opposition to the doctrine of God as a sheer transcendent being, pantheism has emerged as its alternative. As a trenchant critic of traditional theism portraying God as a reified transcendence, the *Jenseitige*, Hegel indeed emphasizes God's immanence in the world and the intimate interrelation of the divine and the human, and for this very reason he has often been suspected of being a pantheist. Those who interpret Hegel's view of God as pantheism cite Hegel's works, including his posthumously published lectures, for the support of this suspicion.[18] However, I claim—and Hegel would certainly concur with me if he were alive today—that the evidence they provide, when used in the way they interpret, is really being misconceived, for their interpretations are very much un-Hegelian; that is, their accusations that Hegel is a pantheist all rest upon a misrepresentation of Hegel's *dialectic*. Indeed, Hegel was fully aware that, when taken in such a way, his conception of God might possibly be equated with pantheism, even including Spinozistic or Schellingian pantheism,[19] and therefore he sought himself to distinguish his own position from that.[20]

Hegel's fundamental problem with pantheism, which claims that God is all in the sense of God being identified with the essence that is in

17. See Williamson, *Introduction to Hegel's Philosophy*, 233–34.

18. For instance, Hegel's passages such as: "Without the world God is not God" (*LPR I*, 308n97); "God is everywhere" (*LPR III*, 290); "Faith in the divine is only possible if in the believer himself there is a divine element which rediscovers itself, its own nature, in that on which it believes, even if it be unconscious that what it has found is its own nature" (Hegel, *Early Theological Writings*, 266).

19. The Schellingian pantheism here refers specifically to Schelling's earlier philosophy, particularly to what is called his "philosophy of identity." Hegel derisively describes Schelling's pantheism in his early philosophy as "the night in which ... all cows are black" (*PS*, 9; §16). Yet it is widely acknowledged that Schelling's earlier pantheistic position was transformed in his later philosophy, where he argues that his pantheism is not incompatible with human freedom or, rather, that they indeed constitutively require each other. For Schelling's transformed pantheistic position advanced in his later philosophy, see Schelling, *Philosophical Investigations*.

20. See *LPR I*, 374–78, *LPR II*, 572–75, *EM*, 267–75; §573 A. In addition, although Hegel tries to distance himself from Spinoza's philosophy, it is also the case that he shows a high regard for Spinoza, saying: "The great merit of the Spinozist way of thinking in philosophy is its renunciation of everything determinate and particular, and its orientation solely to the One—heeding and honoring only the One, acknowledging it alone. This view [*Ansicht*] must be the foundation of every authentic view" (*LHP III*, 122).

all things,[21] lies not in its idea of the universal immanence of God in the world, but rather in its view of God as a mere substance, i.e., as rigid, static, abstract universality, which in turn renders God's relation to the world undynamic and undialectical. In other words, Hegel criticizes pantheism for characterizing God's immanence in the world as an abstract, immediate unity, rather than as a spiritual, mediated unification *in movement*.[22] According to Hegel, this problematic feature of pantheism derives from, as is the case with traditional theism, its inability to go beyond the level of the understanding on which immediacy, positivity, or substantiality is seen to characterize both the essence of a thing and of its relationship to other things—in this case, the essence of God and his relationship to the world (including human beings).

Contrary to the God of pantheism as well as the God of traditional theism, Hegel's God, whose conception is grounded upon the metaphysics of speculative, dialectical reason rather than that of the understanding, is not only substance but also subject or, more exactly, *spirit*. For Hegel, as for pantheists, God is no doubt the *hen kai pan* (the One and All), i.e., absolute universality as such. However, instead of taking up this idea in terms of a philosophy of abstract identity or "mystical monism"[23] as pantheism seems inclined to do, Hegel's speculative philosophy conceives of the God of *hen kai pan* as *true infinity*, which overreaches and includes the finite within itself, and as *absolute, concrete universality*, in which all finite, particular things come into being, live, and pass away as its own moments yet without simply reducing their genuine individuality, concreteness, and differences to the sameness of one substance. In

---

21. According to Hegel, we can only find pantheism of this sort effectively present in any serious philosophy, not pantheism in its literal meaning—for instance, this paper or that table is God; see *LPR I*, 375.

22. For Hegel, "To conceive the immanence of God in the world as a spiritual immanence . . . is the only way to maintain both the integrity and intelligibility of the finite world and the absolute, true Infinity of God" (Min, "Hegel on the Foundation," 76).

23. William Desmond, who is a contemporary representative of the Kierkegaardian critique of Hegel as a pantheist, characterizes Hegel's God portrayed in his philosophy of religion in terms of "mystical monism," which he claims is not the true God of Christian faith but a counterfeit; see Desmond, *Hegel's God*. For Hodgson's critical response to Desmond's critique of Hegel's God, see Hodgson, *Hegel and Christian Theology*, 248–59, where he argues that Desmond's characterization of Hegel's God as a pantheism and mystical monism is a "gross caricature," which is derived from his failure to see Hegel's holism as "an alternative to monism and dualism," and that, contrary to Desmond's criticism, Hegel's God is an authentic reading of original Christian faith.

other words, the identity or unity of God and the world is not an identity of equation but an identity of *inclusion*; that is to say, it is neither one of abstract unity nor one of mystical union, but one of *spiritual unification* in which God as true infinity or concrete universality finds his expressive moments in finite creatures, and each of finite creatures finds its truth and essence in the infinite, universal God.[24] According to Hegel, such a spiritual, inclusive relationship between God and the world is made possible fundamentally because God *is* in his eternal essence "living spirit." Through this conception of God, Hegel not just avoids the charge of being pantheistic, but more importantly *sublates* pantheism into a higher and more transcended form—that is, negating its reified understanding of identity as an abstract, immediate sameness in which individuality has no genuine actuality and freedom, while, at the same time, preserving its pursuit of universality or totality in opposition to sheer dualism. One might call this sublated form of pantheism "panentheism." However, Hegel's panentheism, if allowed to use this term in defining Hegel's God, is in an important sense different from a Whiteheadian panentheism in that the God of Hegel's panentheism is not only relational but, more importantly, truly *dialectical*.[25]

As has been stressed time and again, it is the metaphysics of the understanding that Hegel finds to be the source of all problems inherent in both traditional theistic and pantheistic views on God, where God cannot in any way *genuinely* relate to the world. What is necessary, therefore, is the rise to the metaphysics of speculative, dialectical reason whereby the true relationship between God and the world, based primarily upon the true concept of God, can be brought to light.[26] Consequently, Hegel argues, instead of God and the world (including humans) seen either as standing opposed to each other as claimed in traditional theism or as immediately equating with each other as argued in pantheism, they must be conceived as the unity-in-difference in which the world is an essential *moment* of God, i.e., in which the world is conceived as the

---

24. For Hegel, it must be noted in this regard that God and the world (human beings) are not linked together in the same way that two humans are related to each other on an equal footing and in a mutual recognition.

25. Along the same lines, for instance, the Whiteheadian panentheism, in which there is no sense of the Hegelian dialectic, cannot seriously reflect on and explain the significance of God's creation and incarnation.

26. "To apprehend correctly and determinately in thought what God as spirit is, requires thorough speculation" (*EM*, 263; §564 A).

self-actualization, self-expression, self-revelation, or self-differentiation of God as living Spirit (Absolute Spirit) and thus has its being or essence (*Wesen*) in God:

> It is indispensable that God should be thought in relationship to the world and to humanity inasmuch as he is a *living* God. The relationship to the world is then a relationship to an other, and differentiation or determination is posited with it. So relationship to the world appears initially as a relationship to an other that is outside of God. But in that it is God's own relationship and activity, God's having the relationship [to the world] within himself is *a moment of God himself*. God's connection with the world is a characteristic within God himself... This differentiating within God himself is the point where what has being in and for itself connects with human being, with the worldly realm as such.... The very point of internal differentiation is the point of mediation of the finite or the worldly with God himself. What is finite and human has *its beginning* there within God himself; *its root* is God's concrete nature, the fact that God differentiates himself internally.[27]

A Speculative Interpretation of "Without the World God Is Not God"

It is from this view of God *as* living spirit, not as substance, and, concomitantly, of his relationship to the world *as* an internal, spiritual, dialectical one, not as an external, substantial, monological one, that we should interpret Hegel's infamous statement, "Without the world God is not God," which has often been misconstrued as a typical example of the Hegelian pantheism against the Christian orthodox theistic conception of God, a conception that God does not need the world to be God. By this statement, I claim, Hegel does not simply mean that God is equated with the world, the totality of finite beings, as pantheists insist; nor does he mean that God is dependent upon the world in the same way that the world is dependent upon God as process theologians seem to argue.[28]

---

27. *LHP II*, 321. Emphasis mine.

28. "If we consider this object [God] in relation to others, then we can say that it *is* strictly for its own sake; it has no such relation [to others] and is strictly in and for itself *the unconditioned*, the free, the unbounded, that which is its own purpose and ultimate goal" (*LPR I*, 114).

In my view, there are two interconnected strands of speculative meaning that should be illuminated in this statement beyond our immediate apprehension of it. First, provided that God cannot be truly infinite insofar as he is externally opposed to the finite world, as discussed earlier in Hegel's opposition to traditional theism with the infinite-finite dichotomy, the statement, "Without the world God is not God," implies that God as *true* infinity must *include* the finite world *within* himself as a moment of his life. That is, God without (outside) the world logically contradicts the God of true infinity that has nothing outside itself. If this strand of meaning is grounded upon the argument for a *logically* consistent relationship between God as infinite and the world as finite, where both terms—God and the world—have already been posited from the outset of the argument, then someone might further ask, "Why on earth should there be a world at all?" This *ontological* question leads us to disclose the second meaning of the statement, which is closely linked with Hegel's own speculative interpretation of the Christian doctrine of "creation."

It is widely known that Hegel argues for the "necessity" of creation, which indeed prevents many Christian theologians from going along with him because they consider it contrary to the orthodox doctrine that God created the world purely by the free decision of his will; in other words, from the viewpoint of Christian orthodoxy, it was not necessary that God create the world. However, from the Hegelian point of view, they are rather perpetrating the fallacy of remaining at the level of the understanding (*Verstand*). That is, Hegel may say that they look at "freedom" (or free will) and "necessity" merely as externally opposed to each other in terms of *either-or*—just as with the infinite-finite dichotomy. However, for Hegel, "necessity" is *internally* related to "freedom," each in its truest, most eminent form, in the sense that necessity here refers specifically to *inner* necessity springing from one's *own* nature and will which, as such, is the truest and purest form of freedom as self-determination. Therefore, on Hegel's view, true necessity must not be incompatible with true freedom. If one acts solely out of the necessity of his own intrinsic, constitutive nature without being imposed, conditioned, or stimulated by something other than himself, it would seem quite reasonable to say that he truly enjoys freedom par excellence.[29] Moreover, as emphatically indicated above,

---

29. This conception of freedom as inner necessity is already found in Kant. For Kant, freedom is more than just the power to choose, but it is "the intelligible cause," "the faculty of beginning a state from itself," independent of "necessitation of sensible

Hegel's God is in his eternal nature living spirit whose concept or essence is self-actualization, self-differentiation, self-revelation, self-expression, or self-manifestation. It is in this specific sense of God's inner necessity *as* freedom to posit within himself his other to whom he can communicate himself as spirit, that we need to comprehend Hegel's statements such as "God *needs* the world," "God *should* create the world," and the like. For Hegel, God's creation should be understood as the self-othering of God in his infinite spiritual activity, both free and necessary. Accordingly, the statement, "Without the world God is not God," does not simply mean that God created the world not out of freedom but out of necessity, which renders God finite and dependent on the world, but, rather, implies that the creation of the world is nothing else than the expression of God's inner necessity to reveal himself and, as such, equally the expression of his freedom or self-determining spiritual activity in its eternity. In this sense, Hegel also says, "He [God] does not create the world once for all, but is the eternal creator, the eternal act of self-revelation. This *actus* is what he is."[30] In short, Hegel's God needs the world precisely because he is truly absolute, infinite, and free, not because he is finite, dependent, or incomplete.

If these two spiritually-laden meanings in their logical and ontological terms, which indispensably require speculative, dialectical, or conceptual thinking beyond the merely reflective understanding, are precisely what Hegel intends to present in the statement, "Without the world God is not God," then, it seems to me, there might be no ground for simply denouncing Hegel as un-Christian because it has nothing to do with claiming a pantheistic position, nor does with denying the absolute freedom of God's creative act. In my view, saying that "God would not create a world at all," which orthodox theologians take to be one of the important marks of God's absolute, infinite freedom, seems rather to render God's freedom finite, conditional, or relative by projecting into God the human notion of freedom, a freedom in the specific sense of free choice between two options.[31] Put differently, when they predicate "freedom" of God, they

---

impulses," i.e., "complete spontaneity" as the power to fulfill its own immanent necessity, namely, the moral ought in case of him (*CPR*, A537/B565, A533/B561, A534/B562, A548/B576).

30. *LPR III*, 170.

31. In fact, it is this notion of freedom *as* a freedom of choice that makes human freedom finite, rather than infinite; conditional, rather than unconditional; and relative, rather than absolute.

seem to fail to go through a process of analogical predication with its three moments, which indeed has been highly treasured in Christian theology as an important theological method or preventive measure against all kinds of anthropomorphism: namely, "similarity" by the principle of causality (*omne agens agit simile sibi*), "negation" (negation of all finitude; e.g., God is free not in the way that we humans are free), and "eminence" (reaffirmation by way of pure perfection).

The Triune God as Absolute Spirit

Let us come back to the Hegelian conception of God with its sublation of traditional theism and pantheism. Instead of either completely denying traditional theism and pantheism or just sympathizing with one of them, or just taking a middle position between them, Hegel seeks a more comprehensive view of God by synthesizing or sublating them in a dialectical fashion. Consequently, his concept of God preserves both divine transcendence and immanence; divine transcendence is primarily drawn from traditional theism in terms of the non-identity or difference of God and the world, whereas divine immanence is from pantheism in terms of the identity or unity of God and the world. The outcome of this enterprise is Hegel's concept of God as "Absolute Spirit," which indeed culminates in Christianity.

According to Hegel, God is living *spirit* or, more properly, Absolute Spirit and as such essentially *trinitarian*. To be more specific, in accordance with to the concept of spirit,[32] God as Absolute Spirit is characterized by its dialectical movement with three constitutive *moments*: the in-itself (universality; the kingdom of the Father), the for-itself (particularity; the kingdom of the Son), and the in-and-for-itself (individuality or singularity; the kingdom of the Holy Spirit).[33] God in his first moment is "what is enclosed within itself [*das in sich Verschlossene*] or is in absolute unity with itself," and this, nonetheless, should not be grasped merely as an "abstract universality outside which, and over against which, the particular might still be independent," but rather as the "absolutely full,

---

32. "The concept that has determined itself, that has made itself into its own object, has thereby posited finitude in itself, but posited *itself* as the content of this finitude and in so doing sublated it—that is spirit" (*LPR III*, 270).

33. As synonymous to "moments," Hegel also uses "elements," "spheres," and "kingdoms" in his lectures on the philosophy of religion; see Hodgson, *Hegel and Christian Theology*, 127.

replete universality" out of which development is not yet brought forth.³⁴ When Hegel says, "God is the absolute substance,"³⁵ it precisely refers to this first *moment* of the divine life in its universality, God in his eternity, in his primordial self-unity, before the creation.³⁶ However, God in his very nature as living *spirit* or absolute activity does not remain in his simple identity with himself, which is indeed "only the foundation, one moment"³⁷ in the trinitarian life of God as Absolute Spirit; instead, he sets forth, unfolds, manifests, reveals, actualizes, concretizes, determines, or differentiates himself in particularity, in time and space. Hence, in the second moment, God has himself as an object and becomes for an other by positing an other of himself within himself as his externality, appearance, or manifestation; yet even in this becoming-for-other he remains the absolute substance, the identity with himself.³⁸ Thus, the finite world of nature and the human spirit comes into being as the *created other* of God. Still, God is not truly Absolute Spirit until he unites this other into himself *in love*³⁹ and thereby becomes the "absolute idea," *absolute being-in-and-for-itself*, "taking its former, initial manifestation back into itself, sublating it, coming to its own self, becoming and being *explicitly* the way it is implicitly" in the first moment, the moment of the in-itself

---

34. *LPR I*, 369. Hodgson remarks that the insight into this universal as *internally* self-differentiated, within which all distinctions remain *enclosed*, is made into what the Christian religion calls "the immanent Trinity" as an "inexhaustible generative matrix"; see Hodgson, *Hegel and Christian Theology*, 104. In fact, Hegel himself regards this moment, the kingdom of the Father, as pertaining to the Christian doctrine of the immanent Trinity; see *LPR III*, 362.

35. *LPR I*, 369.

36. In other words, for Hegel, "substance" is an attribute or moment of God as Absolute Spirit. In this respect, pantheism, whether it be Spinozism or Schelling's identity philosophy, can be characterized by the *absolutization* or *reification* of this first moment of the concept of God, namely, that God *is* substance; see *LPR I*, 370, 374.

37. *LPR I*, 371.

38. *LPR I*, 371. I would say that the fundamental difference between human spirit and divine spirit lies in this, that for human spirit, "being-for-an-other" is a sign of finitude because it has the other *over against* itself; on the contrary, for divine spirit it is rather a mark of infinity because it contains the other *within* itself as its *self*-differentiation: "God is the entire totality" (*LPR III*, 199).

39. For Hegel, love requires the trinitarian dialectic of the identity of identity and difference: "love is both a distinguishing and the sublation of the distinction" (*LPR III*, 276). With this dialectical concept of love, Hegel draws the speculative meaning of the Christian statement that "God is love."

(the kingdom of the Father).⁴⁰ Accordingly, in the third moment of the trinitarian dialectic, what is implicit and abstract in the concept of God in its first moment, that is, the absolute unification of "the identity with himself" (universality) and "the otherness of himself" (particularity), is to be explicit and realized; that is to say, God in his third moment is God in his first moment that is sublated and enriched by preserving the second moment within himself.

In short, identity with itself, differentiation or otherness from itself, and reconciliation or unification of identity and otherness within itself: these constitute the three moments of the divine life and history as Absolute Spirit, as the "*infinite*, substantial *subjectivity*."⁴¹ Hegel is convinced that this content of God as Absolute Spirit is revealed in the doctrines of Christianity, and this is precisely why he identifies Christianity as the revelatory/revealed, absolute, or consummate religion, as discussed in the preceding chapter. Indeed, for Hegel, it is the Christian doctrine of the Trinity that truly manifests the concept of God as Absolute Spirit, though couched in the form of representation (*Vorstellung*):

> If "spirit" is not an empty word, then God must [be grasped] under this characteristic, just as in the church theology of former times God was called "*triune*." This is the key by which the nature of spirit is explicated. God is thus grasped as what he is for himself within himself; God [the Father] makes himself an object for himself (the Son); then, in this object, God remains the undivided essence within this differentiation of himself within himself, and in this differentiation of himself loves himself, i.e., remains identical with himself—this is God as Spirit. Hence if we are to speak of God as spirit, we must grasp God within this very definition, which exists in the church in this childlike mode of representation as the relationship between father and son—a representation that is not yet a matter of the concept. Thus it is just this definition of God by the church as a *Trinity* that is the concrete determination and nature of God as spirit.⁴²

---

40. *LPR I*, 176–77.

41. *LPR III*, 169.

42. *LPR I*, 126–27. Emphasis mine. Hegel's triune God is, as Hodgson puts it, "the *inclusive* or *holistic* Trinity" that incorporates both the immanent Trinity (God's ideal self-relations) and the economic Trinity (God's real relations to the world): "God is both self-creating and other-creating, both erotic and agapeic" (Hodgson, *Hegel and Christian Theology*, 130–31, 256). On the immanent-economic Trinity relation for Hegel, see also Prabhu, "Hegel's Concept of God," 84: "To become a concrete and truly spiritual God, the immanent trinity must be re-enacted in the economic trinity in

Consequently, the Hegelian concept of God as Absolute Spirit, which is as such trinitarian, is both transcendent and immanent in relation to the world, and thus truly absolute, infinite, and universal. Contrary to traditional theism and pantheism that see God solely as substance, the former as a transcendent substance which is set over against the world and the latter as an immanent substance which is immediately identical with the world, the God of Hegel is not only substance but also, and more importantly, spirit in its internally-related movements of self-differentiation (the immanentization of being-for-others) and self-possession (the transcendentization of being-for-itself). In God, therefore, the world remains *world*, not God, yet not outside God but *within* God. In this way, Hegel's triune God as Absolute Spirit is absolute universality per se—truly transcendent precisely in virtue of its universal immanence and, by the same token, truly immanent precisely in virtue of its absolute transcendence.[43]

The Significance of Hegel's God for Universal Subjectivity

What does "God" signify in and for human existence? Why is Hegel's God as Absolute Spirit particularly important and relevant to human subjectivity? For Hegel, as has been stressed all along, the human subject must be conceived not just as a substance in the sense of the simple identity of what it is, but as a "spirit," that is, a self-transcending, self-differentiating, self-universalizing *movement toward the Absolute* through the mediation of otherness in history. This Absolute or, more properly, "Absolute Spirit" or "Absolute Idea" is, as stated earlier, none other than another name for the triune God for Hegel.[44] Therefore, human beings are authentically human only in their movement of self-transcendence to God. Furthermore, as argued, this entire movement of the elevation (*Erhebung*) of the human subject to God is driven by an irresistible demand,

---

the form of a worldly incursion. . . . Nevertheless, the two trinities, even if they cannot be separated, must be sharply distinguished, because it is simply false to equate eternal distinction with historical manifestations. The former serves as the ground of the latter."

43. For a succinct exposition of the dialectic of transcendence and immanence in the Hegelian concept of God, see Min, "Hegel's Absolute," 85–87.

44. See Williams, *Hegel on the Proofs*, 241: "The absolute idea is the ultimate category and expression of Hegel's philosophical trinitarianism, and the absolute spirit is the ultimate category of Hegel's theological trinitarianism."

or a primordial orientation, toward Absolute Spirit *immanent* in, or built into, the very structure and nature of the human subject *as* spirit. In other words, according to Hegel, the concept of God is truly *intrinsic to* and *constitutive of* human beings as spiritual subjectivity in the sense that by our very being or nature we *necessarily* look for God, the Absolute or Absolute Spirit. We might call this a sort of the Hegelian transcendental argument for the existence of God on the basis of metaphysical anthropology (the elevation of the human subject to God), that is, "God" as the a priori condition of the possibility for the human subject's restless self-transcending movement toward something greater and more universal than itself.[45] My further question, then, is how we can possibly translate such transcendental reasoning into a Hegelian socio-historical argument for God or, more precisely, for the necessity of the concept of God as Absolute Spirit?

Johann Baptist Metz once said that a theologian, who in its literal sense studies the concept (*logos*) of God (*theos*), is the last remaining universalist.[46] It is, I would say, precisely because "God"—as the primary object of theology—is not merely an abstract, independent, transcendent supreme Being *alongside* other lesser beings, but an *all-encompassing*, *all-inclusive*, *absolute* infinity and universality par excellence as the ultimate ground, source, and goal of all that is, in and through which each being both retains its own individuality and finds itself inseparably and internally related to *every* other being. In the same vein, as discussed earlier, Hegel's God is Absolute Spirit, absolute universality per se, which contains *within* itself the world of nature and finite/human spirits as its self-manifestations in their distinctive otherness, that is, in which *all* beings become *moments* of God in their concrete differences. In this way, Hegel's God is not some abstract impersonal force, or logicized infinite reason, but is *the* concrete universal in its absolute, fullest sense, in which all beings are seen as self-expressive moments of God in their distinctiveness and thus in which they find one another as well as find themselves.

45. In fact, Hegel is concerned not so much with "*whether God exists*," i.e., the proofs for God's existence in its conventional sense—whether it be ontological, cosmological, or teleological (physico-theological) argument—as with "*what God does*," i.e., God's self-manifestation in actuality, and particularly in human beings; see Lauer, "Hegel on Proofs," 444. However, this does not mean that Hegel simply endorses the Kantian denial of the value of the proofs as such; he rather *recasts* them, particularly the ontological proof, which relies heavily on his theory of the "concept" in the *Logic*; see *LPR I*, 414–41; Williams, *Hegel on the Proofs*, 44–145.

46. Metz, "Last Universalists," 51.

Furthermore, as mentioned in the preceding chapter, Hegel insists that the conception of God ("how we conceive of God") is in conformity with the conception of human beings ("how we humans think of ourselves and one another") and vice versa. Therefore, for Hegel, the religious or theological view of God is intrinsically related to the sociopolitico-historical view of human subjectivity—both human individuality and human community: "A slavish human being tends to worship a tyrannical god, and vice versa"; "An inferior god or a nature god has inferior, natural and unfree human beings as its correlates; the pure concept of God or the spiritual God has as its correlates spirit that is free and spiritual, that actually knows God"; "A people that has a bad concept of God has also a bad state, bad government, and bad laws."[47] Hence, only insofar as God is conceived as Absolute Spirit, i.e., absolute universality *per se* in its trinitarian dialectical movement,[48] can the human subject be comprehended as truly spiritual and universal too. In other words, Hegel insists, only in the God who fully reveals himself as Absolute Spirit in the community of human spirits, can human beings find themselves and find one another equally as universal subjectivity. Such human beings equipped with universal subjectivity always tries to make themselves broader and more open to others, and thereby attain the consciousness of humanity as a single community of brotherhood, extending over all times and places: "Subjectivity has given up all external distinctions . . . of mastery, power, position, even of sex and wealth. Before God all human beings are equal."[49]

In short, the concept of God as absolute universality allows human beings to see themselves and one another as universal subjectivity and to act accordingly, which is freed from sheer subjectivism and atomistic, egoistic individualism. For example, rather than being preoccupied with their own individual salvation, they seek and work toward the universal salvation, solidarity, liberation, and emancipation of all. Indeed, for a

47. Min, "Hegel's Dialectic," 11; *LPR II*, 515; *LPR I*, 452. See also *LPWH*, 101.

48. As discussed above, the *absolute* universality of the Hegelian triune God as Absolute Spirit is very different from the *abstract* universality of both the God of traditional theism and the God of pantheism—the former in the sense of a universality as opposed to which the particular has an independent existence and the latter in the sense of a universality which is directly equated with the particular in its empirical existence.

49. *LPR III*, 138. This seems to be Hegel's rephrasing of Gal 3:28: "There is neither Jew nor Greek, there is neither slave nor free, there is neither male nor female; for you are all one in Christ Jesus."

more harmonious, peaceful, and just world, human history has always implicitly, if not explicitly, been longing for such universal subjectivity that, according to Hegel, is fundamentally and ultimately possible under the concept of God as Absolute Spirit. Especially, as stressed in chapter 1, our present globalizing world is crying out for such human subjects with universal consciousness and sensibility more desperately than ever before. For this reason, I am inclined to insist that the Hegelian concept of God must occupy an indispensable place in a new conception of *universal* subjectivity for the age of globalization, just as "in Hegel's philosophy the fulfillment of his quest for reconciliation is grounded in the concept of divine Being."[50]

In conclusion, for Hegel, the concept of God as Absolute Spirit is *internal* and *essential* to the concept of the human subject as *spiritual* and *universal* subjectivity, both transcendentally and socio-historically. Without the Hegelian concept of God properly understood as absolute universality that serves as the transcendental source and the historical telos for human subjectivity in both its individuality and community, we are prone *either* to reduce our subjectivity merely to its aesthetic mode in Kierkegaard's parlance, which is precisely the capitalist view of human beings as mere sensuous consumers, or at best to a Habermasian or Buberian inter-subjectivity of I-Thou relationship, *or* to absolutize its abstract, formal negativity or madness without any sense of goal and direction. In what follows, I will critically reflect on Žižek's reading of Hegelian subjectivity as a contemporary left-Hegelian example of the latter case.

A Critique of Žižek's Reading of Hegelian Subjectivity

Unlike almost all other predominant postmodern thinkers who announce, or even celebrate, the *death* of the subject, the *resurrection* of the subject is at the heart of Žižek's philosophical project. Žižek's concern about and stress on subjectivity is directly aligned with his political question, namely, the question of "How does political change and revolution come to pass?" For Žižek, the postmodern claim of the death of the subject, as already discussed in chapter 1 (section 3), leads fundamentally to the elimination of the possibility of people's political consciousness and action. Hence, in this postmodern context today, Žižek seeks to establish a more refined philosophical understanding of what subjectivity should

50. Williamson, *Introduction to Hegel's Philosophy*, 195.

look like, thereby creating the theoretical foundation of the political subject that is at stake in our age.

Surprisingly enough, Žižek's first move seems anachronistic; that is, he goes back to the Cartesian *cogito*. However, Žižek clarifies that it is "not to return to the *cogito* in the guise in which this notion has dominated modern thought (the self-transparent thinking subject), but to bring to light its forgotten obverse, the excessive, unacknowledged kernel of the *cogito*, which is far from the pacifying image of the transparent Self."[51] Along these lines, Žižek remarks that postmodern philosophers' understanding of the Cartesian subject only as a self-sufficient and self-transparent thinking substance overlooks the important dimension and implications of Descartes's project of radical doubt, i.e., the madness inherent to the *cogito* as the hidden truth of subjectivity.[52] In this way, for Žižek, the Cartesian *cogito* should be conceived as the prototype of the "ticklish" subject—the split, divided, barred subject (in the philosophical sense) and the revolutionary, emancipatory subject (in the political sense)—which he really wants to resuscitate today. We can see Žižek's more full-fledged explorations of the philosophically split and politically revolutionary subject in his reading of Hegel or, more precisely, his Lacan-inspired reading of Hegel. In this regard, it would be necessary to begin our discussion by first examining Žižek's view on the Lacanian subject.

Žižek's Lacanian Subject

Žižek's thought presupposes the basic psychoanalytic concepts of Jacques Lacan, such as the three registers of the Imaginary, the Symbolic, and the Real, the big Other, *objet petit a*, *jouissance*, the act, etc. Furthermore, Žižek re-inscribes Lacan's psychoanalytic notion of the subject into the heart of his conception of a new political subject. Žižek's understanding of the Lacanian subject is clearly revealed in his attempt to distinguish Lacan from so-called post-structuralists.[53] Against the general understanding

51. Žižek, *Ticklish Subject*, xxiv.

52. According to Žižek, the fundamental reason that the *cogito* is generally understood as a self-identical thinking substance lies in Descartes's own inability to hold fast to this hidden truth of subjectivity to the end.

53. In fact, according to Žižek, one of the aims of his first book is to articulate Lacan's radical break with post-structuralism; see Žižek, *Sublime Object of Ideology*, xxx.

of Lacan's theory as belonging to post-structuralism, Žižek endeavors to remove that misleading name tag from Lacan. To do this, he pays special attention to the Lacanian notion of the *Real*. According to Žižek, the Lacanian Real, which is the *excess* prior to and beyond symbolization or signification, is "not a transcendent positive entity, persisting somewhere beyond the symbolic order like a hard kernel inaccessible to it," but rather "just a void, an emptiness in a symbolic structure marking some central impossibility," and thus the Real is something "impossible to *occupy* its position" and yet "even more difficult to *avoid* it."[54] The Lacanian subject persists and performs in the same way that the Real functions: the subject *is* the Real. Hence, for Žižek, the Lacanian subject, different from post-structuralist subjectless subjectivation, cannot simply be reduced to a social-construct, subject-positions, or ideological interpellation; in other words, the subject is not merely subjectivation in the sense of becoming somebody as an effect of non-subjective processes. Rather, Lacan sees the subject as *always-already* split, empty, lacking, or barred ($),[55] prior to its subjectivation and alienation in the socio-symbolic system (the big Other):

> [I]f we make an abstraction, if we subtract all the richness of the different modes of subjectivation, all the fullness of experience present in the way the individuals are "living" their subject-positions, what remains is an empty place which was filled out with this richness; this original void, this lack of symbolic structure, *is* the subject, the subject of the signifier. The *subject* is therefore to be strictly opposed to the effect of *subjectivation*.[56]

Along these lines, for Žižek, the Lacanian subject is also defined as "the answer of the Real to the question asked by the big Other, the symbolic order" and "the void of the impossibility of answering the question of the Other."[57] In other words, "the subject is *nothing but* the impossibility of its own signifying representation—the empty place opened up

---

54. Žižek, *Sublime Object of Ideology*, 195 and 175.

55. For Žižek, it must be noted that this Lacanian matheme $ (the barred or split subject) represents two distinctive yet intertwined things: firstly, subjectivation, extrinsic conditioning, or external alienation in the register of the Symbolic, and secondly, primordial negativity, intrinsic failure, or self-relating, internal alienation in the register of the Real. Importantly, according to Žižek, the latter is more fundamental and primary than the former—not in a chronological sense but in an ontological sense.

56. Žižek, *Sublime Object of Ideology*, 197.

57. Žižek, *Sublime Object of Ideology*, 202.

in the big Other by the failure of this representation."[58] In the process of signification, "there is always a certain remnant, a certain leftover, escaping the circle of subjectivation," and "*the subject is precisely correlative to this leftover: $ ◊ a*. The leftover which resists 'subjectivation' embodies the impossibility which 'is' the subject."[59] Indeed, the Lacanian graph of desire seems to depict this adequately, that the subject *is* the void or gap in the big Other in the sense that it is the leftover or excess in the process of symbolization, signification, or subjectivation.[60] In Žižek's view, this is precisely where the Lacanian conception of the subject surpasses post-structuralism. Simply put, while the post-structuralist notion of the subject remains in the second phase of the graph of desire (identification, signification, or subjectivation—the Symbolic), the Lacanian subject reaches the completed graph (beyond identification—the Real).

In short, in contrast to the post-structuralist view on the subject as reducing subjectivity to the sum total of its particular, historical attributes stemming from its situated existence (socio-symbolic identification), Žižek argues that the Lacanian subject is the void and excess *as* the act or, more precisely, "act before act"[61] (the Real) in its dialectical relation to the big Other (the Symbolic). According to Žižek, it is true that the subject is necessarily permeated, and to some extent subjectivized, by the symbolic order such as language, law, ideology, power, etc.; however, this does not exhaust subjectivity as such. There is always the remainder that subsists, insists, or persists in and beyond the interpellation or socialization of the subject, and, for Žižek, this remainder *is* the subject *as* the act. More precisely, the Lacanian subject is retroactively constituted when an *authentic* act occurs, which Žižek characterizes as that which is within the subject more than the subject itself. Žižek further contends that despite its contingency and unintentionality, the act is "nevertheless accepted as something for which its agent is fully responsible—'I cannot do otherwise, yet I am nonetheless fully free in doing it.'"[62] Žižek thus states that the Lacanian subject is "the *act*, the *decision* by means of which

58. Žižek, *Sublime Object of Ideology*, 236.

59. Žižek, *Sublime Object of Ideology*, 236.

60. For a detailed exposition of the Lacanian graph of desire, see Žižek, *Sublime Object of Ideology*, 95–144.

61. Žižek, *Sublime Object of Ideology*, 247. This primordial and purely formal "act before act" should be distinguished from particular, paradigmatic, and intentional acts.

62. Žižek, *Ticklish Subject*, 462.

CONSTRUCTIVE REFLECTIONS ON HEGELIAN SUBJECTIVITY   191

we pass from the positivity of the given multitude to the Truth-Event and/or to Hegemony."[63] In this way, Žižek reads the Lacanian subject as the possibility of an authentic act, and particularly a political act, which can create a path to a new socio-symbolic order.[64]

Žižek's Hegelian Subject

Žižek refuses the conventional, and particularly postmodernist or post-structuralist, reading of Hegel as an idealist-monist, pan-logicist, or totalitarian thinker.[65] On the contrary, he sees Hegel as a prominent philosopher who strongly affirms negativity, contradiction, madness, arbitrary freedom, impossibility, contingency, difference, and otherness.[66] In the same vein, for Žižek, Hegel's dialectic should be understood on the basis of Lacanian psychoanalysis as the most consistent model of the acknowledgement of the impossibility or not-all of what Lacan calls the Symbolic: "far from being a story of its progressive overcoming, dialectics is for Hegel a systematic notation of the failure of all such attempts."[67] Along these lines, in his reading of Hegel Žižek takes special note of the Hegelian conception of the subject as *radical negativity*; that is to say, Žižek locates the accomplishment of Hegel's philosophy in its affirmation of subjectivity *as* self-relating negativity and madness which is equivalent to the Lacanian Real. Žižek frequently cites two famous passages from Hegel's works that illustrate the pre-synthetic power of negativity constitutive of the Hegelian subject. One is the "night of the world" (*Nacht*

---

63. Žižek, *Ticklish Subject*, 184.

64. See Žižek, "Class Struggle or Postmodernism?," 121: "An act accomplishes what, within the given symbolic universe, appears to be 'impossible,' yet it changes its conditions so that it creates retroactively the conditions of its own possibility."

65. With regard to the postmodernist unanimous outright rejection of Hegel, Michael Hardt even remarks that "the roots of poststructuralism and its unifying basis lie, in large part, in a general opposition not to the philosophical tradition *tout court* but specifically to the Hegelian tradition" (Hardt, *Gilles Deleuze*, x).

66. See Žižek, *Sublime Object of Ideology*, xxx: "The current image of Hegel as an 'idealist-monist' is totally misleading: what we find in Hegel is the strongest affirmation yet of difference and contingency—'absolute knowledge' itself is nothing but a name for the acknowledgement of a certain radical loss." This Žižekian reading of Hegel, however, has been much disputed; for one of the harshest criticisms, see Dews, *Limits of Disenchantment*, 236–58.

67. Žižek, *Sublime Object of Ideology*, xxix.

der Welt) passage from his 1805–6 *Jenaer Realphilosophie* manuscripts,[68] that is, "the night of the world" as "the 'unruliness' of the subject's abyssal freedom which violently explodes reality into a dispersed floating of *membra disjecta* [scattered fragments]."[69] The other is the "tarrying with the negative" passage from the Preface to the *Phenomenology of Spirit*:

> Death ... is of all things the most dreadful, and to hold fast to what is dead requires the greatest force. ... But the life of spirit is not the life that shrinks from death and keeps itself untouched by devastation, but rather the life that endures death and maintains itself in it. Spirit wins its truth only when, in utter dismemberment, it finds itself ... spirit is this power only by looking at the negative in the face, and tarrying with it. This *tarrying with the negative* is the magical power that converts it into being. This power is identical with what we earlier called the subject ... .[70]

For Žižek, this power of radical negativity, or the night of the world as pre-synthetic, abyssal freedom, is precisely what defines the Hegelian subject.

Furthermore, according to Žižek, the famous Hegelian thesis that "substance is essentially subject" needs to be read along the lines of Lacan's notion of the subject as the Real in its dialectical relation to the Symbolic, namely, that substance has the same structure as the subject, and vice versa—the structure of intrinsic incompleteness (not-all) whose crux is radical negativity. In this respect, Žižek argues, what Hegel adds to the Kantian notion of the transcendental constitution of reality is a "gesture of transposing epistemological limitation into ontological fault"; that is, "the gaps and voids in our knowledge of reality are simultaneously the gaps and voids in the 'real' ontological edifice itself."[71] This Hegelian ontologization of the Kantian epistemological limitation also implies, as Lacan holds too, that prior to, or beyond, the synthesis that constitutes the unity of phenomenal reality (the Symbolic), some kind of ontological

---

68. See Rauch, *Hegel and the Human Spirit*, 87: "The human being is this Night, this empty nothing which contains everything in its simplicity—a wealth of infinitely many representations, images, none of which occur to it directly, and none of which are not present. This [is] the Night, the interior of [human] nature, existing here—*pure Self*—[and] in phantasmagoric representations it is night everywhere: here a bloody head suddenly shoots up and there another white shape, only to disappear as suddenly."

69. Žižek, *Ticklish Subject*, 35.

70. *PS*, 19; §32. Emphasis mine.

71. Žižek, *Ticklish Subject*, 63.

madness (the Real) must be posited and presupposed. It is this "*ontological incompleteness of 'reality' itself*"[72] that involves the empty, contingent, impossible position where substance *always-already* fails to complete itself, which is, at the same time, the position where the subject—the subject of self-relating, radical negativity—is to be formed not only as the condition of possibility of substance or reality, but also as the condition of its own impossibility.

In order to better understand Hegel's proposition that "substance is subject," Žižek insists, we should take note of the difference which distinguishes the Hegelian *absolute* subject from the Kantian-Fichtean subject. According to Žižek, the Kantian-Fichtean subject is still finite in the sense that it is the positing subject, the subject of practical activity of mediating and transforming the given objective reality, which is, after all, bound by the presupposed reality. On the other hand, the Hegelian subject is absolute in the sense that it is not "limited, conditioned by some given presuppositions," but itself "posits these very presuppositions" by virtue of "the act of 'choosing' what is already given," i.e., by pretending that the given reality is already its own work and responsibility.[73] Thus the Hegelian subject is a name for this "purely formal, empty gesture," that is, "an act of pure feigning by means of which the subject pretends to be liable for what is happening anyway, without taking part in it."[74] In this sense, the conception of "substance as subject" precisely means that the subject's act of self-relating negativity is not something extrinsic to substance but constitutive of it.[75] Accordingly, for Žižek, the Hegelian subject would emerge where substance fails to integrate itself: the subject is "nothing but the name for this inner distance of 'substance' towards itself, the name for this empty place from which the substance can perceive itself as something 'alien.'"[76]

In conclusion, as with his reading of the Lacanian subject discussed above, Žižek's view on the Hegelian subject as radical negativity ("the night of the world" and "tarrying with the negative"), with the conception of "substance as subject," also has social and political implications. For Žižek, Hegelian subjectivity involves an excessive gesture that throws

---

72. Žižek, *Ticklish Subject*, 69.
73. Žižek, *Sublime Object of Ideology*, 250–51.
74. Žižek, *Sublime Object of Ideology*, 251.
75. Žižek, *Ticklish Subject*, 85.
76. Žižek, *Sublime Object of Ideology*, 257.

the whole social order out of joint.⁷⁷ The destruction of the seemingly organic social order and its harmonious unity is the very moment of the actualization of the subject, which is the way in which substance becomes subject. To put it in the other way, openness to transformations in sociopolitical reality can be possible only by the Hegelian subject; any social substance needs the subject who (mis)recognizes that it can perform an act of creating a new social order.

Critical Reflections

As discussed above, Žižek's Lacan-inspired reading of Hegelian subjectivity underlines the capacity of the subject to resist its complete reduction to any forms or kinds of postmodernist subjectivation. In this regard, Žižek focuses on the investigation and articulation of the structural constitution of the Hegelian subject in its *dialectical* (in Žižek's sense) relation to the Other, evoking the dimension of constitutive gap or radical negativity at the heart of subjectivity, which is described in different terms that have the same connotation—such as split, void, loss, excess, arbitrary freedom, madness, unruliness, disruptive power, and so on. Furthermore, as continuously emphasized, this is not just for a purely philosophical project, but has clear political intentions and implications. In other words, Žižek's theoretical approach to the Lacanian-Hegelian notion of subjectivity is directly linked to his practical agenda for the political subject, that is, his defense of political agency that possibly challenges and overthrows the existing social-symbolic order and system. In a word, Žižek seems to insist, *there is no socio-political change and revolution without the Hegelian subject as radical negativity.*

I agree with Žižek that "negativity" is the kernel of Hegel's conception of subjectivity.⁷⁸ This is contrary to the conventional, and particularly postmodernist, rendering and criticism of the Hegelian subject as a sort of indiscriminately "voracious eater 'swallowing' every object it stumbles upon,"⁷⁹ which is based upon the characterization of Hegel as

---

77. Žižek, *Ticklish Subject*, 111.

78. See *SL*, 835: "It [negativity] is the *simple point of the negative relation* to self, the innermost source of all activity, of all animate and spiritual self-movement, the dialectical soul that everything true possesses and through which alone it is true; for on this subjectivity alone rests the sublating of the opposition between concept and reality, and the unity that is truth."

79. Žižek, *Less Than Nothing*, 398.

a totalitarian thinker. More specifically, the subject *is* negativity in the sense both that, in its being-for-itself, it is irreducible to any determinate moment of its phenomenal actualization and that, in its being-for-others, it does not take things outside itself as simply given in their immediacy. In both senses, which are indeed *dialectically intertwined*, the subject has the capacity to transcend the existing status quo vis-à-vis its own identity and its relation to others. In fact, the subject *as* negativity in its self-transcending movement—and this is explicitly revealed when the subject *acts*—is part and parcel of Hegel's philosophy of spiritual subjectivity described in the *Phenomenology*, which we have long discussed in chapters 3 and 4. According to Hegel, as Žižek correctly stresses, the human subject, distinct from other natural entities including animals, is constituted through a negative self-relation, relating itself to itself negatively or always transcending itself, which is, indeed, made possible *only inasmuch as* it relates to the other; that is, self-relating negativity is always mediated by relation-to-other. In this way, the Hegelian subject as negativity is nothing other than a dialectical movement of being-for-itself and being-for-others. This is certainly a constitutive part of what we mean by Hegelian "spiritual" subjectivity. Along the same lines, Hegel himself defines the essence of "spirit" in the following way:

> *Spirit* can step out of its abstract universality, a universality that is for itself, out of its simple self-relation, can posit within itself a determinate, actual difference, something other than the simple I, and hence a *negative*; and this relation to the other is, for spirit, not merely possible but necessary, because it is through the other and by sublation of it, that spirit comes to authenticate itself as, and in fact comes to be, what it ought to be according to its concept, namely, the ideality of the external, the idea that returns to itself out of its otherness, or, expressed more abstractly, the self-differentiating universal which in its difference is together with itself and for itself.[80]

Furthermore, as pointed out earlier, Žižek's emphatic reading of the Hegelian subject as negativity provides an alternative to postmodern depoliticization with its deconstructive notions of the subject as a mere effect of the Lacanian Symbolic (the system of language, unconsciousness, power, ideology, etc.), in the sense that the Žižekian rendering of the Hegelian subject could open up possibilities of the political subject and its actions. I am of the same opinion on this score, in that Žižek's

---

80. *EM*, 16; §382 Z. Emphases mine. See also *LPR I*, 176–77.

theoretical effort to resuscitate Hegelian subjectivity with a view to giving rise to the political subject is not least all the more relevant to the contemporary postmodern context of capitalist globalization. Global capitalism today seems to be all-inclusive and imperishable, having "endless ability to integrate, and thus cut off, the subversive edge of all particular demands,"[81] especially through playing on implicit ideologies of subjectivation and depoliticization, which indeed prevents us from even dreaming of any utopian hopes. Therefore, it should be necessary to conceive of the new political subject that questions, problematizes, and takes authentic action against the status quo of global capitalism—that is to say, the human subject, individual and collective, that changes *"the very co-ordinates of the 'reality principle',"* redefines "what counts as reality,"[82] and thus initiates the creation of a new social-symbolic order.

What, then, constitutes such a new social-symbolic order? What makes Hegelian subjective acts truly authentic? I believe that these questions must be raised against Žižek and particularly his reading of the Hegelian subject as radical negativity. To put my concluding criticism first: I am inclined to argue that Žižek's undue obsession with subjectivity *as* radical negativity confined to its strictly *formal* gesture is not sufficient enough to fully grasp Hegel's original vision of *spiritual* subjectivity in its depth and richness, which in turn makes Žižek unable to maintain coherence between his views on the Hegelian-philosophical subject (purely formal negative gesture) and the Hegelian-political subject (concrete and decisive act for a new social-symbolic order). Let me further elaborate on this criticism of mine.

When Žižek speaks of a new social-symbolic order or, more precisely, a new economico-political regime, he specifically has in mind a *radical* alternative to the capitalist market economy and the liberal-democratic polity,[83] that is, a new form of communism which faithfully holds fast to what Alain Badiou calls "the 'eternal' Idea of Communism, or the communist 'invariants'—the 'four fundamental concepts'": "strict *egalitarian*

---

81. Žižek, *Did Somebody Say Totalitarianism?*, 117.

82. Žižek, *Did Somebody Say Totalitarianism?*, 167, 172.

83. In his debates with Butler and Laclau, Žižek differentiates himself from the so-called postmodern Left including them, insisting that "they never envisage the possibility of a completely different economico-political regime, but just propose some changes *within* the present capitalist and liberal-democratic system" (Žižek, "Da Capo senza Fine," 223). Incidentally, Žižek's theory of politics has changed over time: roughly speaking, from radical democracy to communism; see Flisfeder, "Communism," 40.

justice, disciplinary *terror*, political *voluntarism*, and *trust in the people*."[84] I personally do not agree that communism can be a genuine alternative to contemporary global capitalism, but I will not be dealing with this issue here because it is beyond the scope of my focus. Rather, my chief concern here lies with the question of whether Žižek's Hegelian subject can serve as the subject of politics in any authentic way, i.e., the political subject that is not only able to break with or subvert the existing order of society, but also capable to envision and work *for* a new one, that is, communism for Žižek. Although Laclau critically remarks that Žižek's "anti-capitalism is mere empty talk,"[85] I would say that his vision of communism, whatever it may be, has at least some minimum content, which is even detectable in the communist invariants stated above, such as egalitarian justice, the emancipation of the excluded, the resuscitation of "the commons,"[86] and so forth. More fundamentally, Žižek's emphasis on anti-capitalism and radical emancipatory politics as such already presupposes the fact that a new order (communism) must be *better than* a currently existing one (capitalism), and this "better than" necessarily involves some evaluation of the *content* of each. In this regard, what Žižek *implicitly* means by the authentic act of the Hegelian subject as radical negativity in the realm of politics must be none other than the concrete, historical act for, or toward, a *better* regime.

However, as we have seen, Žižek conceives of the Hegelian subjectivity as radical negativity in its *purely formal* sense, that is, as the empty, non-historical gesture which opens up an irreducible gap always-already inherent within the social-symbolic order itself, but nonetheless changes nothing at the level of positive content. In other words, according to Žižek, the Hegelian subject, perceived as a heroic confrontation with or the answer of the Real, is only the name for a constitutive void, crack, excess, madness, impossibility, or failure in the Symbolic, and as such its decisive act does not itself contain any concrete content or historical meaning.[87] Now the following questions inevitably arise: How can

84. Žižek, *First as Tragedy*, 125.

85. Laclau, "Structure, History and the Political," 206.

86. Žižek distinguishes three aspects of the commons: the commons of culture, of external nature, and of internal nature; see Žižek, *First as Tragedy*, 91.

87. See Žižek, *Puppet and the Dwarf*, 22: "[T]he decision is purely formal, ultimately a decision to decide, without a clear awareness of what the subject is deciding about; it is a nonpsychological act, unemotional, with no motives, desires, or fears; it is incalculable, not the outcome of strategic argumentation; it is a totally free act,

such formal, empty, non-historical subjectivity fight for and create a new concrete, historical socio-symbolic order, which is, for Žižek, communism? How is it possible to translate the Hegelian-philosophical subject as purely formal, abstract negativity into the Hegelian-political subject as concrete socio-historical agency? Is it not incoherent or inconsistent to say that the former can and should constitute the theoretical basis for the latter?

It seems that Žižek does not provide satisfactory answers to those questions. In my view, the fundamental problem in the Žižekian reading of the Hegelian subject is that he overlooks another very crucial dimension—along with and *intrinsic to* the disruptive power of self-relating radical negation ("Real," "death drive," "the night of the world," etc.)—in the constitution of Hegelian subjectivity, namely, the moment of *teleological* movement. Indeed, this is closely connected with Žižek's understanding of the Hegelian notion of "absolute negativity" as well. As has been discussed previously, Žižek interprets it exclusively as the intervention of the Lacanian Real or the death drive that prevents the positivity, identity, and totality of the Symbolic in a purely formal sense. Žižek also claims that the inner logic of the Hegelian dialectical movement of absolute negativity is "not that from one extreme [thesis] to the opposite extreme [antithesis], and then to their higher unity [synthesis]; the second passage [the negation of negation] is, rather, simply the radicalization of the first [negation]."[88] However, as clearly seen in the preceding chapters, the Hegelian spiritual subjectivity *as* absolute negativity in its dialectical movement is not only the formal act of negating but also, and more importantly, the concrete movement of *sublating*, that is, the dialectical movement *toward* "absolute universality," i.e., the unification of form and content, subject and object, internal and external, thought and being, finite and infinite, individual and social, private and public, and so forth, in which all subjects find themselves and find one another. In this way, Hegel's absolute negativity, which sets in motion dialectical movement, should be conceived fundamentally as a teleological movement with a specific content that is the Absolute.[89] Otherwise, as Hegel himself warns,

---

although he couldn't do otherwise."

88. Žižek, *Ticklish Subject*, 79. See also Žižek, *Sublime Object of Ideology*, 199–200.

89. See *PS*, 10; §18: The subject is "*negativity*, and for this very reason it is the bifurcation of what is simple; or it is the doubling which posits oppositions and which is again the negation of this indifferent diversity and of its opposition. That is, it is only this self-*restoring* sameness, or reflection into itself in otherness—not an *original unity*

the dialectical movement is likely to be understood as having the "merely negative result" by means of "the extinction of the qualitative form determinations in the merely quantitative, mathematical syllogism."[90]

I claim that an important reason why Žižek does not interpret Hegelian subjectivity, absolute negativity, and dialectical movement in teleological terms, and thereby cannot coherently link his reading of the Hegelian philosophical subject with the subject of politics is that he fails to recognize the significance of the concept of God as Absolute Spirit in Hegel's philosophy of subjectivity. It has been stressed time and again in this book that Hegel's God as Absolute Spirit and absolute universality *per se* is *the* telos toward which the human subject strives, moves, and grows through its dialectical relations to others in history.

By this, however, I do not simply mean that Žižek belittles theology like many other left-wing Hegelians. In fact, theology has played an important part in Žižek's works since the beginning of 2000,[91] where he particularly aims to restore what he calls "the subversive kernel of Christianity" *as* the religion of atheism-materialism.[92] Furthermore, according to Žižek, it is Hegel who guides us to see this kernel of Christianity that primarily relates to how to read Christ's crucifixion. For Žižek, the significance of Christ's death, which was already emphasized by Hegel himself, is God's self-emptying (*kenosis*); that is, what dies on the cross is God himself. However, rather than interpreting this death of God (i.e., Christ's crucifixion) as *a moment* in the process *toward* God's universal presence in all his finite, human others as Absolute Spirit in its eternal history of the divine life, which is indeed Hegel's speculative interpretation as we discussed in the preceding chapter, Žižek just takes this story out of its constitutive context, which is essentially *teleological* for Hegel, and claims to have found therein the core of Christianity—the subversive kernel of Christianity as the religion of atheism. Žižek does so precisely by associating the Hegelian notion of the Christian God with the Lacanian Real.

---

as such, or *immediate* unity as such—that is the true. It is the coming-to-be of itself, the circle that presupposes its end as its goal and has its end for its beginning, and which is actual only through this accomplishment and its end."

90. *SL*, 681.

91. For Žižek's theological works, see *Fragile Absolute* (2000), *On Belief* (2001), *Puppet and the Dwarf* (2003), *Monstrosity of Christ* (2009), *Paul's New Moment* (2010), and *God in Pain* (2012).

92. Žižek, *Puppet and the Dwarf*, 6. Žižek's basic claim here is that "the subversive kernel of Christianity" is "accessible *only* to a materialist approach—and vice versa: to become a true dialectical materialist, one should go through the Christian experience."

More specifically, Žižek claims, when Christ died on the cross, what died indeed was the God of the beyond as what Lacan calls the big Other, and now God exists only as the Holy Spirit in the sense of the Lacanian Real, namely, the community of believers "deprived of its support in the big Other" that "decides on the 'objective meaning' of our deeds."[93] In short, by the subversive kernel of Christianity Žižek means precisely that Christianity is the religion of atheism, an atheism not in the vulgar humanist sense, such as Feuerbachian projectionism, but in the sense that "there is no big Other." In this religion of atheism (Christianity) people (believers) freely unplug themselves from the existing social-symbolic order that they have been born into or situated in, which is homologous to Lacan's "Real" and Hegel's "night of the world." In the same vein, for Žižek, the Hegelian Absolute is the fragile absolute, and the Hegelian-Christian God is simply empty and impotent: "God is . . . ultimately the name for the purely negative gesture of meaningless sacrifice, of giving up what matters most to us."[94]

In conclusion, I argue that what Žižek reads into the Hegelian God is not congruous with Hegel's own explication of God; it is too much colored by Lacanian psychoanalysis, particularly Lacan's conception of the Real that is radically non-historical and non-teleological. In other words, Žižek entirely neglects the Hegelian aspect in which God is conceived as the ultimate ground and goal of all human subjects living and acting in history, where they not only find their own individuality but also find one another internally related. After all, Žižek fails to consider the teleological structure as a constitutive component for the concept of Hegelian subjectivity, i.e., the movement of spiritual subjectivity toward God as absolute universality, and is *ipso facto* unable to provide a logical connection between his conception of Hegelian subjectivity as formal, radical negativity and as political, revolutionary agency that struggles for a better regime with emancipatory universal truth.

93. Žižek, *Puppet and the Dwarf*, 171.
94. Žižek, *On Belief*, 150.

CHAPTER 6

Concluding Remarks: Hegelian Spiritual Subjectivity for the Age of Globalization

IN THIS BOOK I have tried to explore Hegel's philosophy of spiritual subjectivity, particularly presented in his *Phenomenology of Spirit*, with a view to ensuring its relevance and necessity to the contemporary, postmodern context of globalization. As I conclude this undertaking, I would like to sum up *why* the current context of globalization crucially needs Hegelian subjectivity as a new anthropological vision about what it means to be authentically human. Before doing that, however, it seems useful to briefly recapitulate the major features of Hegel's conception of spiritual subjectivity that we have discussed thus far, along with its important insights.

A Recap of Hegelian Spiritual Subjectivity

For Hegel, the human subject should be conceived not as a self-identical, self-sufficient, autonomous substance existing in sheer independence of things other than itself (modern subjectivism), nor simply as an other-determined construct existing in utter dependence on the other (postmodern subjectivation), but essentially as a *spirit* existing in and through a dialectical becoming (*Werden*) of being-for-itself (substantial identity with itself) and being-for-others (relation to others) toward the Absolute (absolute universality). That is, it is a self-conscious movement of transcending itself into an ever greater universal subjectivity through its dialectical interactions with others/objects in history. In this respect, the Hegelian spiritual subjectivity *is* the *teleological* (not purposeless or directionless), *dialectical* (not linear-monological—either subjectivistic or objectivistic), and *socio-historical* (not abstract or other-worldly) *process* of self-determination and self-transcendence. By "absolute universality," or "absolute subjectivity," which is the final telos of the human journey, Hegel means precisely the stage in which the human subject in its consciousness and praxis becomes fully broadened or universalized and sees the totality of all that is as intrinsically interrelated in their individual differences, and this can ultimately come to pass only when the human subject conceives of God as Absolute Spirit and thereby of all beings as self-expressive moments of God in his eternal trinitarian movement. In this regard, for Hegel, the entire development process of human subjectivity is, so to speak, the human journey toward God as Absolute Spirit. Indeed, human subjectivity as spirituality implicitly or immanently contains within itself the primordial drive toward God as absolute universality (the *imago Dei* as the *capax Dei*), and this is precisely what fundamentally motivates and promotes the dialectical movement of Hegelian spiritual subjectivity in its entire journey—making it possible to experience contradiction *as contradiction*, with which the subject is always confronted in the process, and to sublate it into a more absolute, inclusive, universal form of spiritual subjectivity, and eventually into absolute subjectivity (i.e., absolutely universal subjectivity). Hence, as opposed to some left-Hegelian treatments of God in Hegel's philosophy of subjectivity, the concept of God is constitutive of and essential to the Hegelian subjectivity as its immanent end (omega) as well as its transcendent origin (alpha). At the same time, as opposed to some right-Hegelian readings, Hegel's God is not equated with the God of traditional theism or deism as an utterly transcendent, remote, substantial, unintelligible Other, but characterized as Absolute Spirit, absolute universality per se, that includes within itself all beings as its self-expressive moments in their distinctive otherness as well as in their interconnected unity.

In short, the three elements of the Absolute or God as absolute universality (the immanent telos), self-conscious identity (being-for-itself), and concrete historical relatedness (being-for-others) are constitutive of the concept of Hegelian spiritual subjectivity in its dialectical movement. As examined earlier, we find paradigmatically in Hegel's *Phenomenology of Spirit* how such Hegelian spiritual subjectivity actually emerges and grows gradually toward absolute universality in and through a dialectical relationship between being-for-itself and being-for-others. The sequence of different stages and forms of consciousness described in the

Phenomenology represents the education (*Bildung*) of the human subject from subjectivity-in-itself (subjectivity in the womb) through subjectivity-for-itself (the birth of subjectivity) to subjectivity-in-and-for-itself (the growth of subjectivity with its ultimate culmination in absolute subjectivity). Simply put, this entire journey is the process of objectifying, disciplining, maturing, broadening, universalizing, or spiritualizing human subjectivity, with a series of sublations in its dialectical relations to otherness in the concrete world. In this way, the Hegelian subject is always to think, will, and act for something larger and greater than itself as it constantly relates itself to others, not in a monological way that simply reduces or subordinates their otherness to its own identity—which is narcissistic, self-centered, egoistic, oppressive, imperialistic, and totalitarian—but rather in a *dialectical* way that relentlessly disciplines and transcends itself into a more universal being that can open to, embrace, and recognize others *as* sharing sameness, i.e., as participating in the same origin and end (God), in their distinctive otherness. In this respect, the Hegelian subject is neither solely a self-determining substance nor solely an other-determined construct, neither exclusively a theocentric piety nor exclusively an anthropocentric hubris, but rather the very synthesis of all these aspects in their *sublated* forms.

In a sense, I would say, the spiritual subjectivity that Hegel envisions in his philosophical-theological anthropology represents the human life that exemplifies Jesus's teachings in Mark 12:29–31: "The first is, 'Hear, O Israel: the Lord our God, the Lord is one; and you shall love the Lord your God with all your heart, and with all your soul, and with all your mind, and with all your strength.' The second is this, 'You shall love your neighbor as yourself.' There is no other commandment greater than these." These two commandments are not separate from, or independent of, each other, but thoroughly interconnected, interpenetrating, interpermeating, and interdependent: I can *truly* know and love God not in isolation but in solidarity with all others or neighbors that are God's creatures like myself. By the same token, I can *truly* relate to and love all others or neighbors only in the light of God as absolute universality, the source and end of all that is. To this, Hegel adds an important philosophical qualification: the subject's attaining this *authentic* knowledge of, relationship to, and love for God and all others (neighbors) requires the *process* of experience in actuality, oftentimes a difficult, challenging, frustrating, and even despairing one—"experience" here in the Hegelian sense of the "*dialectical* movement which consciousness [the subject] exercises on itself, both on its knowledge and on its object, *insofar as, for consciousness, the new, true object issues* from this movement."[1] Once again, the Hegelian subject as spirit is the one that constantly strives to enlarge its capacity to know, embrace, and love *all*, both in their universality and in their particularity, by the dialectical—self-negating, self-transcending, and, at the same time, self-preserving—process of relating itself to others in history toward absolute universality in accordance with the immanent telos or primordial urge built into its very structure of being-human.

The Significance of Hegelian Subjectivity in the Context of Globalization

As indicated above, the Hegelian vision of spiritual subjectivity is different from modern anthropocentric subjectivism as well as postmodern subjectless subjectivation, and should instead be conceived as the sublated synthesis of these two perspectives, namely, as the dialectical movement of a modern "being-for-itself" (substantiality) and a postmodern "being-for-others" (relationality) toward an ever greater concrete universality in its culmination in the concept of God as Absolute Spirit. I have constantly reiterated that the primary intention or goal of this book in discussing and unpacking Hegel's philosophy of subjectivity is to ensure that this sort of Hegelian spiritual subjectivity is not only relevant but also crucially necessary in the contemporary, postmodern context of globalization. In what follows, as concluding remarks, let me revisit my main argument for this.

As discussed in chapter 1, the emerging new conditions, challenges, and problems brought about by globalization today compel us to envision a new humanity, equipped with a more mature ethico-political intelligence, sensibility, and volition to change the course of globalization—which, in effect, increasingly works just for the growing power and interests of the privileged few—in the direction of creating a global community of co-existence and co-prosperity for all. However, the current process of globalization driven by neoliberal capitalism, with the imperialism of the market as its very nature, is eager to celebrate—and indeed continues to produce even now in every corner of the globe—humans *without* spirituality and subjectivity, namely, mere hedonistic, individualistic consumers who are not willing to go beyond the confines of their

---

1. PS, 55; §86.

own sensuous desires and private interests. In other words, capitalist globalization today turns the human individual into a consumer and the human society into an anonymous crowd of consumers, and this transformation, or better yet, deformation of humanity into a mere consuming being represents the most effective way to promote de-humanization, de-ethicalization, and de-politicization and thereby to maximize the unbridled power of global capitalism without much difficulty and resistance. To make matters worse, contemporary philosophical conceptions of human beings are generally represented by the postmodernist thesis of the "death of the subject," and this, unfortunately enough, is likely to justify the above-stated anthropology of capitalist globalization on a theoretical, philosophical level. That is to say, postmodernist anthropology, irrespective of its real purport or strategic intent, falls into the *abstract* negation of human subjectivity as such (i.e., the nullification of the human capacity for self-determination, self-reflection, and self-transcendence) and, in turn, may serve as a philosophical legitimation for the normative image of human beings required by capitalist globalization, namely, global consumers constituted exhaustively by the *extrinsic* logic of sheer capitalistic excesses and sensuous, materialistic desires without a depth of interiority in their self-reflection and self-transcendence. It is in this context that I emphatically argue for a new (post-)postmodern conception of subjectivity for the age of globalization.

Hence, philosophically speaking, the new conception of human subjectivity I propose is characterized by the overcoming of such postmodern *subjectlessness*. This "overcoming" here, however, should be understood not in the sense of pure negation or rejection but in the Hegelian sense of "sublation." That is, it *negates* the inadequacy of the postmodern death of the subject in its immediate sense (the abstract negation of subjectivity per se) and *transcends* into a new form of (post-)postmodern subjectivity relevant and necessary to the context of globalization, in which it also *preserves* some postmodern adequacy or legitimacy up to a point, i.e., the critique of modern subjectivism and the acknowledgment of "relation," "difference," or "otherness" in the formation and development of subjectivity. Therefore, this newly conceived subjectivity is certainly at odds with both the postmodernist conception of subjectivity as subjectivation and the modernist conception of subjectivity as subjectivism; it is instead a *dialectical* unification of the two, *sublated*, in its teleological and sociohistorical movement—namely, the dialectical movement of the subject's relation to itself (modernity) and its relation to others (postmodernity) toward a greater universality.

In this connection, I have presented three important *interlocking* elements constitutive of the new conception of subjectivity for the age of globalization: "self-transcending drive toward universality" (the sense of the *We*), "self-determined or autonomous action" (the sense of the *I*), and "solidary relationship with others" (the sense of the *You, (S)he, or They*). If we only emphasize the first element to the exclusion of the other two, the human subject may make globalization into a totalitarian empire, whose presumed universal common good will soon turn out to be nothing but particular, private interests of some individuals or some groups that happen to take power. If we exclusively underscore the second element, the human subject may lead globalization to the frenzy of self-interested individuals and groups with arbitrary wills and opinions, and in turn to the tyranny or imperialism of a few powerful hands. If we exclusively celebrate the third element, the human subject may reduce globalization to a mere bundle of others, each in fact prioritizing and promoting the concerns and interests most relevant to one's own particular, distinctive otherness and difference (e.g., identity politics), which will eventually turn into a chaotic, nihilistic agora of fragmented voices and desires.

In short, to make globalization conducive to enhancing the potential for universal human rights, justice, peace, sustainability, co-responsibility, and interdependence, rather than increasingly reinforcing the prerogatives of the privileged few (the economically, politically, culturally, religiously, ecologically, and/or technologically powerful), we absolutely need a new type of the human subject, that is, an authentic cosmopolitan or global citizen who is restlessly universalizing oneself through self-determined ethico-political actions in solidarity with others to advance the common good for all members of the global community. I insist that this newly proposed conception of human subjectivity finds its philosophical archetype in Hegel's philosophy of subjectivity *as* spiritual subjectivity. The Hegelian spiritual subjectivity, as I have stated all along, can be defined as the dialectical movement of its three constitutive moments in their internal relations, i.e., "the Absolute or absolute universality" (the immanent goal), "being-for-itself" (substantial identity with itself), and "being-for-others" (relation to others), each of which is homologous with the above-mentioned three constitutive elements of the proposed new

CONCLUDING REMARKS 207

subjectivity respectively.² It is for this very reason that I have emphatically argued in this book that the Hegelian vision of spiritual subjectivity should be revisited and reexamined with a new historical sensibility and exigency to seek an antidote for today's excessive individualistic liberalism and materialistic nihilism based on globalizing capitalism so that it may play a pivotal role in conceiving a contemporary anthropology relevant and necessary to the context of globalization.

---

2. For an easier comparison between these two, see the following table:

	Hegel's Spiritual Subjectivity	**A Proposed Subjectivity for Globalization**
Teleological Moment	The Absolute (absolute universality)	Self-transcending drive toward universality
Subjective/ Substantial Moment	Being-for-itself	Self-determined or autonomous action
Objective/Relational Moment	Being-for-others	Solidary relationship with others

Bibliography

Anderson, Walter Truett. *Reality Isn't What It Used to Be: Theatrical Politics, Ready-to-Wear Religion, Global Myths, Primitive Chic, and Other Wonders of the Postmodern World*. San Francisco: Harper & Row, 1990.
Baudrillard, Jean. *The Consumer Society: Myths and Structures*. Translated by Chris Turner. London: Sage, 1998.
Bauman, Zygmunt. *Consuming Life*. Cambridge: Polity, 2007.
Baynes, Kenneth, et al., eds. *After Philosophy: End or Transformation*. Cambridge: Massachusetts Institute of Technology Press, 1987.
Beck, Ulrich. *What Is Globalization?* Translated by Patrick Camiller. Cambridge: Polity, 2000.
Beiser, Frederic C. *Hegel*. New York: Routledge, 2005.
Best, Steven, and Douglas Kellner. *Postmodern Theory: Critical Interrogations*. New York: Guilford, 1991.
Bevans, Stephen B. *Models of Contextual Theology*. Rev. ed. Maryknoll, NY: Orbis, 2002.
Bisticas-Cocoves, Marcos. "The Path of Reason in Hegel's Phenomenology of Spirit." In *Phänomenologie des Geistes*, edited by Dietmar Köhler and Otto Pöggeler, 165–84. Berlin: Akademie Verlag, 1998.
Boas, Taylor C., and Jordan Gans-Morse. "Neoliberalism: From New Liberal Philosophy to Anti-Liberal Slogan." *Studies in Comparative International Development* 44, no. 2 (June 2009) 137–61.
Bohm, David. "Postmodern Science and a Postmodern World." In *The Post-Modern Reader*, edited by Charles Jencks, 383–91. New York: St. Martin's, 1992.
Butler, Judith. *The Psychic Life of Power: Theories in Subjection*. Stanford, CA: Stanford University Press, 1997.
Caputo, John D., ed. *Deconstruction in a Nutshell: A Conversation with Jacque Derrida*. New York: Fordham University Press, 1997.
———. *Prayers and Tears of Jacques Derrida: Religion without Religion*. Bloomington: Indiana University Press, 1977.
Chen, Shaohua, and Martin Tavallion. "The Developing World Is Poorer Than We Thought, but No Less Successful in the Fight against Poverty." *The Quarterly Journal of Economics* 125, no. 4 (November 2010) 1577–1625.
Croce, Benedetto. *What Is Living and What Is Dead of the Philosophy of Hegel*. Translated by Douglas Ainslie. New York: Russell & Russell, 1969.
Das, Dilip K. *Two Faces of Globalization: Munificent and Malevolent*. Northampton, MA: Edward Elgar, 2009.

Davis, J. E. "The Commodification of Self." *Hedgehog Review* 5, no. 2 (2003) 41–49.
Dean, Jodi. *Žižek's Politics*. New York: Routledge, 2006.
Dean, Kathryn. *Capitalism and Citizenship: The Impossible Partnership*. New York: Routledge, 2003.
Derrida, Jacques. *Margins of Philosophy*. Translated by Alan Bass. Chicago: University of Chicago Press, 1982.
———. *Of Grammatology*. Translated by Gayatri Chakravorty Spivak. Corrected ed. Baltimore, MD: Johns Hopkins University Press, 1974.
———. *Of Spirit: Heidegger and the Question*. Translated by Geoffrey Bennington and Rachel Bowlby. Chicago: University of Chicago Press, 1989.
———. *Positions*. Translated by Alan Bass. Chicago: University of Chicago Press, 1981.
———. *Specters of Marx: The State of the Debt, the Work of Mourning and the New International*. Translated by Peggy Kamuf. New York: Routledge, 1994.
Descartes, René. *A Discourse on the Method*. Translated by Ian Maclean. Oxford: Oxford University Press, 2006.
———. *Meditations on First Philosophy*. Translated by Michael Moriarty. Oxford: Oxford University Press, 2008.
Desmond, William. *Hegel's God: A Counterfeit Double?* Aldershot: Ashgate, 2003.
Dews, Peter. *The Limits of Disenchantment—Essays on Contemporary European Philosophy*. London: Verso, 1995.
Dreyfus, Hubert L., and Paul Rabinow. *Michel Foucault: Beyond Structuralism and Hermeneutics*. Chicago: University of Chicago Press, 1982.
Dufour, Dany-Robert. *The Art of Shrinking Heads: The New Servitude of the Liberated in the Era of Total Capitalism*. Translated by David Macey. Cambridge: Polity, 2008.
Eribon, Didier. *Michel Foucault*. Translated by Besty Wing. Cambridge: Harvard University, 1991.
Fichte, Johann Gottlieb. *The Science of Knowledge*. Translated by Peter Heath and John Lachs. Cambridge: Cambridge University Press, 1982.
Flisfeder, Matthew. "Communism." In *The Žižek Dictionary*, edited by Rex Bulter, 40–43. Durham, NC: Acumen, 2014.
Forster, Michael N. *Hegel's Idea of a Phenomenology of Spirit*. Chicago: University of Chicago Press, 1998.
Foucault, Michel. *The Archaeology of Knowledge and the Discourse on Language*. Translated by Alan Sheridan. New York: Vintage, 1982.
———. *The Birth of the Clinic: An Archaeology of Medical Perception*. Translated by Alan Sheridan. New York: Vintage, 1994.
———. *Discipline and Punish: The Birth of the Prison*. Translated by Alan Sheridan. New York: Vintage, 1995.
———. *The History of Sexuality*. Translated by Robert Hurley. 3 vols. New York: Vintage, 1988–90.
———. *Madness and Civilization: A History of Insanity in the Age of Reason*. Translated by Richard Howard. New York: Vintage, 1988.
———. *The Order of Things: An Archeology of the Human Sciences*. Translated by Alan Sheridan. New York: Vintage, 1994.
———. *Power/Knowledge: Selected Interviews and Other Writings, 1972–1977*. Translated by Colin Gordon et al. Edited by Colin Gordon. New York: Pantheon, 1980.
———. "The Subject and Power." *Critical Inquiry* 8, no. 4 (Summer, 1982) 777–95.

Fritzman, J. M. *Hegel*. Cambridge: Polity, 2014.
Fromm, Erich. *On Disobedience and Other Essays*. New York: Seabury, 1981.
———. *The Revolution of Hope: Toward a Humanised Technology*. New York: Harper & Row, 1968.
———. *To Have or to Be?* New York: Continuum, 2002.
Gadamer, Hans-Georg. *Hegel's Dialectic: Five Hermeneutical Studies*. Translated by P. Cristopher Smith. New Haven, CT: Yale University Press, 1976.
Giddens, Anthony. *Runaway World: How Globalization Is Reshaping Our Lives*. 2nd ed. New York: Routledge, 2003.
Goldman, Robert, and Stephen Papson. *Sign Wars: The Cluttered Landscape of Advertising*. New York: Guilford, 1996.
Grenz, Stanley J. *A Primer on Postmodernism*. Grand Rapids, MI: Eerdmans, 1996.
Hardt, Michael. *Gilles Deleuze: An Apprenticeship in Philosophy*. Minneapolis: University of Minnesota Press, 1993.
Harris, H. S. *Hegel's Ladder*. 2 vols. Indianapolis: Hackett, 1997.
Hartshone, Charles. *Man's Vision of God*. Hamden: Archon, 1964.
Harvey, David. *A Brief History of Neoliberalism*. Oxford: Oxford University Press, 2005.
Heartfield, James. *The "Death of the Subject" Explained*. Sheffield: Sheffield Hallam University Press, 2006.
Hebron, Lui, and John F. Stack Jr. *Globalization: Debunking the Myths*. 3rd ed. Lanham, MD: Rowman & Littlefield, 2017.
Hegel, G. W. F. *The Difference between Fichte's and Schelling's System of Philosophy*. Translated by H. S. Harris and Walter Cerf. Albany: State University of New York, 1977.
———. *Early Theological Writings*. Translated by T. M. Knox. Philadelphia: University of Pennsylvania Press, 1975.
———. *Elements of the Philosophy of Right*. Translated by H. B. Nisbet. Cambridge: Cambridge University Press, 1991.
———. *Encyclopedia of the Philosophical Sciences in Basic Outline: Part I: Science of Logic*. Translated and edited by Klaus Brinkmann and Daniel O. Dahlstrom. Cambridge: Cambridge University Press, 2010.
———. *Faith and Knowledge*. Translated by Walter Cerf and H. S. Harris. Albany: State University of New York, 1977.
———. *Lectures on the History of Philosophy, 1825–1826*. Translated by Robert F. Brown. 3 vols. Oxford: Oxford University Press, 2009.
———. *Lectures on the Philosophy of Religion*. Translated by R. F. Brown, P. C. Hodgson, and J. M. Steward. 3 vols. Berkeley: University of California Press, 1984–1987.
———. *Lectures on the Philosophy of Religion: One-Volume Edition, The Lectures of 1827*. Translated by R. F. Brown, P. C. Hodgson, and J. M. Steward. Berkeley: University of California Press, 1988.
———. *Lectures on the Philosophy of World History: Manuscripts of the Introduction and The Lectures of 1822–1823*. Translated by Robert F. Brown and Peter C. Hodgson. Oxford: Oxford University Press, 2011.
———. *Natural Law: The Scientific Ways of Treating Natural Law, Its Place in Moral Philosophy, and Its Relation to the Positive Sciences of Law*. Translated by T. M. Knox. Philadelphia: University of Pennsylvania Press, 1975.
———. *Phänomenologie des Geistes*. Hamburg: Felix Meiner Verlag, 1952.

———. *Phenomenology of Spirit*. Translated by A. V. Miller. Oxford: Oxford University Press, 1977.
———. *The Phenomenology of Spirit*. Translated by Michael Inwood. Oxford: Oxford University Press, 2018.
———. *The Phenomenology of Spirit*. Translated by Terry Pinkard. Cambridge: Cambridge University Press, 2018.
———. *Philosophy of Mind: Part Three of the Encyclopedia of the Philosophical Sciences (1830)*. Translated by W. Wallace and A. V. Miller. Revised by Michael Inwood. Oxford: Oxford University Press, 2007.
———. *Philosophy of Nature: Part Two of the Encyclopedia of the Philosophical Sciences (1830)*. Translated by A. V. Miller. Oxford: Oxford University Press, 2004.
———. *Science of Logic*. Translated by A. V. Miller. New York: Humanities, 1969.
———. *System of Ethical Life (1802/3) and First Philosophy of Spirit (Part III of the System of Speculative Philosophy 1803/4)*. Translated by H. S. Harris and T. M. Knox. Albany: State University of New York Press, 1979.
Held, David, et al. *Global Transformations: Politics, Economics, and Culture*. Stanford, CA: Stanford University Press, 1999.
Hellmann, Thorsten. "Advanced Economies Benefit from Globalization Much More Than Developing Countries and NICs." *Bertelsmann Stiftung*, March 24, 2014. https://www.bertelsmann-stiftung.de/en/press/press-releases/press-release/pid/advanced-economies-benefit-from-globalization-much-more-than-developing-countries-and-nics.
Hodgson, Peter C. *Hegel and Christian Theology: A Reading of the Lectures on the Philosophy of Religion*. Oxford: Oxford University Press, 2005.
Hopper, Paul. *Understanding Cultural Globalization*. Cambridge: Polity, 2007.
Hwang, Jinsu. "Spiritual Action: Hegel's Philosophy of Action Based on *Phenomenology of Spirit*." PhD diss., Claremont Graduate University, 2011.
Hyppolite, Jean. *Genesis and Structure of Hegel's Phenomenology of Spirit*. Translated by Samuel Cherniak and John Heckman. Evanston, IL: Northwestern University Press, 1974.
"Income Inequality, USA, 1913–2019." *World Inequality Database*, March 21, 2020. https://wid.world/country/usa.
Jacobi, Friedrich Heinrich. "On Transcendental Idealism." In *Kant's Early Critics: The Empiricist Critique of the Theoretical Philosophy*, translated and edited by Brigitte Sassen, 169–75. Cambridge: Cambridge University Press, 2000.
Jaeschke, Walter. *Reason in Religion: The Foundations of Hegel's Philosophy of Religion*. Translated by J. M. Stewart and Peter Hodgson. Berkeley: University of California Press, 1990.
Jameson, Frederic. *Postmodernism, or, The Cultural Logic of Late Capitalism*. Durham, NC: Duke University Press, 1991.
Kant, Immanuel. "Critique of Practical Reason." In *Practical Philosophy*, translated and edited by May J. Gregor, 133–271. Cambridge: Cambridge University Press, 1996.
———. *Critique of Pure Reason*. Translated by Paul Guyer and Allen Wood. Cambridge: Cambridge University Press, 2000.
———. "Religion within the Boundaries of Mere Reason." In *Religion and Rational Theology*, translated and edited by Allen W. Wood and George di Giovanni, 39–215. Cambridge: Cambridge University Press, 1996.
Köher, Gernot. "Global Apartheid." *Alternatives* 4, no. 2 (1978) 263–75.

Kojève, Alexander. *Introduction to the Reading of Hegel: Lectures on the Phenomenology of Spirit*. Translated by James H. Nichols Jr. New York: Basic, 1969.

Laclau, Ernest. "Structure, History and the Political." In *Contingency, Hegemony, Universality: Contemporary Dialogues on the Left*, edited by Judith Butler et al., 182–212. London: Verso, 2000.

Lauer, Quentin. "Hegel on Proofs for God's Existence." *Kant-Studien* 55, no. 4 (1964) 443–65.

———. *Hegel's Concept of God*. Albany: State University of New York Press, 1982.

———. *A Reading of Hegel's Phenomenology of Spirit*. 2nd ed. New York: Fordham University Press, 1993.

Lawlor, Leonard. *Derrida and Husserl: The Basic Problem of Phenomenology*. Bloomington: Indiana University Press, 2002.

Leighton, J. A. "Hegel's Conception of God." *The Philosophical Review* 5, no. 6 (1896) 601–18.

Lumsden, Simon. *Self-Consciousness and the Critique of the Subject: Hegel, Heidegger, and the Poststructuralists*. New York: Columbia University Press, 2014.

Lyotard, Jean-François. *The Postmodern Condition: A Report on Knowledge*. Translated by G. Bennington and B. Massumi. Minneapolis: University of Minnesota Press, 1984.

Megill, Allan. *Prophets of Extremity: Nietzsche, Heidegger, Foucault, Derrida*. Berkeley: University of California Press, 1985.

Melnick, Arthur. *Kant's Theory of the Self*. New York: Routledge, 2009.

Metz, Johann Baptist. "The Last Universalists." In *The Future of Theology: Essays in Honor of Jürgen Moltmann*, edited by Miroslav Volf, Carmen Krieg, and Thomas Kucharz, 47–51. Grand Rapids, MI: Eerdmans, 1996.

Milbank, John, et al. *Paul's New Moment: Continental Philosophy and the Future of Christian Theology*. Grand Rapids, MI: Brazos, 2010.

Miller, James. *The Passion of Michel Foucault*. New York: Simon & Schuster, 1993.

Min, Anselm K. "The Deconstruction and Reconstruction of Christian Identity in a World of Différance." In *The Task of Theology: Leading Theologians on the Most Compelling Questions for Today*, edited by Anselm K. Min, 29–55. Maryknoll, NY: Orbis, 2014.

———. "Hegel on the Foundation of Religion." *International Philosophical Quarterly* 14, no. 1 (1974) 79–99.

———. "Hegel's Absolute: Transcendent or Immanent?" *The Journal of Religion* 56, no. 1 (1976) 61–87.

———. "Hegel's Dialectic of the Spirit: Contemporary Reflections on Hegel's Vision of Development and Totality." In *Language and Spirit*, edited by D. Z. Phillips and Mario von der Ruhr, 8–38. Hampshire: Palgrave Macmillan, 2004.

———. "Sin, Grace, and Human Responsibility: Reflections on Justification by Faith Alone in the Age of Globalization." *Neue Zeitschrift fur Systematische Theologie und Religionsphilosophie* 59, no. 4 (2017) 572–94.

———. *The Solidarity of Others in a Divided World: A Postmodern Theology after Postmodernism*. New York: T&T Clark International, 2004.

———. "The Speculative Foundation of Religion: A Study in Hegel's Transcendental Metaphysics." PhD diss., Fordham University, 1974.

Navickas, Joseph L. *Consciousness and Reality: Hegel's Philosophy of Subjectivity*. The Hague: Martinus Nijhoff, 1976.

Nietzsche, Friedrich. "On Truth and Lie in a Nonmoral Sense (1873)." In *On Truth and Untruth: Selected Writings*, translated and edited by Taylor Carman, 15–49. New York: HarperCollins, 2010.

———. *The Will to Power*. Translated by Walter Kaufmann and R. J. Hollingdale. New York: Random House, 1967.

Onions, C. T., et al. *The Oxford Dictionary of English Etymology*. Oxford: Clarendon, 1966.

Pinkard, Terry. *Hegel's Naturalism: Mind, Nature, and the Final Ends of Life*. Oxford: Oxford University Press, 2011.

———. *Hegel's Phenomenology: The Sociality of Reason*. Cambridge: Cambridge University Press, 1994.

"Poverty Headcount Ratio at $1.90 a Day (2011 PPP) (% of Population)." *World Bank Open Data*, June 23, 2021. https://data.worldbank.org/indicator/SI.POV.DDAY.

Powell, Jason. *Jacques Derrida: A Biography*. New York: Continuum, 2006.

Prabhu, Joseph. "Hegel's Concept of God." *Man and World* 17 (1984) 79–98.

Rauch, Leo. *Hegel and the Human Spirit: A Translation of the Jena Lectures on the Philosophy of Spirit (1805–1806) with Commentary*. Detroit, MI: Wayne State University Press, 1983.

Rawls, John. *A Theory of Justice*. Cambridge: Harvard University Press, 1971.

Rockmore, Tom. *Before and After Hegel: A Historical Introduction to Hegel's Thought*. Berkeley: University of California Press, 1993.

Rose, Margaret. "Defining the Post-Modern." In *The Post-Modern Reader*, edited by Charles Jencks, 119–36. New York: St. Martin's, 1992.

Rousseau, Jean-Jacques. *The Social Contract*. Translated by Christopher Betts. Oxford: Oxford University Press, 1999.

Roy, Ravi K., et al., eds. *Neoliberalism: National and Regional Experiments with Global Ideas*. London: Routledge, 2006.

Saad-Filho, Alfredo, and Deborah Johnston, eds. *Neoliberalism: A Critical Reader*. Ann Arbor, MI: Pluto, 2005.

Sachs, Andreas, et al. *Globalization Report 2020: Who Benefits the Most from Globalization?* Gütersloh: Bertelsmann Stiftung, 2020.

Saussure, Ferdinand de. *Course in General Linguistics*. Translated by Wade Baskin. New York: Philosophical Library, 1959.

Schelling, F. W. J. *Philosophical Investigations into the Essence of Human Freedom*. Translated by Jeff Love and Johannes Schmidt. Albany: State University of New York Press, 2006.

Shorrocks, Anthony, et al. *Global Wealth Report 2017*. Zurich: Credit Suisse Research Institute, 2017.

Sloterdijk, Peter. *In the World Interior of Capital: For a Philosophical Theory of Globalization*. Cambridge: Polity, 2013.

Steger, Manfred B. *Globalism: The New Market Ideology*. Lanham, MD: Rowman & Littlefield, 2002.

———. *Globalization: A Very Short Introduction*. 4th ed. Oxford: Oxford University Press, 2017.

Steger, Manfred B., and Ravi K. Roy. *Neoliberalism: A Very Short Introduction*. Oxford: Oxford University Press, 2010.

Stern, Robert. *The Routledge Guidebook to Hegel's Phenomenology of Spirit*. London: Routledge, 2013.

Stiegler, Bernard. *For a New Critique of Political Economy*. Translated by Daniel Ross. Cambridge: Polity, 2010.
Stiglitz, Joseph E. *Globalization and Its Discontents*. New York: W. W. Norton, 2003.
Taylor, Charles. *Hegel*. Cambridge: Cambridge University Press, 1975.
———. *Hegel and Modern Society*. Cambridge: Cambridge University Press, 1979.
Tholuck, Friedrich August Gottreu. *Die Lehre von der Sünde und vom Versöhner, oder die wahre Weihe des Zweiflers*. Hamburg: Friedrich Perthes, 1825.
"Trade (% of GDP)." *World Bank Open Data*, 2021. https://data.worldbank.org/indicator/NE.TRD.GNFS.ZS.
Turner, Rachel S. *Neo-Liberal Ideology: History, Concepts and Policies*. Edinburgh: Edinburgh University Press, 2008.
Weedon, Chris. *Feminist Practice and Poststructuralist Theory*. Cambridge: Blackwell, 1987.
Whitehead, Alfred North. *Process and Reality: An Essay in Cosmology*. New York: Free, 1978.
Williams, Robert R. *Hegel on the Proofs and the Personhood of God: Studies in Hegel's Logic and Philosophy of Religion*. Oxford: Oxford University Press, 2017.
Williamson, Raymond Keith. *Introduction to Hegel's Philosophy of Religion*. Albany: State University of New York Press, 1984.
Winfield, Richard Dien. *Hegel's Phenomenology of Spirit: A Critical Rethinking in Seventeen Lectures*. Lanham, MD: Rowman & Littlefield, 2013.
Wolf, Martin. *Why Globalization Works*. New Haven, CT: Yale University Press, 2004.
Xavier, Marlon. *Subjectivity, the Unconscious and Consumerism: Consuming Dreams*. Cham: Palgrave Macmillan, 2018.
———. "Subjectivity Under Consumerism: The Totalization of the Subject as a Commodity." *Psicologia & Sociedade* 28, no. 2 (May/August 2016) 207–16.
Žižek, Slavoj. "Class Struggle or Postmodernism? Yes, Please!" In *Contingency, Hegemony, Universality: Contemporary Dialogues on the Left*, edited by Judith Butler et al., 90–135. London: Verso, 2000.
———. *The Courage of Hopelessness: A Year of Acting Dangerously*. Brooklyn, NY: Melville House, 2017.
———. "Da Capo senza Fine." In *Contingency, Hegemony, Universality: Contemporary Dialogues on the Left*, edited by Judith Butler et al., 213–62. London: Verso, 2000.
———. *Did Somebody Say Totalitarianism?* London: Verso, 2001.
———. *First as Tragedy, Then as Farce*. London: Verso, 2009.
———. *The Fragile Absolute: or, Why Is the Christian Legacy Worth Fighting For?* London: Verso, 2000.
———. *Less Than Nothing: Hegel and the Shadow of Dialectical Materialism*. London: Verso, 2012.
———. *The Monstrosity of Christ: Paradox or Dialectic?* Cambridge: Massachusetts Institute of Technology Press, 2009.
———. *On Belief*. London: Routledge, 2001.
———. *Organs without Bodies: On Deleuze and Consequences*. New York: Routledge, 2004.
———. *The Puppet and the Dwarf: The Perverse Core of Christianity*. Cambridge: Massachusetts Institute of Technology Press, 2003.

———. "The Real of Sexual Difference." In *Reading Seminar XX: Lacan's Major Work on Love, Knowledge, and Feminine Sexuality*, edited by Suzanne Barnard and Bruce Fink, 57–75. Albany: State University of New York Press, 2002.

———. *The Sublime Object of Ideology*. 2nd ed. London: Verso, 2008.

———. *The Ticklish Subject: The Absent Centre of Political Ontology*. 2nd ed. London: Verso, 2008.

———. *Trouble in Paradise: From the End of History to the End of Capitalism*. Brooklyn: Melville House, 2014.

———. *Violence*. New York: Picador, 2008.

Žižek, Slavoj, and Boris Gunjević. *God in Pain: Inversions of Apocalypse*. New York: Seven Stories, 2012.

Žižek, Slavoj, and Glyn Daly. *Conversations with Žižek*. Cambridge: Polity, 2004.

Žižek, Slavoj, et al. *The Neighbor: Three Inquiries in Political Theology*. Chicago: University of Chicago Press, 2005.

Index

absolute, the, xvi, xviii, 46, 48, 52, 54, 56, 57, 80, 85n135, 87, 149, 157n256, 164, 165, 184, 185, 198, 201, 202, 206, 207
absolute ego, Fichtean, xviii, 17, 37, 44–46, 49, 54
Absolute Idea, 182, 184
Absolute Knowing, xviii, xix, 56, 77n99, 81n117, 88, 148, 150, 166–69
Absolute Spirit, xviii, xix, 23, 52, 56, 87, 88, 125, 126, 148, 149, 150, 151, 159, 161, 162, 163, 164, 166nn288–89, 167, 168, 169, 171, 178, 181–87, 199, 202, 204
acosmism, 172n8
act, the, 190, 191, 193, 197
action, cognitive, 59, 61, 64, 66, 68
  concept of, 59n17, 83–85, 110n92, 113, 114, 115–20, 127–28, 142–47, 148n226
  conscientious, 144, 145, 146
  determinate, 145
  ethical/political, xiii, 1, 30, 31, 33, 34, 56–57, 195, 206
  immediate, 71, 92, 109
  mediating, 84
  moral, 142, 143, 144, 145
  self-determined or autonomous, xv, 35, 57, 206, 207
activity, absolute, 182
  autonomous, 46
  cognitive, 61
  conceptual, 59, 61, 64, 67, 68

formative, 75, 76; *see also* labor
immanent, 18, 76
law-giving, 122
observational, 93, 101
practical, 193
pure, 45, 154
reflective, 58, 64
self-conscious, 153
self-positing, 46, 48
spiritual, 180
transcendental, 44, 48
unconscious, 136
adaptation, 96n41
Aeschylus, 156
aestheticization, xiv, 13
alienation, xv, 34, 131, 134, 135, 149, 158, 159, 160, 163, 189
Althusser, Louis, 17n52, 21
Anerkennung. See recognition
antagonism, 32
anthropology, xiv, xvii, 2, 3, 10, 11, 13, 14, 18, 28, 34, 56, 185, 203, 205, 207; *see also* globalization, anthropology of
Antigone, 126n149, 128
antinomy, 42, 142
apartheid, global, 8
appearance, 31, 41, 45, 65, 66, 67, 94, 105, 108, 113, 162n275, 182
Apple, 13n37
Aquinas, Thomas, 173n9
archaeology, 15n43, 19n59, 21
Aristophanes, 157
Aristotle, 173n9, 51n60, 116n111

217

INDEX

atheism, 117n111, 172, 174, 199, 200
Aufhebung. See sublation
Aufklärung. See Enlightenment, the
Augustine, 173n9

Badiou, Alain, 196
Barthes, Roland, 17n52
beautiful soul, 146–48
Beck, Ulrich, 2
becoming, 52, 117n113, 201
begreifendes Denken. See conceptual thinking
being-for-itself, xvi, 51, 57, 63, 64, 65, 73, 74, 75, 77, 80, 82, 84, 85, 86, 96, 98n49, 102, 107, 108, 110n92, 115, 119, 132n171, 133, 145, 158, 159, 184, 195, 201, 202, 204, 206, 207
being-for-others, xvi, 51, 57, 63, 64, 65, 80, 86, 96, 98n49, 106, 119, 120, 132, 144, 145, 159, 184, 195, 201, 202, 204, 206, 207
Beiser, Frederic C., 51n60, 116n111, 172n6
Bertelsmann Stiftung, 6
Bevans, Stephen B., xviin6
big Other, the, 188, 189, 190, 200; *see also* Symbolic, the
Bildung, 68, 131, 203; *see also* cultivation; education
Brehier, Emile, 116n109
Buddhism, Western, 28, 32–33
Butler, Judith, 28, 196n83

capax Dei, 202
capitalism, xiv, 11, 12n35, 28, 31, 33, 197, 207
  anti-, 197
  consumer, 12n35
  global, xiii, xiv, xvii, 4, 8–9, 12–14, 27–28, 30–33, 196–97, 205; *see also* globalization, capitalist
  late, 33

neoliberal, 3–5, 8–10, 12, 14, 204; *see also* neoliberalism
categorical imperative, 12, 121n134
category, 23n83, 48, 105, 107n80, 135, 184n44
certainty, absolute, 38
Christ, Jesus, 81, 160, 161, 162, 163, 174, 186n49, 200
Christianity, 81, 82n118, 84n128, 158n264, 159, 160, 161, 163, 164, 165, 166, 170, 181, 182, 183, 199, 200; *see also* religion, absolute/consummate/revealed
citizenship, 11n30
  cosmopolitan, xiii, 1, 11, 35, 56, 206
Clayton, Philip, ix
cogito, 17, 38, 58n15, 188
coherence, principle of, 151n238
commodity, xiv, 12, 13, 14
common good, ix, xv, 35, 206
communism, 4n6, 196, 197, 198
conceptual thinking, 50, 77n99, 163n281, 165, 180
conflict, 1, 10, 34, 128, 140, 147
conscience, 142–48
consciousness, acting, 146, 147, 148
  active, 100
  base, 133–44, 147n223
  Christian, 81n115
  ethical, 121, 123
  honest, 119
  individual, 83, 121, 123
  Jewish, 81n115
  judging, 146
  moral, 140n201
  noble, 133–34, 147n223
  pure, 45, 82, 134–35, 163n281
  religious, 81, 85n137, 150n234, 151
consumer, xiv, 9, 12, 13, 14, 18, 27, 28, 34, 187, 204, 205
consumerism, 11, 12
consumption, 11, 12, 71, 72, 147n225
contradiction, 50, 51, 56, 59, 62, 63, 75, 77, 80, 81, 88, 90, 104,

110n92, 111, 117, 119, 122,
    136, 140, 141, 142, 145, 146,
    147, 158, 191, 202
  inner, 55, 67, 79, 143
  structural, 62, 83
co-prosperity, xv
  co-existence and, xiii, 1, 8, 34,
    204
corporations, multinational. *See*
    MNCs
creation, divine, 160, 163, 171n3,
    177n25, 179, 180, 182
Credit Suisse Research Institute, 7
crucifixion, 163, 199
cult, 154–55, 163
cultivation, 35, 131, 132, 133, 134,
    134
culture, capitalist, 10n28, 11, 12n35,
    14
  consumerist, 11
  world of, 125, 131n166, 134,
    135, 139, 144; *see also*
    subject, the, cultural

Dalferth, Ingolf U., ix
Daly, Glyn, 32
Dean, Kathryn, 11n30
death drive, 73n80, 198
death of the subject, xiv, xvii, 1, 14,
    17, 18, 26, 27, 28, 33, 34,
    187, 205
death of man, 18–21, 26
deconstruction, 21–27, 30, 33
deduction, 38
  transcendental, 41n20, 42
Deleuze, Gilles, 15, 28
democracy, 26, 30n112, 137n192,
    196n83
depoliticization, xiv, 29, 30n112, 32,
    195, 196, 205
Derrida, Jacques, xvii, 15, 17n52, 18,
    21–27, 29, 30
Descartes, René, xviii, 17, 38–39, 46,
    47, 48, 49, 50, 55
description, 93–94
desire, xiv, 12, 13, 14, 27, 33, 70–75,
    82, 83, 84, 108, 130, 190,
    197n87, 205, 206

Desmond, William, 176n23
destiny, 128, 129, 156, 157
devotion, 82
dialectic, 9, 29, 50, 57, 60, 61, 62n34,
    64n46, 71n66, 84, 108n85,
    110, 116n110, 119, 120, 133,
    136, 147n223, 158n259, 168,
    173n9, 175, 177n25, 184n43,
    191
  master-slave. *See* master-slave
    dialectic
  transcendental, 42
  trinitarian, 182n39, 183
difference, absolute, 146
  cultural, 31–32
  identity and, 50, 182n39
  inner, 67
  natural, 130
  otherness and, 17, 206
  political, 32
  structuralist/linguistic, 23–24,
    29
  unity-in-, 177
differentia(e), 93–95
différance, 24–26, 29, 30
Ding an sich. See thing-in-itself
discourse, 16, 17, 18, 19, 20, 21, 26,
    27, 31, 163
discrepancy, 77, 92, 145, 164, 169
  inner, 62, 67
dissembling replacement, 141–42
diversity, 31, 34, 63, 198n89
dividing practices, 21
divine law, 126–28, 131
division, xv, 34, 80, 83, 100n55,
    107n81
domination, xiii, 14, 21, 23, 33,
    73n78
doubt, 38, 56, 78, 79, 188
dualism, 163, 172, 176n23, 177
  Cartesian, 38n11
  subject-object, xviii, 36, 39,
    47, 48
  subjectivism and, 47–50, 52

economy, xiv, 4, 5, 6, 8, 11, 32, 33,
    196
education, 35, 76n95, 203,

emancipation, 21, 26, 186, 197
empiricism, 63, 90, 116n111
enjoyment, 31, 83, 84, 108, 109, 133n171, 134
Enlightenment, the, 17n52, 19, 21, 125n147, 135–37, 139, 174n12
Entzweiung. See division
episteme, 21
epistemology, 37, 40, 44
essence, absolute, 136, 139, 140, 149, 152, 157, 158, 159n266,
   concrete, 150n234
   determinate, 116
   divine, 153, 155, 157, 161
   eternal, 171n3, 177
   ethical, 122
   extrinsic, 92
   human, 136
   individual, 108
   inner, 105, 106, 108, 113
   intrinsic, 94, 117
   negative, 140n201, 144
   objective, 75, 132
   simple, 67
   singular, 82
   spiritual, 106, 120, 121, 124, 149, 155, 157
   subjective, 124
   true, 64, 65, 105, 148, 151, 152, 168
   universal, 93, 132n171, 148n226, 149, 153
evil, 33, 113, 147, 158
   radical, 148n226
excess, 29, 33, 131, 189, 190, 194, 197, 205
experience, xviin6, 23, 24, 26, 40, 42, 44, 45, 63, 68, 72n77, 75, 77, 78n104, 79, 80, 82, 83, 92, 95n36, 101, 104, 105, 107, 111, 113, 118, 120, 122, 134, 138n194, 155, 168, 174, 189, 199n92, 203
exploitation, 31n117, 32

Fackenheim, Emil, 172n6

faith, xvii, 24, 47, 113, 134–36, 139, 150n233, 161, 162, 164, 166n289, 168n295, 175n18, 176n23
Fall, the, 160
family, 126–28, 129, 131, 132
fantasy, 16n46, 31, 32
fascism, 26, 33
Father, the, 160, 163, 181, 182n34, 183
Feuerbach, Ludwig, 81n114, 172, 200
Fichte, Johann Gottlieb, xviii, 17, 37, 39, 44–46, 47, 48, 49, 50, 54, 55, 57, 90n14, 139n195, 193
Findlay, John, 172n6
forgiveness, 147, 148, 149n229, 150
Forster, Michael N., 55n6
Foucault, Michel, xvii, 15, 17n52, 18–21, 22, 26, 29
foundation, transcendental, 25, 41
foundationalism, 16, 22
freedom, 26, 72n77, 76, 77, 78, 79, 86, 129, 130, 137n189, 140, 141, 149n228, 175n19, 177, 191, 192, 194
   absolute, 131, 137–39
   abyssal, 192
   divine, 179–80
   negative, 76n96, 137n189
French Revolution, 49n56, 137n190, 138n194, 139n195
Friedman, Milton, 4n6
Fritzman, J. M., 60n22
Fromm, Erich, 12
fundamentalism, 31
Für-sich-Sein. See being-for-itself.

Gadamer, Hans-Georg, 67n60
Gall, Franz Josef, 102n61
gap, 6, 7, 8, 29, 49, 64, 105, 132n170, 137, 164, 190, 192, 194, 197
Garaudy, Roger, 172n6
GDP, 5n9, 5n12, 6
genealogy, 19
Gewissen. See conscience
global community, xiii, 1, 11, 204, 206

INDEX

globalization, xiii–xx, 1–14, 27, 28, 31, 33, 34, 35, 36, 56, 171, 187, 201, 204–7
   anthropology of, 3, 10, 11, 13, 56
   capitalist, xiii, xiv, xvii, 1, 2, 8n22, 12, 13, 14, 18, 27, 28, 34, 196, 205; *see also* capitalism, global
   context of, xiii, xv, xvii, xix, xx, 1, 2, 27, 28, 34, 35, 56, 171, 201, 204, 205, 207
   cultural, 9–13
   economic, 3–9, 10
God, death of, 18, 157, 199
   Hegel's concept of, xix, 149, 150, 151, 158–69, 170–87, 199, 200, 202, 203, 204; *see also* absolute spirit
   triune, 181, 183n42, 184, 186n48; *see also* God, Hegel's concept of; absolute spirit
Goethe, Johann Wolfgang von, 108n84, 109n89, 146n220
grammatology, 25
gross domestic product. *See* GDP

happiness, 107, 141–42
happy consciousness, 157, 158n259
Hardt, Michael, 191n65
Harris, H. S., 158n264
Hartshone, Charles, 174n15
Hayek, Friedrich August von, 4n7
Held, David, 3, 6n13
hen kai pan, 176
Hodgson, Peter C., 176n23, 182n34, 183n42
Holy Spirit, the, 159, 162, 181, 200
Homer, 156
Homo Consumens, 12
homogenization, 9n24, 31
hope, xiv, 30, 34, 78, 81
Houlgate, Stephen, 172n6
hubris, anthropocentric, 33, 203
human law, 126–28, 131
human rights, 26, 206
human sciences, 20, 21
human subjectivity, xiii–xviii, xx, 1, 2, 11, 17n52, 18, 27, 28, 33, 47, 53n66, 57, 59, 64n46, 68, 87, 150, 171, 184, 186, 187, 202, 203, 205, 206
   erosion of, xiv, xvii, 27
   new conception of, xiii, xv, xvi, xvii, 205
humanism, 172
Hyppolite, Jean, 58n12, 76n95, 78n104, 80, 97n47, 109n89, 110n91, 112n98, 113, 116n109, 118n118, 123

idealism, 90, 95n36
   German, 125n147, 139n195
   subjective, 17, 44n37, 46n48, 90n14
   transcendental, 90n14
identity, self-conscious, xvi, 202
   substantial, 201, 206
identity politics, 31, 206
ideological apparatuses, 21
ideology, 4, 9, 11, 14, 17, 28, 33, 138, 190, 195
imago Dei, 160, 202
immanence, divine, 158, 172, 173n9, 175, 176, 181, 184
imperialism, xiii, xiv, xv, 9n24, 18, 31, 204, 206
impossibility, 29, 30, 189, 190, 191, 193, 197
impossible, the, 29–30
inclination, xiv, 12, 23, 100, 107n81, 121n134, 140
incarnation, divine, 81, 82, 83, 157n256, 160–63, 177n25
individualism, 107n81, 112, 130n164, 186
individuality, as the principle of actuality, 114, 144n212
inequality, 7, 8, 31n117, 32
infinite-finite dichotomy, 173, 174, 179
infinity, 67, 71n66, 76, 79, 87, 89, 140n201, 169, 173, 176, 177, 179, 182n38, 185
   bad, 173
injustice, 8, 31n117

INDEX

institution, 8n23, 19n59, 20, 138n293, 149
interdependence, xv, 5, 9, 206
interiority, xiv, 12, 76, 92, 94, 101, 102, 103, 105, 119, 152, 155, 205
International Monetary Fund, 8n23
Internet, 4, 10, 14
intolerance, 31n117, 32
intuition, 23n78, 38, 40, 41, 42, 44, 60n22, 75, 108, 163n281, 166, 168n295
    intellectual, 45, 141n204
    sensible, 40, 41, 49

Jacobi, Friedrich Heinrich, 44, 144n213
Jameson, Fredric, 27
Jenseitige, 81, 175
Jobs, Steve, 13n37
Judaism, 81
judgment, 15n45, 133, 146n222, 147, 148n226, 165n287
    infinite, 103, 104
justice, xv, 1, 29, 30, 128n155, 206
    economic, 8
    egalitarian, 196–97

Kant, Immanuel, xviii, 17, 37, 39–44, 45, 46, 47, 48, 49, 50, 54, 55, 57, 60n22, 88, 89n8, 89n10, 90n14, 97n47, 119n120, 121n134, 123, 124, 129, 139–44, 148n226, 179n29, 185n45, 192, 193
Kaufmann, Walter, 172n6
Keynes, John Maynard, 5n11
Kierkegaard, Søren, 14, 168n295, 176n23, 187
Kojève, Alexander, 73n82, 172n6
Köher, Gernot, 8n22
Kroner, Richard, 172n6
Kultus. *See* cult

labor, 74–76, 83, 84, 89, 132n171, 154n246; *see also* activity, formative

Lacan, Jacques. xix, 17n52, 73n80, 188–91, 192, 193, 194, 195, 198, 199, 200
Laclau, Ernest, 196n83, 197
language, xiv, 11, 17, 20n60, 22–27, 47, 61nn30–32, 146n222, 153, 154, 156, 160, 190, 195
Lauer, Quentin, 62n34, 160n271, 166n289, 171
Lavater, Johann Kaspar, 102n61
law, logical, 100, 105
    moral, 43n36, 121n134, 124, 139n197
    psychological, 100, 101, 105
law of the heart, 107, 109–12, 114
Lawlor, Leonard, 22n78
leftover, 190,
Levinas, Emmanuel, 29
Lévi-Strauss, Claude, 17n52
liberalism, 31, 207
liberalization, 4, 9
Lichtenberg, Georg Christoph, 102
logocentrism, 22–23
logos, 22, 25, 166n289, 185
lord of the world, 130–31
love, 127n151, 162, 174, 182n39
Lukács, Georg, 172n6
Lyotard, Jean-François, 16, 17n52

madness, 20, 111, 147n225, 187, 188, 191, 194, 197
Marcuse, Herbert, 172n6
master-slave dialectic, 70, 73–75, 147n223
McTaggart, John, 172n6
mediation, xviii, xix, 52, 54, 57, 60, 61, 62n36, 69, 70, 87, 91, 107, 127, 144, 153, 178, 184
metanarrative, 16
Metz, Johann Baptist, 185
Middle Ages, the, 82n118, 125n147, 132n167
Min, Anselm K., ix, 2, 11, 130n164, 151n238
MNCs, 5, 8, 12
modernism, xv, xvi, 34
modernity, 15n45, 17, 18, 47, 206
monism, 172

mystical, 176
morality, 43n36, 46, 88, 107n81, 119n120, 125, 139–45, 147, 165n288
movement, dialectical, xviii, 34, 47, 50, 51, 52, 54, 56, 57, 76, 78, 80, 84, 85, 86, 87, 91n16, 150, 154n246, 157, 158n259, 159, 167, 168, 169, 171, 181, 186, 195, 198, 199, 202, 203, 204, 205, 206
   self-conscious, xv, xix, 102, 135, 201
   self-differentiating, 106
   self-transcending, xv, 91, 117, 185, 195
   self-universalizing, 184
   socio-historical, 47, 50, 57, 205
   teleological, xvi, 47, 50, 52, 54, 57, 150, 168, 169, 171, 198, 205
   trinitarian, xix, 159, 160, 163, 167, 186, 202
multiculturalism, 28, 31–32
multiplicity, 12, 16, 31, 78, 151

Navickas, Joseph L., 53n66
Nazism, 26
necessity, dead, 111
   inner, 179–80
   lawful, 96, 100, 102, 103
negation, abstract, 28, 34, 78, 205
   determinate, 28n97, 64n45, 85
   negation of, 159, 198
negativity, absolute, xvi, 52, 71n66, 72n74, 73n80, 87, 117, 118, 135, 144, 198, 199
   abstract, xvin5, 198
   radical, xix, 170, 191–93, 194, 196, 197, 200
   self-relating, 191, 193, 195
neo-liberalism, 4
New Age spiritualism, 28, 32–33
Nietzsche, Friedrich, 16n48, 18
nihilism, xiii, 11, 13, 14, 207
Novalis, 146n220

objectivism, 15, 16, 116n111, 166

objectivity, universal, xvi, 56, 149
Olson, Alan, 172n6
ontologization, 29, 192
opposition, binary, 25
oppression, 23, 34
order, symbolic, 9, 189, 190, 191, 194, 196, 198, 200
organism, 96–99, 100, 104
otherness, brute, 92, 143
   messianic, 29
   sublated, 77, 92

panentheism, 177
pantheism, xix, 117n111, 172, 173–77, 178, 181, 182n36, 184, 186n48
peace, xv, 1, 11, 150n232
perception, 55n4, 58, 62–64, 65, 68, 93, 107n80
philosophy, contextual, xvi–xvii
   modern, 36, 37, 38, 39, 46, 47, 48, 49, 52, 54
   speculative, 166, 172n7, 176
phonocentrism, 22–23, 24n85
phrenology, 102, 103, 105
physiognomy, 102, 103, 105
piety, theocentric, 203
Pinkard, Terry, 55n3, 55n5, 148n226
pleasure, 107, 108–9, 110, 111, 112, 114
plurality, 16, 31, 41n22, 61, 138
politics, xiv, 31, 33, 196n83, 197
   subject of, 32, 197, 199; see also subject, the, political
positivism, 91n18
postmodernism, xiv, xv, xvi, xvii, 1, 14–18, 21, 27, 28, 33, 34
postulate, 43n36, 141, 143
poverty, 84n128
   global, 6, 7, 8
Prabhu, Joseph, xi, 183n42
predicament, 55, 62, 79, 90, 122, 128, 131, 144, 147, 164
   self-contradictory, 92, 108
predicate, 119, 120, 137
presence, metaphysics of, 22–23
predication, analogical, 181
psychiatry, 20

psychoanalysis, 191, 200
pure duty, Kantian, 139–44
pure insight, 134–37, 139

Quantum Theory, 16n47

racism, 26, 31
Rauch, Leo, 192n68
Rawls, John, 128n155
Real, the, 188, 189, 190, 192, 193, 197, 200
reason, active, 91, 104, 105–14, 115
　certainty of, 90
　dialectical, 176, 177
　law-giving, 121–22, 123
　law-testing, 121, 122, 123
　moral, 143
　observing, 91–105, 106, 107n80, 108, 115
　practical, 43n36, 46
　pure, 42, 43, 90, 91
　self-actualizing, 91, 114–24
　socialized, 88, 106, 115
　sound, 121
　speculative, 42, 44, 165, 168n295
　theoretical, 43n36, 46
　truth of, 90
　universal, 106, 107, 120, 123
recognition, 72–74, 145, 150
　legal, 129, 130
　mutual, 72, 106, 150, 177n24
reconciliation, 49n56, 50, 82, 118, 125, 147, 148, 149n229, 150, 159, 160, 163, 164, 165, 183, 187
relation(ship), dialectical, xvi, xviii, 49, 52, 55, 190, 192, 199, 202, 203
　power, 19, 20
　solidary, xv, 35, 57, 206, 207
　transcendental, 39
relationality, 204
Relativity Theory, 16n47
religion, xix, 11, 33, 81n117, 88, 134n178, 137, 148, 150–64, 165, 167, 169, 172, 182, 199, 200

absolute/consummate/revealed, 81n117, 157n258, 158–64, 165, 166, 167, 183; *see also* Christianity
　art-, 152, 153–58, 159
　concept of, 151, 152, 159, 160, 161, 162
　moral, 241n204
　natural, 152–53, 157n256, 159
　philosophy of, ix, xi, 176n23, 181n33
representation, 24n85, 45, 60n22, 96, 77, 105, 136, 151, 153, 159n267, 160, 162n275, 163n281, 164, 166, 167, 168n295, 169, 183, 189, 190
representational thinking/thought, 50n57, 163, 164, 165
res cogitans. *See* thinking substance, Cartesian
res extensa. *See* extended substance
resurrection, 162, 163
revolution, 4, 30n111, 187, 194
　Copernican, 17, 39, 44n40
Rousseau, Jean-Jacques, 74n84, 110n91, 137, 138n193, 139n195, 146n220

Sache selbst, 118–20, 121
Saussure, Ferdinand de, 17n52, 23, 24n84
Schelling, F. W. J., 93n25, 175, 182n36
Schiller, Friedrich, 109n89, 146n220
Sein-für-Anderes. *See* being-for-others
self-actualization, 117, 118, 119, 120, 134, 135, 178, 180
self-affirmation, 84
self-alienation, 80, 131, 132
self-conceit, 111
self-contradiction, 71, 90, 123
self-determination, xiv, 14, 47, 87n3, 145, 171, 179, 202, 205
self-differentiation, 178, 180, 182n38
self-expression, 149, 160, 178, 180
self-manifestation, 88, 180, 185n45s

self-reconciliation, 87n3
self-reflection, xiv, 205
self-renunciation, 84
self-revelation, 54, 162, 178, 180
self-transcendence, xiv, xvi, 1, 14, 54, 171, 184, 202, 205
sense-certainty, 55n4, 58, 60–62, 64, 68, 93, 136n187
signification, 23, 189, 190
signified, 23–25
  transcendental, 23
signifier, 23–25, 189
sinnliche Gewißheit. See sense-certainty
Sittlichkeit, 106, 107, 115, 119n120, 139, 149
Sitz im Leben, xvii, 1, 4
skepticism, 70, 76, 78–80, 90, 129n160, 130, 131, 158n259
Sloterdijk, Peter, 8n22
solidarity, xiii, xv, 1, 35, 186, 203, 206
solipsism, 90n13
Solomon, Robert, 172n6
Son, the, 159, 162, 163, 181, 183
Sophocles, 128, 156
speculation, 50n59, 177n26
spiritual animal kingdom, 115–21, 122n137
spiritual subjectivity, Hegelian, xv, xvi, xviii, xix, 1, 35, 47, 50, 51, 52, 54, 55, 56, 57, 85, 86, 87, 88, 149n230, 166, 168, 170, 185, 195, 196, 198, 200, 201–7
spiritualization, xiv, 151, 159
spontaneity, 40, 140n198, 180n29
state/political power, 132–34, 139
Steger, Manfred B., 3n4, 3n5, 4n6, 6n12
Stiegler, Bernard, 12n35
Stiglitz, Joseph E., 8
Stirling, James, 172n6
stoicism, 70, 76–78, 129, 130, 158n259
Strauss D. F., 175
structuralism, 17n52, 20n61, 23

post-, 18n55, 28, 188n53, 189, 190
subject, the, death of. *See* death of the subject
  desiring. 70–73, 75, 79, 89; *see also* desire; master-slave dialectic
  cultural, 125, 131–39, 144, 149
  ethical, 126–31, 144, 149
  laboring, 70, 74–76, 89; *see also* labor; master-slave dialectic
  moral, 125, 129, 139–48, 149, 150, 165
  philosophical, 150, 164–69, 170, 196, 198, 199
  political, 188, 194, 195, 196, 197, 198
  practical rational. *See* reason, active
  religious, 150–64, 165, 167, 170
  self-defining, 37n3
  split. *See* unhappy consciousness
  theoretical rational. *See* reason, observing
  thinking. *See* stoicism; skepticism
  transcendental, 25, 44
  the, turn to, xviii, 36, 37, 38, 39, 46, 47, 54
  universal, 35, 87, 118, 120, 121, 134n177, 168
  universal-individual rational. *See* self-actualizing reason
  Žižek's Lacanian, 188–91, 193; *see also* Lacan, Jacques
  Žižek's Hegelian, 191–200
subjection, 18, 26, 131
subjectivation, xv, 12n35, 13, 18, 26, 189, 190, 194, 196, 201, 204, 205
subjectivism, xv, xviii, 15, 17, 27, 34, 39, 47, 48, 49, 50, 52, 87, 116n111, 166, 172, 186, 201, 204, 205
subjectivity, absolute, xvi, xix, 88, 125, 143, 148–50, 168, 169, 170, 202, 203
  authentic, xviii, 51, 55

subjectivity, absolute (*continued*)
  communal-spiritual, xix, 124, 125, 126, 131, 139, 144, 147, 149
  cosmopolitan, 35
  critical, xiv, 28
  Derrida's deconstruction of, 21–27, 29, 30
  excess of, 33
  individual-rational, xix, 89, 124, 125
  moral, 88, 139, 143
  self-conscious, xviii, 57, 73n80, 74, 86
  spiritual. *See* spiritual subjectivity, Hegelian
  postmodern, xvii, 27, 34
  post-postmodern, 34, 36, 205
  universal, xvi, xix, 18, 19, 21, 56, 86, 88, 146n222, 148, 149, 153, 158, 159, 162, 169, 170, 184, 186–87, 201, 202
subjectivity-for-itself, xvi, 58, 69, 70, 86, 171, 203
subjectivity-in-and-for-itself, xvi, 86, 171, 203
subjectivity-in-itself, xvi, 57, 60, 62, 64, 171, 203
subjectlessness, xiv, 18, 28, 34, 205
subjectum, 17
sublation, xv, xviii, xix, 36, 39, 47, 55, 59, 62, 64, 67, 68, 71, 104, 167, 173, 181, 182n39, 195, 203, 205
substance, 27, 38n9, 48, 54, 60n24, 86, 132, 133, 137, 139, 149, 156n250, 157, 158, 159, 161n272, 165, 173, 176, 178, 182n36, 184, 192, 193, 194, 201, 203
  absolute, 72n77, 166, 182
  ethical, 106, 115, 120, 121, 122, 123, 125, 127, 128, 129, 131, 132
  extended, 38
  infinite, 38
  natural, 129
  objective, 139
  social/political, 131, 138, 194
  spiritual, 106
  thinking. *See* thinking substance, Cartesian
  universal, 106, 127, 132, 139, 149
substantiality, 41n22, 144, 146, 176, 204
supplement, ideological, xiv, 32
Symbolic, the, 188, 189n55, 190, 192, 197, 198; *see also* big Other, the
symbolization, 189, 190
synthesis, 41, 74, 89, 118, 139, 192, 198, 203, 204

Taylor, Charles, 51n63, 71n68, 81n114
teleology, 97
terror, 49n56, 138, 139, 197
text, 25, 26
  context and, xvii, 2
theism, traditional, xix, 172, 173–77, 179, 181, 184, 186n48, 202
theology, contextual, xvi, xviin6
thing-in-itself, 45, 46, 48, 89
thinking substance, Cartesian, xviii, 17, 37, 38–39, 46, 54, 188
Tholuck, Friedrich August Gottreu, 174n16
to-come, 29, 30
tolerance, 31–32
totalitarianism, 26, 130n164
totality, dialectical, xv, xvi, 34
trace, 24, 29
transcendence, xvn1, xvin5, 58n15, 76, 135, 144
  divine, 158, 172, 173, 175, 181, 184
transcendental self, Kantian, xviii, 17, 20, 37, 39–44, 46, 47n49, 49, 54
Trinity, the, 159n267, 182n34, 183
truth, correspondence theory of, 15n45
  objective, 17, 22, 25
  rational, 15n45
  universal, 15, 153, 169, 200

tyranny, 130, 206

unconscious, the, xiv, 17, 127
understanding, 40–44, 48, 49, 50, 55n4, 58, 62n37, 64–68, 71n66, 76n96, 87n2, 93, 95, 97n47, 107n80, 167, 168n295, 172n7, 173, 176, 177, 179, 180
unhappy consciousness, 70, 80–85, 131, 150n233, 158
unification, xvi, 23n78, 40, 48, 49, 50, 51, 52, 54, 56, 80, 87, 142n207, 151, 159, 160, 162, 164, 165, 176, 177, 183, 198, 205
universal, abstract, 61, 119
  concrete, 168, 185
universality, absolute, xvi, xix, 52, 56, 57, 162, 176, 184, 185, 186, 187, 198, 199, 200, 201, 202, 203, 204, 206, 207
  abstract, 61, 109, 124, 129, 130, 138, 139, 144, 148, 154, 176, 181, 186n48, 195
  concrete, 34, 120, 124, 148, 149, 176, 177, 204
  formal, 122n137, 123, 124, 129, 130, 139, 144
  self-transcending drive toward, xv, 35, 56, 206, 207
unruliness, 192, 194
utility, 137

Verstand. See understanding

violence, 14, 31, 130
  conceptual, 23
virtue, 107, 112–14, 150n232
void, 29, 32, 76n96, 156, 163, 189, 190, 192, 194, 197
Volk, 61n32, 106n75, 112n98, 126, 153
Vorstellung. See representation

Wahrnehmung. See perception
way of the world, 101, 112–14
wealth, 7, 8, 9, 132–34, 139, 186
Weedon, Chris, 19n60
Weltlauf. See way of the world
Werden. See becoming
Wesen. See essence
Whitehead, Alfred North, 174, 177
will, general, 107n81, 137n191, 138n193, 139
  individual, 85, 137, 139
  universal, 85, 137, 138
Williams, Robert R., 184n44
Winfield, Richard Dien, 62n37, 90n13, 129, 156n250, 166n291
World Bank, 5n9, 6, 8n23
World Inequality Database, 7
World Trade Organization, 8n23

yearning, 82, 147n225

Zeitgeist, xvii, 1, 15
Žižek, Slavoj, xvii, xix, 8n22, 28–33, 73n80, 104n71, 170, 187–200

www.ingramcontent.com/pod-product-compliance
Lightning Source LLC
Chambersburg PA
CBHW051055230426
43667CB00013B/2300